LONDON
SECRET WALKS

Explore the City's Hidden Places

by Graeme Chesters

Survival Books • Bath • England

First published 2012

Copyright © Survival Books 2012
Cover design: Di Bruce-Kidman
Cover photo: © Magdalena Bujak (🖥 www.shutterstock.com)
Maps © Jim Watson

Survival Books Limited
Office 169, 3 Edgar Buildings
George Street, Bath BA1 2FJ, United Kingdom
☎ +44 (0)1935-700060
✉ info@survivalbooks.net
🖥 www.survivalbooks.net

British Library Cataloguing in Publication Data
A CIP record for this book is available
from the British Library.

ISBN: 978-1-907339-51-6

Printed in Singapore by International Press Softcom Limited

Acknowledgements

S pecial thanks are due to Peter Read for commissioning this book, Robbi Forrester Atilgan for editing and additional research, Alex Browning and David Woodworth for proof-reading, Di Bruce-Kidman for the DTP and cover design, Jim Watson for the superb maps and – dare I forget – Louise, my long-suffering wife, for answering my computer queries and continuing with the pretence that writing is a proper job.

Last, but not least, a special thank you to the many photographers who provided images (listed on page 318) – the unsung heroes – whose beautiful images add colour and bring London to life.

Editor's Notes

Please note the following regarding the walks in this book.

♦ The walk lengths are approximate, as is the time required to complete them – shown as a half or full day – particularly if you make a lot of stops (coffee, lunch, museums, shopping, etc.). You can, of course, terminate any walk at any point and combine a number of walks to make a longer walk.

♦ All walks start at or near a tube or railway station and directions are provided to the nearest station at the end of each walk. There's a tube map inside the rear cover. Buses aren't listed as there are simply too many to include them all.

♦ The maps aren't drawn to scale but the length of walks is shown. Overall maps are included on pages 8-13 so that you can see the location of the walks on a larger map of London.

♦ The opening hours of many sights and museums (etc.) are listed. Bear in mind that these are liable to change. Where opening times are erratic or not stated, a telephone number is included. Where there's an entry fee, the fee for an adult is quoted. There are usually (but not always) reduced fees for children, families and concessions, e.g. pensioners, students and the unemployed. If no fee is listed, then entry is free.

♦ Recommended 'pit stops' (Food & Drink) have been included in all walks - shown in blue on maps and in the text. If you're planning to stop at one of the pubs, restaurants or cafés listed, bear in mind that many only serve lunch between say noon and 2.30pm and dinner from 6 or 7pm. Many pubs are also open in the mornings for coffee, etc. Some establishments don't open at all in the evenings or at weekends (which is noted), particularly in the City of London. When not listed, pub/restaurant opening times are the 'standard' times, e.g. noon-2.30pm and 6-11pm, although some are open all day (and may also serve food all day). Telephone numbers are shown when bookings are accepted or advisable, otherwise booking isn't usually necessary (or even possible).

Contents

Little Venice

Introduction

Walking makes a lot of sense in London, whether it's for pleasure, exercise or simply to get from A to B. Although the city has a comprehensive public transport system, it's also one of the world's most expensive and very crowded, so walking is often the quickest and most enjoyable way to get around – at least in the centre – and it's also free and healthy! London's reputation for rain is largely unfounded – it actually enjoys lower annual rainfall than New York, Rome and Sydney – and is rarely too hot or too cold to make walking uncomfortable (but take your brolly just in case).

London has a somewhat haphazard street pattern (to put it mildly), the result of having grown organically over 2,000 years, rather than being planned logically like some modern cities. As a result, many attractions are off the beaten track, away from the major thoroughfares and public transport hubs. This favours walking as the best way to explore them, as does the fact that London is a visually interesting city with a wealth of stimulating sights between destinations; you don't see a lot from the seat of a cab or bus – and see nothing at all when cocooned in a tube train!

The starting point for this book was Samuel Johnson's advice to his friend Boswell in the 18th century, on the occasion of the latter's arrival in London: "survey its innumerable little lanes and courts." By extension, wander off the beaten tourist track and you'll find a world of fascinating sights, as you would expect in a city as large and old as London. My aim was to compile a list of these hidden attractions and construct walks around them – which resulted in the 25 walks contained in this book.

Most of the walks can be done in half a day or less, depending, of course, on how quickly you walk and how long you spend at the highlighted sights, particularly the pubs and restaurants. The walks don't always follow the most logical route, but that's deliberate and part of the fun: the aim is to maximise enjoyment and provide a flavour of the area, rather than to get from the start to finish as quickly as possible.

Writing this book has been a fascinating, educational and enjoyable journey, which has had the added bonus of returning me to the weight I was when I got married (16 years ago). I hope you find the walks as engaging, rewarding and stomach-flattening as I have.

Graeme Chesters
June 2012

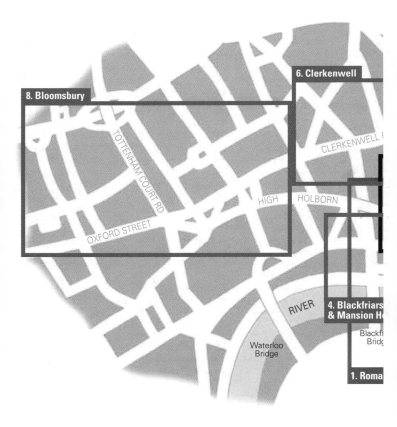

8. Bloomsbury

6. Clerkenwell

CLERKENWELL

TOTTENHAM COURT RD

HIGH   HOLBORN

OXFORD STREET

RIVER   **4. Blackfriars & Mansion H**

Blackf
Brid

Waterloo
Bridge

1. Roma

Walks 1-8

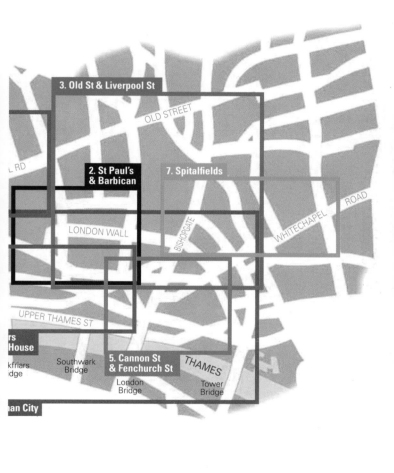

16. Regent's Park

Regent's Park

MAP

15. Mayfair

OXFOR

BAYSWATER ROAD

Hyde Park

PARK LANE

KNIGHTSBRIDGE

Hyde
Co

SLOANE ST

EATO

KING'S ROAD

Battersea
Bridge

Albert
Bridge

Ch
Br

11. Belgravia & Chelsea

Walks 9-16

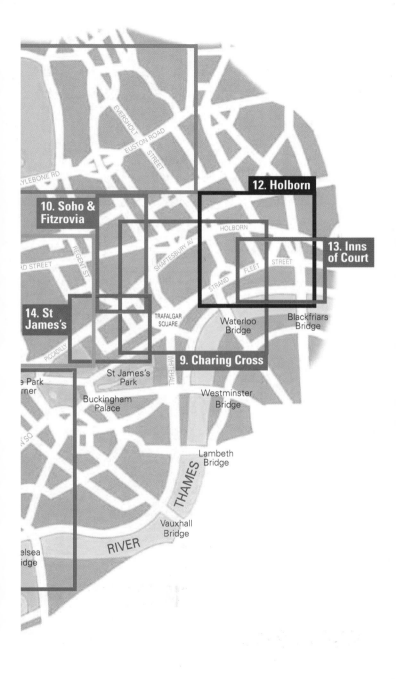

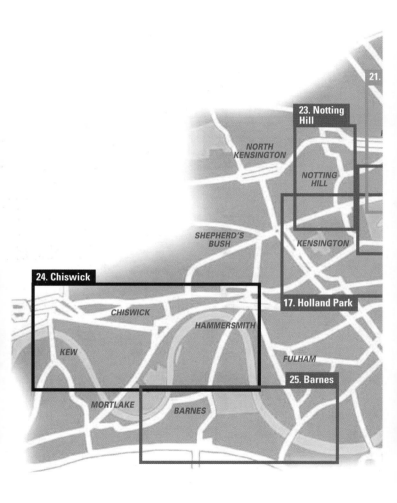

Walks 17-25

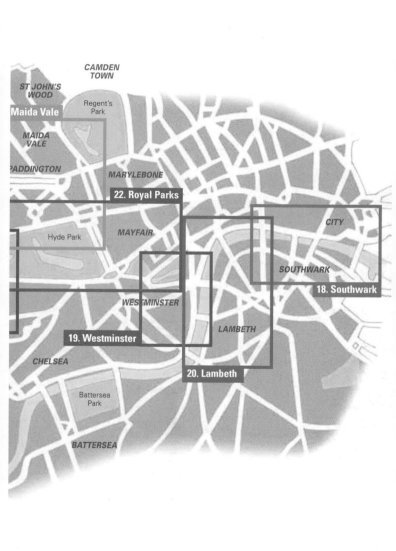

1 St Magnus-the-Martyr

2 All Hallows by the Tower

3 Trinity Square Gardens

4 Roman wall

5 All Hallows on the Wall

6 St Alphage Garden

7 Roman wall

8 London's Roman Amphitheatre

9 Roman wall – and turret

10 Museum of London

11 St Bride's

12 Black Friar

13 Planet of the Grapes

14 Roman Mithraeum

15 London Stone

● Places of Interest ● Food & Drink

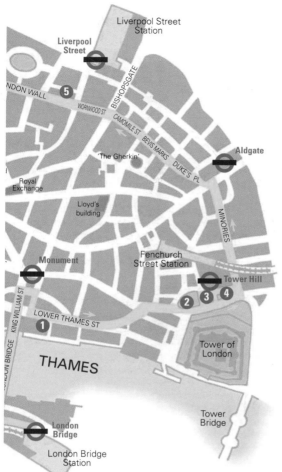

Liverpool Street
Station

Liverpool Street

LONDON WALL

WORNWOOD ST

BISHOPSGATE

CAMOMILE ST

BEVIS MARKS

DUKE'S PL

Aldgate

'The Gherkin'

Royal
Exchange

Lloyd's
building

MINORIES

Monument

Fenchurch
Street Station

Tower Hill

KING WILLIAM ST

LOWER THAMES ST

THAMES

LONDON BRIDGE

London Bridge

London Bridge
Station

Tower of
London

Tower
Bridge

ROMAN
LONDON

WALK 1

Distance: 3.84mi (6.19km)
Duration: full day
Start: London Bridge station
End: Cannon Street station

Modern London has been shaped by generations of architects, entrepreneurs and immigrants – not to mention a few invaders – but the city's f rst stones were laid by the Romans, who founded the city in around 50AD. Londoners may regard their city as being as ancient and noble as Athens or even Rome itself, but there's little evidence of major, permanent settlement on the site before the Roman conquest of Britain in 43AD.

The wider Thames Valley had been occupied for millennia before the founding of London; archaeologists have uncovered signs of human habitation dating back at least 500,000 years. But the Romans probably founded the f rst proper urban settlement on the site of modern London. Before this, all that existed were a few sacred sites and a hill fort or two. London's location was chosen because it was the lowest easy bridging point of the River Thames, which was wider and shallower then. There was also a way through the marshes to the south and two convenient hills, at St Paul's and Cornhill, which rose safely above the f oodplain and provided useful vantage points

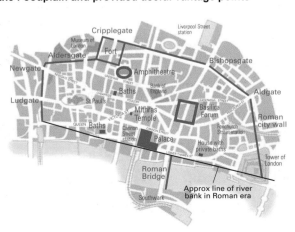

ROMAN LONDON

Start Walking…

To explore the remains of Roman London, leave London Bridge station and follow the signs for London Bridge itself. As you cross the River Thames, to the right are the Art Deco splendour of Hays Wharf, HMS Belfast, Tower Bridge and Canary Wharf; ahead are two of London's iconic structures, the Monument and the Gherkin (30 St Mary Axe), while to the left you can see the dome of St Paul's Cathedral and, in the distance, the Post Office Tower. When you reach the north bank, you're close to the spot where London was founded.

The first London Bridge was probably wooden, built between 100 and 400AD by the Romans, and a number of bridges have come and gone over the centuries, some swept away by floods or destroyed by fire or even frost. The current concrete structure was built 1967-72 to replace John Rennie's five stone arches which had spanned the river since the late 1820s; the Rennie bridge was sold to a US oil magnate and shipped to the US stone-by-stone to be rebuilt in Lake Havasu City, Arizona.

In previous centuries, London Bridge was crowded with houses and shops, some reaching seven storeys high; the last ones weren't demolished until 1758-62. For a time, traitors' heads were displayed above bridge gatehouses, a macabre tradition which began in 1305 with the head of Scottish independence leader William ('Braveheart') Wallace.

Billingsgate porters were known for their distinctive hats, which they wore from 1415 onwards to mark the English defeat of the French at the Battle of Agincourt. The hats resembled the leather helmets worn by the English archers who were instrumental in the victory.

On the north bank, the first street on the right is Monument Street, the site of the impressive, gold-topped Monument, built to commemorate the Great Fire of London in 1666. Continue down Monument Street and turn right into Fish Street Hill, so-called because it was one of the City streets where the retail sale of fish was authorised. At the bottom is Lower Thames Street, the site of the famous Billingsgate Market from the 14th century until 1982, selling food, wine, and later, fish (it's now on the Isle of Dogs in East London).

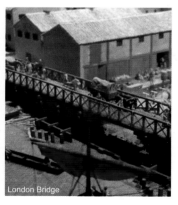

London Bridge

WALK 1

Ahead, across Lower Thames Street, is the parish church of **St Magnus-the-Martyr** ①, (Tue-Fri, 10am-4pm) named after a hapless Norwegian earl who was murdered by his cousin in 1110. A church was founded here in the 10th century and rebuilt by Wren after the Great Fire. It's here that we find our first evidence of Roman London in the church forecourt up against a pillar: a hefty portion of timber which, according to the sign, is 'from Roman wharf AD75, found Fish Street Hill 1931'; some experts think it's from a bridge rather than a wharf.

On leaving the church, turn right and head east along Lower Thames Street. The road swings to the left and becomes Byward Street, which gets its name from the daily bywords, or passwords, that are still issued to staff at the nearby Tower of London. At the lights, cross to the large traffic island ahead to reach **All Hallows by the Tower** ②. This ancient, Grade I listed church is London's oldest, established by the Saxon Abbey at Barking on the site of a Roman building.

> All Hallows was lucky to survive the Great Fire in 1666. It was so close to the inferno that diarist Samuel Pepys famously climbed the spire to watch the fire lay waste to the city.

Inside is a Saxon arch from 675AD, with Roman tiles visible at the top, typical of the architectural recycling in London as civilisations succeeded one another. The arch is next to a small flight of stairs leading down to the atmospheric Crypt Museum. At the bottom of the stairs on the left is a large section of well preserved, tessellated Roman pavement from the floor of a 2nd-century domestic house. The museum has plenty of other Roman finds – bowls, keys, lamps, needles, pots and more – as well as casts of Roman tombstones; the originals are in the British Museum. There's also an informative model of Roman London and exhibits from later phases of the church, including some striking Saxon carvings. The church's gorgeous baptismal

All Hallows by the Tower ②
Mon-Fri, 8am-6pm, Sat-Sun, 10am-5pm, except during services.

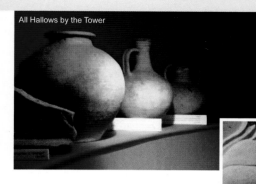

All Hallows by the Tower

Trinity Square Gardens

font cover (1692) by the renowned Dutch wood carver Grinling Gibbons – Sir Christopher Wren's favourite – is regarded as one of London's finest carvings.

Behind the church, Gloucester Court provides a splendid view of the Tower of London. But leave exploration of the Tower to another day and cross to the north side of Byward Street to enter Trinity Square and **Trinity Square Gardens** ❸. The gardens have a poignant monument to the merchant seamen and fishermen killed in the two World Wars: around 12,000 in WWI and 24,000 in WWII; their names are inscribed on a series of plaques.

Cross the square to Tower Hill tube station to find another unexpected reminder of the Romans: a tall section of **Roman wall** ❹ located down some steps to the right. Built around 200 AD of Kentish ragstone, it's part of a wall that ran in a two-mile arc from Tower Hill to Blackfriars, enclosing 330 acres (134ha) of land. In front stands a life-sized, 19th-century statue of Trajan (Emperor AD98-117). The wall here rises to 35ft (10.6m), although only the lower section up to around 15.5ft

(4.4m) is Roman; the stonework above is medieval. The Roman build is better constructed than the medieval wall above and includes layers of red tiles to strengthen it.

On the far side of the wall, you can enjoy a vista which combines ancient and modern London, as the Roman structure shares the skyline with a distant view of The Shard (London's newest skyscraper) on the south bank by London Bridge station. Walk through the small park by the wall and turn left up The Minories, named after an order of nuns of the same name founded in 1293. Despite its religious connections, this street was described in the 18th century as a 'hotbed of brothels and gin palaces'.

At the top, another left turn takes you into Aldgate High Street. Aldgate was the most easterly of the six original city gates built by the Romans, and the road which passed through it led directly to Colchester, another important Roman city. Cross a second set of lights into Dukes Place and continue as it becomes Bevis Marks, a corruption of Buries Marks, the town house of the Abbot of Bury St Edmunds, which stood here. On the left is Bevis Marks The Restaurant, which is one of London's best kosher restaurant, next to the elegant synagogue (see page 49).

Bevis Marks leads into Camomile Street, which follows the line of the old Roman wall; it was named after the medicinal plant which grew here. Turn left down St Mary Axe for a view of the curvaceous Gherkin and, at the end of the road, the distinctive Lloyds of London building. St Mary Axe is named after a church that was demolished in the 16th century – the axe referred to is from a gory legend about 11,000 murdered virgins. Retrace your steps to Camomile Street, turn left and, at the end, cross Bishopsgate, named for another Roman gate where the London to Lincoln road called Ermine Street began. Continue ahead, now on Wormwood Street which becomes London Wall.

In 1993, an IRA bomb exploded on Bishopsgate, killing one, injuring 44 and doing damage costing £1bn. The buildings which rose from the ruins now include some of the City's most spectacular 'skyscrapers'.

The church of **All Hallows on the Wall** 5 is on the right, built against a section of Roman wall; as at Tower Hill, the upper parts

Roman wall

All Hallows on the Wall ⑤
Most Fridays, 11am-3pm,
☎ 020-7588 2638

FOOD & DRINK

12 **Black Friar:**
Nicholson's pub with award-winning ales, good honest pub grub – great pies!

13 **Planet of the Grapes:**
Wine bar with some 450 wines, plus meat and cheese platters and traditional 'pub' grub.

of the wall are medieval. Inside the church you can see where the Roman tower was, in the vestry. The church is first mentioned at the start of the 12th century and was partly destroyed in the Great Fire, but later rebuilt.

Leaving the church, turn right along London Wall. You may expect to see few signs of anything Roman in this vista of concrete and glass but as you approach the Museum of London, there's a high section of Roman wall on the right by the bland tower block of St Alphage House. It sits in the small, tranquil **St Alphage Garden** ⑥, in what was once a yard of St Alphage Church, of which only part of a wall and some windows survive.

Continue along London Wall as far as Wood Street on the right, where wood was sold in medieval times; there's another remnant of **Roman wall** ⑦ here in a small garden. At the northern end of Wood Street is the site of the insensitively-named Cripplegate, which was one of eight medieval gates at the edge of the City. Its name derives either from the Anglo-Saxon *crepel*, meaning tunnel, or from the crippled beggars who plied their sad trade here, although the gate was demolished in around 1760.

Walk back along Wood Street, cross London Wall and carry on along the southern part of Wood Street. Just before Love Lane – a haunt of prostitutes in medieval times – to the left, in the middle of the road, is a private house that was once the tower of a Wren church. Swing left down

London's Roman Amphitheatre

Love Lane and at the end is the Guildhall.

Follow the route to the right heading anticlockwise from Aldermanbury, past St Lawrence Jewry (see page 36) on Gresham Street. Turn left into Guildhall Yard for the entrance to the Guildhall Art Gallery (Mon-Sat, 10am-5pm, Sun, 12-4pm). The Gallery's basement houses the imaginatively displayed remains of **London's Roman Amphitheatre** ⑧. It's an evocative presentation in a cool, dark environment, with a clever use of lighting.

> London's Amphitheatre, discovered in 1988, was built originally of wood in around AD70 and renovated in the 2nd century, with brick walls and tiled entrances. While it was no Coliseum, it was an impressive structure, able to accommodate between 6,000 and 7,000 spectators, at a time when London's total population was only some 20,000.

Returning to Wood Street, walk north and turn left along London Wall and left again along Noble Street. It boasts the longest and most striking section of **Roman wall – and turret** ⑨, which provides an indication of just how large and impressive the structure must originally have been.

Return to London Wall, cross over and ahead is another section of wall in a garden next to 140 London Wall; the wall here is mainly medieval, built on a Roman base. Past the garden is a sign for the **Museum of London** ⑩ (10am-6pm), the world's largest urban history museum. The entrance is situated at first-floor level on a traffic island ahead; take the stairway on the right, just past 140 London Wall.

Battersea Shield, Museum of London

ROMAN LONDON

Don't be misled by the museum's unprepossessing concrete exterior, as it's excellent; the gallery devoted to Roman London is alone worth a visit. The museum opened in 1976 and is an amalgamation of the collections of the London and Guildhall Museums. Its displays cover the history of the Thames Valley from deep prehistory to the present; its location, overlooking a section of Roman wall, is appropriate, linking the museum to the past it so comprehensively maps.

When you leave the museum, go straight ahead and take the escalator down to ground level and Aldersgate. Heading south, Aldersgate becomes St Martin's le Grand with St Paul's Cathedral looming large ahead. At the end, turn right into Newgate Street, named after a Roman gate (one of six which date back to Roman times), which was the original site of Newgate Prison. The notorious jail was later expanded onto the site of the Old Bailey and remained in use until the early 20th century. Swing left down Old Bailey and turn right along Ludgate Hill, heading for Fleet Street.

Ludgate might be the source of London's name: legend tells that Brutus, grandson of the Trojan king Aeneas, built a city, New Troy, on Ludgate Hill in 1100BC. So the story goes, this was rebuilt in 113BC by King Lud, although another version has him build just a gate in 66BC. It was renamed Caerlud, city of Lud, which was later corrupted to Caerlundein, then Londinium and finally London.

Turn left off Fleet Street down St Bride's Lane to visit the church of **St Bride's** ⑪. The crypt under the church contains the remains of a 2nd-century Roman pavement and building, as well as traces of no fewer than seven previous

St Bride's ⑪
Mon-Fri, 8am-6pm, Sat, hours vary,
Sun, 10am-6.30pm

23

St Brides

churches on the site. The fairly scant Roman remains are at the back and can be viewed with the aid of a mirror.

The church sits on an old pagan site dedicated to Brigit, or Brighde, a Celtic fertility goddess. In the 6th century a church was built to St Bridget, an Irish saint, the first of eight churches here. St Brides is sometimes known as the journalists' church, due to its position on Fleet Street, the former heart of the British newspaper industry.

The famous spire of St Brides which measures around 230ft (70m) was the tallest structure in London when it was added to Sir Christopher Wren's original design in 1701-3. It's said to have inspired a pastry chef, William Rich, to design the tiered wedding cake still popular today; he could see the steeple from his window.

Return to Fleet Street, head east and turn right down New

Bridge Street and left along Queen Victoria Street. On the corner of the two streets is one of London's most striking pubs, the Grade II listed **Black Friar** ⓬. Built in 1875 near the site of the 13th-century Dominican Priory which gives the area its name, Blackfriars, its shape resembles a slab of cheese or an iron. The pub is decorative externally, but the real glory is its interior, which is splendidly over-the-top and Art Nouveau in character. We're fortunate still to have it as there were plans to demolish the pub in the '60s; it was saved by that great champion of historic buildings, the Poet Laureate Sir John Betjeman.

Leaving the pub, head left along Queen Victoria Street, passing the Church of Scientology London at number 46 on the left. Walk a little way further to take in a great view of St Paul's Cathedral on your left. As you continue along Queen Victoria Street, the Gherkin and the Lloyds of London building

St Paul's Cathedral

appear ahead. When you pass Mansion House tube station on the right, to the left is **Planet of the Grapes** ⑬. It's at the bottom of Bow Lane, on the corner with Queen Victoria Street (number 74-82), and is a bright basement wine bar with a short, inventive menu and over 450 wines. There are also a couple of tables outside at pavement level which are good vantage points from which to observe this lively junction.

Continue left along Queen Victoria Street and towards the end of this long thoroughfare, the ruins of the **Roman Mithraeum** ⑭ are visible on your right. The Mithraeum was discovered in 1954 during post-war rebuilding work and the subsequent archaeological dig attracted great public interest, with crowds of up to 30,000 at times. It's a temple to the god Mithras, of Persian or Anatolian origin, who was popular with Roman soldiers. The Mithraeum was actually discovered a short distance away, on the banks of the River Walbrook; it was moved to its current location due to building considerations, but there's talk of returning it to the original site.

The temple was built in the mid-3rd century and was of modest size, 60ft by 25ft (18.3m x 7.6m). It had a sunken nave, to

Roman Mithraeum

London Stone

reflect the fact that Mithras slew a bull in a cave, thereby unleashing power and wisdom into the world; the rebuild, however, is at ground level. In the 4th century, the temple was rededicated, probably to Bacchus, god of wine and ecstasy, which seems appropriate in pleasure-seeking London.

When the site for Number One Poultry (see page 45) – opposite the Roman Mithraeum – was developed, some important archaeology came to light, including a wooden drain along a main Roman road which was dated to 47AD, which provided the most accurate date for the founding of Roman London.

Before the main junction just past the Mithraeum, take a sharp right down Walbrook, named after the ancient river it runs

along, which was the Romans' main water supply. Turn left down Cannon Street, and if you're sharp-sighted enough you may spot one of London's oddest, most myth-shrouded and least visually interesting relics, the **London Stone** 15; unprepossessing, it's displayed behind bars at knee-level opposite a branch of Boots the Chemist.

> Cannon Street has no connection with guns and artillery but rather is named for the candle makers who lived there in the 12th century. It was original named Candelwrithe Street, which became Candlewick Street and, finally, Cannon Street.

The Stone is a smallish lump of weathered limestone with a pair of grooves in the rounded top. Some

Cripplegate fort tower

Roman Wall

commentators think it's part of a Roman marker stone, from which distances were marked; others think (probably wishfully) that it's from an ancient stone circle that stood on Ludgate Hill. Whatever, it's old and has come to be seen as symbolising the authority and power of London. The first written reference to it is in the early 10th century, in a book of Athelstan, King of the West Saxons. For many years the London Stone was a significant site, where deals were made and oaths sworn, so its current status as an often-overlooked curiosity is quite a comedown and a salutary way to end this exploration of the remains left in London by a long-fallen empire.

To reach Monument tube station, continue ahead along Cannon Street and the station is on the right, past the junction with King William Street.

Roman centurians

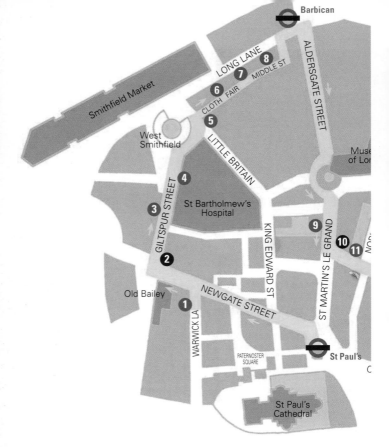

1. Cutlers' Hall
2. Viaduct Tavern
3. Golden Boy of Pye Corner
4. Statue of Henry VIII
5. Tudor Gatehouse
6. 41 Cloth Fair
7. 43 Cloth Court
8. East Passage
9. Postman's Park
10. Piccolo Bar
11. St Annes and St Agnes
12. 25 Gresham Street
13. Wax Chandlers' Hall
14. 10 Gresham Street
15. Guildhall
16. St Lawrence Jewry
17. 5 Aldermanbury Square
18. St Mary Aldermanbury
19. St Alban Tower
20. 100 Wood Street
21. 88 Wood Street
22. St Olave Silver Street Garden

Places of Interest ● Food & Drink

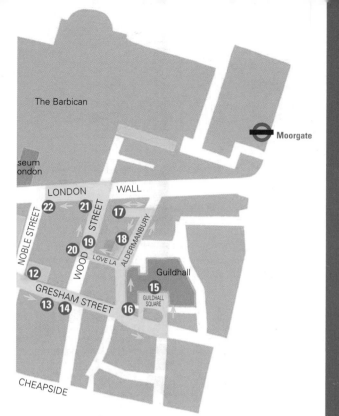

The Barbican

Moorgate

seum
ondon

LONDON   WALL

22 21 17
NOBLE STREET

STREET
19 18
20 ALDERMANBURY
LOVE LA

WOOD
12   Guildhall

GRESHAM STREET   15
GUILDHALL
SQUARE
13 14   16

CHEAPSIDE

ST PAUL'S & BARBICAN

WALK 2

Distance: 1.45mi (2.34km)
Duration: half day
Start/end: St Paul's tube station

The City is a tiny area of London. Its small scale is ref ected in its nickname 'The Square Mile' – it actually covers 1.12mi² (2.90km²) – but this ancient corner of the modern metropolis attracts a huge amount of interest. In medieval times the City was London. The City is a minor geographical part of Greater London, but its boundaries have remained almost unchanged in the last 500 years and it's still the beating heart around which the capital continues to spread.

The term 'City' has also come to mean the UK's financial services industry, which continues its long history of being based in the area. The City's residential population is only some 12,000, but around 350,000 work here, mainly in financial services.

The City's many places of interest are often packed into small, diff cult-to-navigate areas; hence the f ve separate walks devoted to it in this book. Walk 1 covers Roman London, while walks 2 to 5 cover the northwest, northeast, southwest and southeast quarters, and can be walked separately or together, to join up the 'grid'. There's inevitably some crossover between the walks, not so much of sites highlighted and discussed but of the streets traversed; this is unavoidable in a city like London that grew haphazardly rather than being built to a logical grid plan like, for example, New York.

Our f rst exploration of the City takes in its northwestern corner, the area between Smithf eld Market and the Guildhall, where narrow medieval streets jostle with gleaming modern buildings and a wealth of small churches wait to be discovered.

ST PAUL'S & BARBICAN

Start Walking…

Leave St Paul's tube station by the exit for St Paul's Cathedral. Turn left along Newgate Street until you reach Warwick Lane on the left, named after the Earls of Warwick, who had a house here in the 14th century. It's the site of the attractive, red-brick **Cutlers' Hall ❶**, the headquarters of the Cutlers' Company, our first example of an ancient City Livery Company.

There are 108 of these trade associations, most known as the 'Worshipful Company of' followed by their particular craft, profession or speciality. Like much in the City, they first developed in the Middle Ages as guilds: groups of tradesmen who banded together to protect their interests by regulating their trades, exerting control over labour conditions, wages and, most importantly, the import/export and sale of goods. Some of the Companies still have a professional role today, e.g. the Apothecaries' Company which awards postgraduate qualifications in some medical specialities, but most are now mainly charitable and social organisations.

Some Companies still operate a Hall, where members and their guests are entertained and business is transacted. Around 40 Companies have Halls in the City of London, including the Cutlers' Company. Its first building (in 1285) was on Poultry, from where it moved to a site on Cloak Lane and then to the current location on Warwick Lane in the 1880s.

Back to Newgate and cross over to visit the **Viaduct Tavern ❷** on the corner with Giltspur Street.

Viaduct Tavern

Cutlers' Hall

It's an ornate Victorian gin palace of the best sort, built in 1869 and named after the Holborn Viaduct. The magnificent interior sets this pub apart, including a beaten metal ceiling and elaborate woodwork and glass; the cellars were allegedly once part of Newgate Prison and can be viewed on request outside busy hours.

A right turn takes us up Giltspur Street. This ancient thoroughfare was once called Knightrider Street after the knights who rode along it to the tournaments in Smithfield wearing the gilt spurs that were manufactured here.

Giltspur Street was the place where the 1381 Peasants' Revolt came to a sticky end. Richard II met Wat Tyler and other leaders of the revolt on this street to discuss the peasants' dissatisfaction over the 'poll tax' but William Walworth, then Lord Mayor of London, took matters into his own hands, distracted Tyler and stabbed him to death.

The first left turn off Giltspur Street is the Cock Lane which gets its name from past association with carnal matters: in 14th-century London, it was one of few places where licensed prostitutes could solicit business. Look up at the wall of the building on the right to spot the **Golden Boy of Pye Corner** ❸, a cherub who was installed in 1910 to mark the westernmost reach of the Great Fire of London. The fact that the fire began in Pudding Lane and ended in Pie Corner led some to claim that it was divine punishment for the sin of gluttony.

Stroll up Giltspur Street to West Smithfield. In the Middle Ages this was an open space used for public entertainment such as jousting, sports – and executions. One infamous execution was that of the Scottish nationalist William 'Braveheart' Wallace, who was convicted of treason at Westminster Hall in 1305. He was dragged through the streets to West Smithfield, 'partly' hanged on the gallows, taken down and allowed to recover briefly, before his intestines were pulled from his body in front

statue of Henry VIII

St Barts features in several films, including *Four Weddings and a Funeral* (the fourth wedding, in which Hugh Grant almost marries Anna 'Duckface' Chancellor). The impressive medieval gatehouse is surmounted by a half-timbered Tudor building displaying impressive craftsmanship, built for Sir Philip Scudamore in the 16th century. Pass through the gate along Bartholomew Passage and look back to admire its reverse which has a beautiful patina of age.

of the crowd. His head ended up on a pike on London Bridge.

Curve to the right around West Smithfield and the gateway to St Bartholomew's Hospital's Minor Injuries Unit is on the right, with an impressive arch that displays London's only **statue of Henry VIII** ④. The gateway was built in 1702 by Edward Strong, while the statue is by Francis Bird and shows the king sporting an impressive codpiece. Continue ahead and at the end on the right is Little Britain. This street was built on land owned by the Dukes of Brittany and, from the late 15th century, was noted for its bookselling and printing industries. Charles Dickens sited the gloomy offices of the lawyer Mr Jaggers in *Great Expectations* in Little Britain.

To the left of Little Britain is an impressive **Tudor gatehouse** ⑤ that leads to the Priory Church of St Bartholomew the Great, which dates from 1123 and is one of London's oldest churches; Great

FOOD & DRINK

2 Viaduct Tavern: Friendly Fuller's pub with excellent beers and good old fashioned pub fayre (roasts). Closed weekends.

10 Piccolo Bar: Italian chain of cafés serving inexpensive pasta dishes, sandwiches and jacket potatoes. Closed weekends.

Turn right out of Bartholomew Passage, with Smithfield Market ahead, and right again down Cloth Fair, one of a series of atmospheric medieval streets.

Postman's Park

East Passage ⑧. At the end of Middle Street, turn left into Cloth Street then right along Long Lane before taking a sharp right into Aldersgate. Keep to the right of the street and past the roundabout, turn into the small park on the right. This is **Postman's Park** ⑨ (8am to dusk or 7pm), one of the City's largest parks – although still small – and the site of the poignant Memorial to Heroic Self Sacrifice (see box). The name Postman's Park reflects its popularity with workers from the nearby Post Office headquarters.

On leaving the park, turn right along St Martin's le Grand and left along Gresham Street, named after Sir Thomas Gresham, founder of the Royal Exchange and Gresham College. At number 7 on the left is the friendly, popular **Piccolo Bar** ⑩. It's part of a small

It's named after the annual Bartholomew Fair, held over three days around 24th August (St Bartholomew's Day) from 1133-1855. A short way along Cloth Fair at its junction with narrow Cloth Court on the left, **number 41** ⑥ is a rare surviving 17th-century merchant's house. Nearby, **43 Cloth Court** ⑦ is the former home of the late Poet Laureate Sir John Betjeman, who did much to preserve Britain's architectural heritage. He moved here in 1955, enchanted by the area's medieval street pattern and narrow alleys, but left in 1977 when he could no longer tolerate the noise of lorries serving nearby Smithfield Market.

Where Cloth Fair becomes Middle Street, on the left is another narrow medieval street,

The Memorial to Heroic Self Sacrifice dates from 1900 and was the brainchild of George Frederic Watts, a popular Victorian artist and philanthropist. He wanted to commemorate ordinary people who died saving others. The memorial comprises a series of plaques on a long wall under a loggia (parts are Grade II listed). The plaques are attractive, in the style of William Morris-style with Arts and Crafts lettering. The inscriptions are simple, brief and moving.

LEIGH PITT.
REPROGRAPHIC OPERATOR.
AGED 30. SAVED A DROWNING
BOY FROM THE CANAL AT
THAMESMEAD, BUT SADLY
WAS UNABLE TO SAVE
HIMSELF · JUNE · 7 · 2007

Italian chain, serving inexpensive dishes and sandwiches to take away or eat in the small dining room downstairs. Just past it, on the corner of Gresham Street and Noble Street, is the pleasant garden of **St Anne and St Agnes** ⑪, a Lutheran establishment. The first mention of a church on this site was in 1137, but it burned down in 1548 and was rebuilt. The second church was destroyed in the Great Fire, after which Wren built the current structure.

On the opposite corner to St Anne and St Agnes is the impressive number **25 Gresham Street** ⑫, by N. Grimshaw, built in 2002. It's a graceful structure with interesting external textures, tucked behind the remains of St John Zachary's Church. The church was destroyed in the Great Fire and the churchyard is now a sunken garden adjacent to the building's main entrance.

Continue along Gresham Street and at number **6** on the right is the historic **Wax Chandlers' Hall** ⑬, while its contemporary neighbour at **number 10** ⑭ is by Norman Foster. Number 10 was built 1996-2003 in an understated style to blend in with the area's older buildings; it's eight storeys high, made of glass and steel, with limestone cladding anchoring it to its surrounds. The Wax Chandlers' Company was established in 1358 and was originally based on the beeswax trade; today it's connected with 'modern applications of wax', such as furniture polish. The Company has owned the site since 1501 and this is the sixth hall here.

Further along Gresham Street and past the church of St Lawrence Jewry (see below) on the left is the entrance to the **Guildhall** ⑮, which has been the administrative base of the Corporation of the City of London for over 800 years. The name comes from its original function as a place where geld, i.e. money, was collected as tax. As well as having an administrative role, the Guildhall has long been a cultural venue: the Polish composer Chopin gave his last public performance here and it's where the UK's most important

Gresham Street

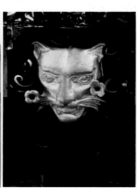

Guildhall

literary award, the Booker Prize, is presented. There's also an excellent Guildhall Art Gallery (Mon-Sat, 10am-5pm, Sun, 12-4pm), which houses the collection of the Corporation of London, assembled since the 17th century. Around 250 works are on display at any one time, out of a total collection of some 4,500, which includes works by Constable, Landseer, Millais and Rossetti.

On leaving the Guildhall, return to Gresham Street and turn right. Immediately on the right is the above-mentioned **St Lawrence Jewry** 16 (usually 8am-6pm), a Grade I listed church with a small, pretty water garden in front. The term Jewry refers to the area that was set aside for Jews before they were expelled from England in 1291. The first church was built here in 1136, named after St Lawrence, a deacon of Rome who was put to death in 258AD; it was rebuilt by Wren in 1671-77, with a handsome decorated east wall.

After the church, turn right along Aldermanbury, which means alderman's manor and dates to the 14th century. Follow it until you reach Aldermanbury Square for the imposing 18-storey **number f ve** 17, by Eric Parry Architects, completed in 2007. It contains 2,500 tonnes of stainless steel in the exterior, which is partly decorative but also conceals an external structural frame that allows the interior to be a column-free space.

Walking back along Aldermanbury, on the right is the peaceful, shady garden of **St Mary Aldermanbury** 18, opened in 1970. St Mary (see box) was another Wren church, a simple, spire-less building constructed after the Great Fire.

> St Mary Aldermanbury was badly damaged during WWII and most of what remained was, bizarrely, shipped to Fulton, Missouri, and reassembled there as a memorial to Winston Churchill.

ST PAUL'S & BARBICAN

Turn right along Love Lane and into Wood Street for some interesting buildings. In fact, there's a charming architectural anomaly literally in the middle of Wood Street: **St Alban Tower** ⑲, a private residence on a traffic island in a building that was originally the tower of a Wren church, destroyed in a bombing raid in 1941. By way of contrast, the nearby number **100 Wood Street** ⑳ is a modern building by another iconic British architect, Norman Foster. The two structures are typical of London, where the old coexists comfortably alongside the new. The Wood Street façade of number 100 is deliberately simple and conservative, as planning requirements dictated that it mustn't clash with its surroundings or be taller than the Wren tower house. The tower (Grade 1 listed) is all that remains of St Alban's church, built by Sir Christopher Wren in 1685 in Perpendicular Gothic style, the rest being destroyed during the Blitz of 1940.

At the northern end of Wood Street is the striking 18-storey **number 88** ㉑, on the corner with London Wall. It was built between 1993 and 2001, and is by renowned architect Sir Richard Rogers, who was also responsible for the Pompidou Centre in Paris and the nearby Lloyds of London headquarters.

Turn left along London Wall and on the corner with Noble Street on the left is the small **St Olave Silver Street Garden** ㉒. It's on the site of the 12th-century parish church of the silversmiths, also destroyed in the Great Fire and never rebuilt. Its legacy is a shady and peaceful garden, one of over 150 green sites in the City managed by the Corporation of London's Open Spaces Department, and a tranquil spot at which to end our walk.

To return to St Paul's tube station, continue left along London Wall, turn left along St Martin's le Grand, and follow it to the end.

St Alban Tower

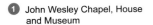

1. John Wesley Chapel, House and Museum
2. Armoury House
3. Britannic House
4. Salters' Hall
5. St Alphage Garden
6. Salters' Garden
7. Cripplegate
8. Armourers' Hall
9. Girdlers' Hall
10. Old Dr Butler's Head
11. Frederick's Place
12. Number One Poultry
13. St Margaret Lothbury
14. 7 Lothbury
15. Bank of England Museum
16. Simpsons Chop House
17. St Michael in Cornhill
18. 54-55 Cornhill
19. St Helen's Bishopsgate
20. Hoop and Grapes
21. Aldgate
22. Bevis Marks Synagogue
23. Heron Tower
24. Turkish Baths

Places of Interest   Food & Drink

Liverpool
Street
Station

**Liverpool
Street**

N WALL

OLD BROAD STREET

BISHOPSGATE

WORMWOOD ST

CAMOMILE ST

BEVIS MARKS

DUKE'S PL

Aldgate

HIGH

ALDGATE

LEADENHALL STREET

STREET

'The
Gherkin'

Lloyd's
building

24

23

19

22

21

20

17 **18**

sbury
rcus

PL

 val
ange

HILL

CHURCH ST

MBARD ST

OLD STREET
& LIVERPOOL
STREET

Distance: 2.49mi (4.01km)
Duration: half day
Start: Old Street tube station
End: Liverpool Street station

OLD ST & LIVERPOOL ST

The north-eastern corner of the City is bordered by City Road and Moorgate to the west, and Bishopsgate and Liverpool Street station to the east; its northernmost point is Old Street, while in the south it extends past Cornhill. At f rst glance, this part of London appears dedicated to the veneration of money; it's dominated by those twin temples to f nance and commerce, the Bank of England and the Royal Exchange, and populated by 'suits' dealing in stocks and shares. Our walk reveals some rather more spiritual attractions, including Britain's oldest synagogue, one of John Wesley's original chapels and some charming churches. One, St Helen's Bishopsgate, could claim to be London's oldest place of worship, its site dating back to pre-Christian times.

This is a district of great contrasts, where historic chop houses sit alongside modern sushi bars, and the halls of medieval city companies – the armourers, the salt traders, the makers of girdles and belts – are overshadowed by thrusting modern architectural icons such as Norman Foster's Gherkin and James Stirling's Number One Poultry.

Our walk takes in many of the better-known sights, from the absorbing Bank of England Museum and the ugly if appealing Barbican, as well as some more unexpected pleasures, such as the terracotta devils that glare down over Cornhill and what must be London's smallest Turkish baths.

Gherkin

OLD ST & LIVERPOOL ST

Start Walking...

We leave Old Street tube station by exit 4 and walk south down the left side of City Road, which was built in 1761. Old Street itself is much older and dates back to the 13th century or even earlier, and was the 'old' route from Aldersgate to the northeast of England. The first place of interest on City Road is the handsome **John Wesley Chapel, House and Museum** ❶, a short distance south of Old Street on the left. John Wesley (1703-91) founded the Methodist movement and the chapel opened in 1778, designed by noted architect George Dance the Younger. Wesley lived in the house next to it for the last 11 years of his life and is buried in the graveyard at the back.

Armoury House

century **Armoury House** ❷, the faux-castle headquarters of the Honourable Artillery Company, the oldest British Army regiment still in existence and based here since 1642. The regiment dates from 1296, but was officially incorporated in 1537 when Henry VIII gave a charter to a body of citizen archers, who later used artillery. The HAC's main role has traditionally been the defence of London, but it has also fought with distinction in foreign wars.

As you keep walking, City Road becomes Finsbury Pavement and then Moorgate. Finsbury Pavement was once a fashionable promenade and provided walkers with a dry route across the marshy area of Moorfields. The area outside the City walls was open fenland which gave it the name Finsbury. Nearby Moorgate takes its name from the medieval City gate which opened

John Wesley Chapel, House and Museum ❶
Mon-Sat, 10am-4pm,
Sun, 12.30-1.45pm

Turn left out of the Wesley Chapel and soon, on the right, is 18th-

Britannic House   Salters' Hall gates   Salters' Garden

on to the fens (or moors). Built in 1415, the gate was demolished in 1762 and its stones used to strengthen London Bridge to prevent it being swept away by tides.

At 100 Moorgate, next to Moorgate tube station, is **Britannic House** ❸, an attractive building with some interesting carvings. Designed by Sir Edwin Lutyens in the early '20s, it won a City Heritage Award and is regarded as the best of his large commercial buildings. The statue of Britannia on the corner is by Sir Francis Derwent Wood.

At the next major junction, take a right into busy London Wall and then right again into Fore Street. This is where author Daniel Defoe was born. Fore Street skirts the southern edge of the Barbican, which is a striking example of modern urban development to some, a concrete eyesore to others. Love it or loathe it, it dominates the skyline in this corner of the City. At number 4 Fore Street are the impressive gates of **Salters' Hall** ❹, the HQ

of the Salters' Company which was established in 1394. They've had a number of halls but the current one was designed by Sir Basil Spence and opened in 1976.

> Salt was a vital commodity in medieval times and was imported from western France and distributed by the Company's salters. Its importance as a commodity dates back to the Romans; the salt rations they received, the *sal*, is the basis of the word salary.

At the end of Fore Street, turn left down Wood Street and left again into **St Alphage Garden** ❺. Go down the small flight of wooden steps and you enter **Salters' Garden** ❻, an attractive, tranquil space, the silence disturbed only by the tinkling of fountains, with elegant planting and an impressive backdrop of a section of Roman wall.

Retrace your steps, pausing at Roman House at the junction of St Alphage Garden and Wood Street to read the plaque marking the site of **Cripplegate** ❼. This was one

Armourers' Hall

Girdlers' Hall

of the old medieval City gates and was demolished in 1760 so the street could be widened.

Turn left along Wood Street, cross London Wall at the end, walk left along it and turn right down Coleman Street, an ancient thoroughfare which use to be home to charcoal burners or 'coalmen'. **Armourers' Hall** ⑧ is on the left, advertising its presence with an eye-catching coat of arms. The Armourers' Company

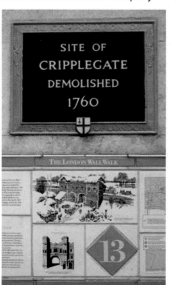

dates from 1322 and has used this site since 1346. The Hall survived the Great Fire but was rebuilt twice subsequently; the present building dating from 1840 is by J. H. Good, and contains an important collection of Dutch and Elizabethan paintings.

Continue down Coleman Street and turn right along Basinghall Avenue; the Basings were a wealthy City family in the 13th century. On the right is the attractive, elegant **Girdlers' Hall** ⑨. The girdlers – who made belts and girdles – have not had much luck with their halls – the first (1431) was destroyed in the Great Fire and the subsequent one flattened during the Blitz, although the current building – designed by C. Ripley – has stood undamaged since 1960. Its garden boasts an ancient mulberry tree.

At the end of Basinghall Avenue, take a sharp left down Basinghall Street. Opposite number 71 take the time to explore the narrow, atmospheric alleyway called Mason's Avenue, after the Masons' Company. At the end schedule a pit stop at the splendidly named **Old Dr Butler's Head** ⑩. It was founded in the early 17th century by Dr William Butler who was court physician to James I, despite having no medical training.

> One of Dr Butler's less 'creative' cures was a pint of his own ale. More bizarre, and less enjoyable, was his practice of discharging a pistol next to his patients' heads and dunking them in the Thames (those who complain about the NHS, please take note).

Carry on down Basinghall Street and turn left at the bottom into Gresham Street, before making an immediate right into Old Jewry, which was the site of the Great Synagogue until 1272; this area was set aside for Jews until their expulsion from England in the late 13th century. Turn right into **Frederick's Place** ⑪, a cul-de-sac with two Corporation of London blue plaques: one for Prime Minister Benjamin Disraeli and the other for accountant Edwin Waterhouse (of PricewaterhouseCoopers fame). Frederick's Place is noted for its attractive terraced houses, built by the Adam brothers in 1776, and was once the site of a house

owned by Sir John Frederick, Lord Mayor of London in 1661.

FOOD & DRINK

10 Old Dr Butler's Head: Shepherd Neame pub with a great selection of cask ales and traditional pub food. Closed weekends.

16 Simpsons Chop House (☎ 020-7626 9985): Old-fashioned chop house with bars and grill room serving traditional English fayre; breakfast and lunch only. Closed weekends.

20 Hoop and Grapes: Historic Nicholson's pub serving superb ales and good pub grub (sea bass, BBQ ribs, sausage and mash), including breakfast. Closed weekends.

BENJAMIN DISRAELI
PRIME MINISTER
IN 1868 AND 1874-1880
WORKED
IN THIS BUILDING
1821-1824

Frederick's Place

Turn right down Old Jewry and left along Poultry which is where the City's vendors of domestic fowl used to set up shop. Today it's dominated by the majestic **Number One Poultry** 12 which resembles an ocean liner landlocked on the City's streets.

This is one of London's better postmodern buildings, designed by James Stirling in the second half of the 20th century, although some commentators think it's stodgy and outdated. As is typical of postmodernism, the building's imagery is reference-rich: the turret is like a submarine's conning tower, while the clock is fashioned after the Fascist-era central post office in Naples.

At the junction ahead, turn left up Princes Street and right along Lothbury. The name may come from 'lod', a drain or cut leading into a larger stream the Walbrook in this instance, or Lod which is short for the splendidly-named Albertus Loteringus, a canon of St Paul's who lived here at the time of the Norman conquest. Lothbury may also have developed from Lottenbury, a place where founders cast candlesticks and other copper items. Founders were certainly here in the early Middle Ages, but by the 18th century merchants and bankers had moved in and the south side of Lothbury is occupied by the Bank of England.

Opposite the Bank's imposing stone walls is **St Margaret Lothbury** 13 (Mon-Fri, 7.15am-5.15pm), an attractive church surrounded by office buildings. There's been a church here since 1181 or 1197 (sources vary); this one is by Sir Christopher Wren and dates from 1686-90, with

Number One Poultry

St Margaret Lothbury

7 Lothbury

an attractive, nicely-proportioned interior. Of particular note is the baptismal font, the work of Grinling Gibbons (1648-1721); born and trained in Holland, he was widely regarded as the best wood carver working in England in the late 17th century. His work can be found in many places, including St Paul's Cathedral, Blenheim Palace and Hampton Court Palace.

Next to St Margaret Lothbury is the stylish **7 Lothbury** ⑭, the winner of a City Heritage Award. It was designed in 1866 by G. S. Clarke the Elder and is the City's best example of Victorian Gothic architecture. The pink and white colours of the exterior result from mixing different-coloured stones rather than using paint or stucco, and the building also has interesting carved and sculpted detail.

Turn right down Bartholomew Lane and you're soon standing at the entrance to the fascinating **Bank of England Museum** ⑮ (Mon-Fri, 10am-5pm).

> There are several theories are to how Threadneedle Street got its name. It may come from the Three Needles in the coat of arms of the Needlemakers' Company or the thread and needle used by the Merchant Taylors.

The museum tells the story of the Bank (nicknamed the Old Lady of Threadneedle Street)

from its foundation in 1694 to its current role as the UK's central bank. Displays include Roman and modern gold bars, and you can test the weight of one: at 28lb (12.7kg) it's surprisingly, but reassuringly, heavy. There's also a display about Kenneth Grahame, author of *Wind in the Willows*, who worked at the bank for 30 years and thwarted an armed robbery in 1893.

When you leave the museum, turn right along Bartholomew Lane, left along Threadneedle Street and right behind the Royal Exchange building to reach Cornhill. Cross it, turn right and tucked away to the left is the short Ball Court, which is home to **Simpsons Chop House** ⑯. Simpsons is a rare, well-preserved example of what was once a City institution: the chop and coffeehouse, where businessmen gathered in the 17th and 18th centuries. Established in 1757, the building dates from the late 17th or early 18th century, with a 19th-century ground floor shop front.

Leaving Ball Court, turn right along Cornhill and soon on the same side of the street is the attractive church of **St Michael in Cornhill** ⑰ (Mon-Fri, 8.30am-5pm). It stands near the site of a church founded by King Lucius in AD 179 – the oldest known site of Christian worship in London. The church is first mentioned in 1055, but the present structure is by Sir Christopher Wren, built 1670-72,

with a tower by his pupil Nicholas Hawksmoor dating from 1718-22. The church is noted for its excellent acoustics and has a long musical tradition.

Cornhill is one of the three hills in the City; the others are Tower Hill and Ludgate Hill. In earlier times, Cornhill was the location of a Roman basilica and, later, a medieval grain market, after which it's named. Today, it hosts an unusually large number of opticians.

Look up to view the attractive red-brick frontage of **54-55 Cornhill** ⑱ and the striking devils

St Michael in Cornhill

Simpsons Chop House

observing the street from their splendid vantage point. The building, by Ernest Runze, dates from 1893 and is clad in Doulton terracotta. The devils were designed by Victorian architect W. J. Neatby and are supposedly his revenge on the rector of nearby St Peter's, who forced the architects to revise their plans because the originals impinged on church land.

Bevis Marks Synagogue 22
Mon, Wed and Thu, 10.30am-2pm, Tue and Fri, 10.30am-1pm, Sun, 10.30am-12.30pm, £4 adults.

At the end of Cornhill, turn left along Bishopsgate, which in Tudor and Elizabethan times was an upmarket residential area, home to a number of rich merchants. A quick right into St Helen's Place, named after the eerie-sounding Black Nuns of St Helen's, whose hall was located here, leads to the twin-naved church of **St Helen's Bishopsgate** 19 (Mon-Fri, 9.30am-12.30pm and some afternoons). This compact, pretty place of worship contains more monuments than any other London church, except Westminster Abbey.

This is thought to be an ancient religious site: the first church is reputed to have been built on the site of a pagan temple by the Emperor Constantine when he converted to Christianity in the 4th century. The present church dates from the 12th century, although there have been many alterations since, and it was restored in 1994-7 following the IRA bombings in 1992 and 1993 (the first in St Mary Axe, the second on Bishopsgate).

Norman Foster's (Baron Foster of Thames Bank) Gherkin, one of London's newest architectural icons, sits directly behind St Helen's, appearing to emerge from the church's roof.

Walk behind the church to St Mary Axe, turn right along it and left along Leadenhall Street, which takes its name from a mansion with a lead roof owned by the Neville family in the 14th century. Cross to the right and as you reach the end of Leadenhall Street, cross at the traffic lights into Aldgate High Street. Further along on the right opposite Aldgate tube station is the **Hoop and Grapes** 20, which claims to be the City's oldest licensed premises, with foundations dating from the 13th century. The current building, timbered and slightly wonky, dates back to the 16th or 17th century, while the cellars are reputed to contain a (now-sealed) tunnel leading to the Tower of London.

Cross Aldgate High Street, walk back past Aldgate tube and

cross at the next set of traffic lights, heading for Sir John Cass's Foundation Primary School. There's a plaque on the school's wall about **Aldgate** 21, one of the six original Roman City gates. The Saxons knew it as Ealdgate.

Next to the school is Dukes Place, possibly named after a mansion once owned by Thomas Howard, the Duke of Norfolk, leads into Bevis Marks, On the left in a courtyard is the attractive, 18th-century **Bevis Marks Synagogue** 22 (Mon, Wed and Thu, 10.30am-2pm, Tue and Fri, 10.30am-1pm, Sun, 10.30am-12.30pm, £4 adults). This is Britain's oldest synagogue (next door is the synagogue's kosher restaurant), built in 1701 for an influx of Jews from the Iberian Peninsula. City authorities insisted that the entrance be on a side street, as they were worried about the reaction of locals.

On leaving the synagogue, turn left and follow the street as it becomes first Camomile Street and then Wormwood Street. Before you cross Bishopsgate, look back to view the sky-scraping **Heron Tower** 23, located at 110 Bishopsgate and owned by property development company Heron International. Completed in 2011, it rises to 755ft (230m), including a 91ft (28m) mast, making it the tallest building in the City.

> In 2012, Heron Tower was London's third-tallest tower, after One Canada Square (also called, incorrectly, Canary Wharf) and The Shard at London Bridge, the tallest building (so far) in the European Union.

From Wormwood Street, turn right down Old Broad Street, a fashionable place to live in the 16th and 17th centuries. Turn right into Bishopsgate Churchyard and complete the walk at the decorative, anomalous **Turkish Baths** 24 building, a hidden gem tucked away in a small square surrounded by tall office blocks. It was built in 1895 for Nevill's Turkish Baths Limited to house a new Turkish bath, which were popular and commonplace in Victorian London. It's one of London's more unusual buildings, designed in the decorative Ottoman style. The baths remained open until 1954, after which the building was used for storage and subsequently became a restaurant.

To reach the Liverpool Street station, continue ahead and turn left along Bishopsgate; the station is on the left soon after.

Heron Tower

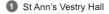

1. St Ann's Vestry Hall
2. Small garden
3. Apothecaries' Hall
4. Blue plaque commemorating Blackfriars Priory
5. Wardrobe Place
6. City of London Youth Hostel
7. The Old Deanery
8. Côte
9. Angel head sculptures
10. Amen Court
11. Temple Bar
12. Paternoster Square
13. Shepherd and Sheep sculpture
14. Christchurch Greyfriars Garden
15. St Vedast Garden
16. 150 Cheapside
17. Bow Lane
18. St Mary-le-Bow
19. 21 and 22/23 College Hill
20. Blue plaques
21. Stained glass window of Dick Whittington and his cat
22. Salvation Army International Headquarters
23. College of Arms
24. St Benet's Church
25. Black Friar

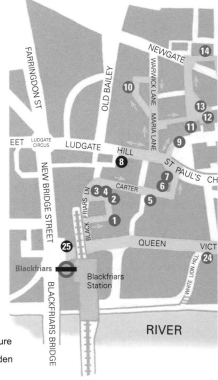

● Places of Interest   ● Food & Drink

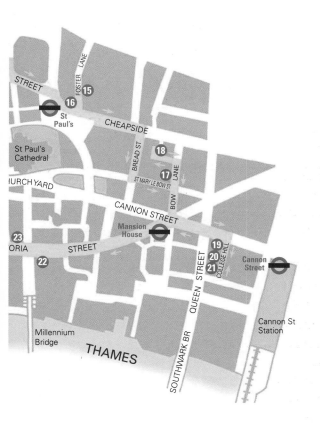

BLACKFRIARS & MANSION HOUSE

Distance: 1.78mi (2.86km)
Duration: half day
Start/end: Blackfriars station

The City's south-western quarter hugs the River Thames from Blackfriars to Monument, with Cheapside and Cornhill marking its northern reaches. This part of the City has a number of highlights, not least St Paul's Cathedral, which stands on the apex of Ludgate Hill, one of the highest points in the city. Sir Christopher Wren's graceful dome has dominated the London skyline for 300 years and still does, despite the modern skyscrapers which have reared up around it.

Our walk also takes us past the venerable Mansion House, off cial home of the Lord Mayor of London – not to be confused with the publically elected Mayor of London who is tucked away south of the river at City Hall – and through Blackfriars, named for the cloaks of the Dominican Friars who moved their priory to the area in the 13th century.

Many famous (and infamous) people have walked these streets before you. We follow their footsteps to discover some less obvious attractions, such

as the remains of a playhouse which William Shakespeare once owned, the church whose bells called Dick Whittington (and his cat) back to off ce in London, and the streets where Guy Fawkes plotted the downfall of James I in 1605 by blowing up the House of Lords. We end at a pub which has been a favourite watering hole of writers, poets and, more recently, Fleet Street's f nest.

Start Walking…

Leaving Blackfriars station, turn left and cross busy Queen Victoria Street, which was built 1867-71 and is an unusually straight thoroughfare by London's standards. Turn right up Blackfriars Lane and right again into Playhouse Yard. This was the original site of the Blackfriars Playhouse which was built in the 1590s by James Burbage in some of the disused Blackfriars Priory buildings. Shakespeare had a share in the theatre and his company, The King's Players, performed here. It was demolished in 1655 and only a fragment of wall survives.

At the end of Playhouse Yard is Church Entry, which once led to the church of St Ann Blackfriars, destroyed in the Great Fire. Follow this narrow passageway to view **St Ann's Vestry Hall** ❶ on the right. The Grade II listed Hall was built by Bannister Fletcher

& Sons in 1905, with a façade in the Edwardian Baroque style. It has a rather poignant sign on the front declaring 'Ancient Monuments Society, Friends of Friendless Churches', which refers to two organisations run from this location.

Just after the hall, a short flight of steps on the left descends to a **small garden** ❷ (8am-7pm, or dusk if earlier). This shady spot marks the site of the church nave of the original medieval Dominican Priory of Blackfriars which stood here until it was dissolved in 1538 by Henry VIII, having moved from Holborn in 1276. Turn and reprise your route back to Blackfriars Lane, where another right turn brings you to the **Apothecaries' Hall** ❸. The Apothecaries bought the site in 1632. Their original Hall was destroyed by the Great Fire and rebuilt in 1688 by Thomas Lock, and remains almost unaltered today, except for some modifications in 1779 and 1927.

St Ann's Vestry Hall

Apothecaries' Hall

WALK 4

Turn right again into Carter Lane, which is named after two 14th-century residents, Stephen and Thomas Le Charatter; on the right-hand corner is a **blue plaque commemorating Blackfriars Priory** ❹ (see above). We are now in one of the most attractive and historic parts of the City, with lots of delightful medieval streets leading off Carter Lane, although this area is little known except to workers in the nearby offices and trading houses. It's also an area steeped in history: Guy Fawkes and his co-conspirators plotted their Gunpowder Plot here at Hart's Horn Tavern, though the pub has long gone.

The Old Deanery

Further along Carter Lane on the right is **Wardrobe Place** ❺, on the site of the former garden of the King's Wardrobe (see box). Wardrobe Place is a wide, attractive court with plane trees and some late 17th- or early 18th-century houses. It's a fine example of the once-common City residential courts, which were (and still are) very civilised places to live.

The King's Wardrobe was a large 14th-century house used by Edward III to store his ceremonial robes, which was destroyed in the Great Fire. The Wardrobe was also where medieval monarchs kept their armour, gold and precious stones.

At number 36 Carter Lane, on the corner with Dean's Court which leads off to the left, is an unusual and eye-catching late 19th-century building in the Italianate style. It's the former St Paul's Choir School, now restored and home to the **City of London Youth Hostel** ❻. Turn left down Dean's Court, which dates from 1670, for a short walk to the site of **The Old Deanery** ❼. Designed by Sir Christopher Wren, it used to be the official residence of the Dean of St Paul's and is now the palace of the Bishop of London.

At the top of Dean's Court, turn left along Ludgate Hill. It's named after the Lud Gate, which some sources claim was built by King Lud in 66BC, although it's more likely to have been the gate to a Roman burial ground in what is now Fleet Street. At number 26 is **Côte** ❽, a branch of the deservedly popular and well-regarded chain of French bistros. On leaving Côte, return the way you came along Ludgate Hill, cross the road and head towards St Paul's Cathedral and into St Paul's Churchyard to view the **angel head sculptures** 9; five large sculpted angel heads (Emily Young, 2003) carved of Purbeck stone, which sit atop columns set beneath the portico of 100 Juxon House.

From St Paul's Churchyard, and with the cathedral behind you, turn right and head west a short distance along Ludgate Hill. Turn right down Ave Maria Lane, which is first mentioned in 1603; the name may be from a stage in the processions of the St Paul's Cathedral clergy. Just after Ave Maria Lane becomes Warwick Lane, on the left is elegant **Amen Court** 10, apparently named for the prayers said at nearby St Paul's.

Amen Court is a surprising, tranquil haven in the heart of the City. This horseshoe-shaped street's late 17th-century houses provide accommodation for

Amen Court

the cathedral's canons and other staff. The Campaign for Nuclear Disarmament (CND) was founded here in 1958 in the flat of John Collins, canon of St Paul's. Amen Court is private and belongs to the cathedral, so isn't officially open to the public, but if you're discreet you can walk around it. A second entrance to Amen Court further along Warwick Lane has an impressive gatehouse.

> Amen Court is said to be haunted by the black dog of Newgate. This canine apparition was said to appear before executions took place at the nearby prison and, apparently, can sometimes be spotted crawling along the court's ivy-clad walls.

Return down Ave Maria Lane and take the pedestrianised passageway on the left, with a large, modern sculpture in the middle (Angel's Wings, Thomas

angel head sculptures

Temple Bar

St Vedast Garden

Heatherwick), to a square at the end. To the right is **Temple Bar** ⑪, which sits in **Paternoster Square** ⑫. Temple Bar originally marked the westernmost point of the City, and was situated accordingly. It's first mentioned in 1293, when it was just a chain between wooden posts. A gate had been erected by the mid-14th century and was rebuilt by Sir Christopher Wren in the 1670s; traitors' heads were displayed on it until 1746. The handsome gate was removed in 1878 due to traffic congestion and for a century was kept on an estate in Hertfordshire; it was rebuilt on Paternoster Square in 2004.

The square itself was named after the Pater Noster makers (turners of rosary or prayer beads) who used to live here. From the 17th century until 1889 it was home to a less tranquil trade when it was the site of Newgate Meat Market, where 600 sheep and 50 bullocks were slaughtered daily. Today, this traffic-free square offers splendid views of St Paul's Cathedral. It boasts a 75ft (23m) high column of Portland stone, topped by a gold-leafed urn which is illuminated at night; a decoration rather than a memorial. Across the square is a fine sculpture, **Shepherd and Sheep** ⑬, by Dame Elizabeth Frink (1930-93).

Leave Paternoster Square by the far side, with the cathedral behind you, emerging onto Newgate Street. This is named after the medieval gate which guarded the main route west out of the City, and which was also used as a jail until one was built on the site of the Old Bailey in the 1420s. Straight ahead, across the road, is the pretty **Christchurch Greyfriars Garden** ⑭, on the site of the nave of Christchurch Greyfriars which was destroyed during the Blitz.

FOOD & DRINK

8 Côte
(☎ 020-7236 4399): French bistro chain serving classic dishes such as steak frites and moules marinières and good wines at reasonable prices.

25 Black Friar: Nicholson's pub with award-winning ales, traditional pub grub – great pies!

From the garden, turn left along Newgate Street and cross a couple of pedestrian crossings until you reach Cheapside, where you turn up Foster Lane on your left. Foster is apparently a corruption of St Vedast, to whom the church on the street is dedicated; he was a 6th-century French Bishop of Arras. **St Vedast Garden** ⑮ is on the right of Foster Lane, reached through a small entrance past the main church door (Mon-Fri, 8am-6pm). It's a secluded courtyard garden with

a number of commemorative plaques and a wall-mounted section of Roman pavement which was found below the floor of St Matthew Friday Street, demolished in 1886. The garden declares itself 'a place for quiet and reflection', a rare treat in the frenetic financial centre of London. There's been a church here since 1100, the current one being rebuilt by Wren after the Great Fire.

Returning down Foster Lane and at the end on the right opposite St Vedast church is **150 Cheapside** ⑯, a building by Michael Aukett. It's a solid rather than ground-breaking construction, but was required to blend in with its historic surroundings. Nine storeys high, it's sleek and contemporary, built of glass and Portland Stone. Cheapside itself

150 Cheapside

Bow Lane

is much older and was London's main market in medieval times, ceap or chepe being an old term for market. There was a decisive battle here on 20th December 1066 (two months after the Battle of Hastings) – dubbed the Battle of London – between the Saxons, led by Edgar the Aetheling, and William the Conqueror's Normans.

> Cheapside has a rich heritage as the birthplace of some famous Londoners, including one-time Archbishop of Canterbury Thomas à Becket and cookery writer Mrs Beeton.

Turn left along Cheapside, cross over and swing right down Bread Street. This was once an important route from Cheapside market to Queenhithe Dock and was the site of London's medieval bread market. The poet John Milton was born here, as a blue plaque attests. Turn left down Watling Street, which is first mentioned in 1230 and is probably an offshoot from the major Roman highway of the same name that ran between Dover and St Albans via London.

Atmospheric **Bow Lane** 17 cuts across Watling Street and gives an idea of what the City must have been like in the 17th century. Bow Lane used to be called Cordwainer Street after the *cordonniers* (French for shoemakers) who traded here; today it's one of the City's most attractive thoroughfares. Take the left turn into Bow Lane to find Bow Churchyard, the site of **St Mary-le-Bow** 18.

St Mary-le-Bow 18
Mon-Wed, 7.30am-6pm, Thu, 7.30am-6.30pm, Fri, 7.30am-4pm.

BLACKFRIARS & MANSION HOUSE

St Mary-le-Bow

St Mary-le-Bow is the most prominent of the City's 39 churches and only those born within the sound of its bells can call themselves a true Cockney. Legend has it, the sound of these bells drew Dick Whittington back to London from Highgate to become the City's Lord Mayor. The first church here was built in around 1080 on marshy land and had to be reinforced with bow arches, hence the name; the Norman crypt remains. The church was rebuilt by Wren after the Great Fire and the 216ft (66m) spire is one of his most striking.

Follow Bow Lane to its southern end, crossing Watling Street and heading towards Mansion House, then turn left and cross Queen Victoria Street to the south side of Cannon Street. Turn right down College Hill and admire the architecturally-interesting buildings at **numbers 21 & 22/23 19**, which are notable for their fine 17th-century stone gateways.

This street has a number of **blue plaques 20**, two of which commemorate Dick Whittington (1354-1423), merchant, Member of Parliament, four times Lord Mayor of London and also sheriff of London. He lived in College Hill and in 1422 was buried at St Michael Paternoster Royal church at the bottom on the left, which he had built. It's worth a visit, if only for the attractive **stained glass window of Dick Whittington and his cat 21**. College Hill derives its name from the fact that Mr Whittington built the College of St Spirit and St Mary to ensure that his soul went to heaven.

Return to Cannon Street, turn left and on reaching Queen Victoria Street continue past Mansion House tube station until you come to the **Salvation Army International Headquarters 22**, on the left. This chic building was completed in 2005. Glass is used extensively to provide openness and transparency; through it you can see the raked concrete legs that support the upper floors, an interesting visual touch. Opposite, by way of contrast, is the **College of Arms 23**, the elegant 17th-century home of the royal heralds.

Salvation Army HQ

It was first granted a charter in 1484 and is still active, examining and recording pedigrees and granting coats of arms.

St Benet's Church 24, which is further west and on the south side of the street, is a small, beautiful, Grade I listed building, which is almost square and resembles a Dutch country church. The graceful tower is surmounted by a dome and cupola topped by a ball and weather vane, while the interior has Corinthian columns and a beautiful altarpiece. Much of the church remains as when Sir Christopher Wren designed it over 300 years ago, although there's been a church on the site for much longer (since 1111). It's sometimes known as St Benet's Welsh church – this dates to 1879, when Queen Victoria granted Welsh Anglicans the right to worship here in perpetuity in their own language; this has continued every Sunday since.

If you fancy a drink or a bite to eat at the end of your walk, then the historic **Black Friar** 25 pub, mentioned in Walk 1 (see page 24), is highly recommended. To reach it continue west along Queen Victoria Street and it's at number 174 on the corner of New Bridge Street.

Blackfriars station is almost opposite the pub.

St Benet's Church

St Michael Paternoster Royal, Dick Whittington window

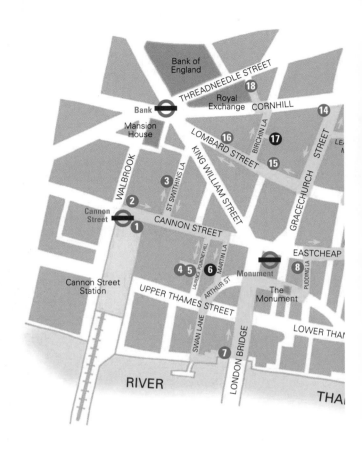

1. Cannon Place
2. Walbrook Building
3. New Court Project
4. 1 and 2 Laurence Pountney Hill
5. Rectory House
6. The Old Wine Shades
7. Fishmongers' Hall
8. Pudding Lane
9. Number 33-35 Eastcheap
10. St Dunstan-in-the-East Church Garden
11. Minster Court
12. St Olave's Church
13. Leadenhall Market
14. St Peter's Cornhill
15. Banners and coats-of-arms
16. Gresham grasshopper
17. George & Vulture
18. Royal Exchange Building

● Places of Interest   ● Food & Drink

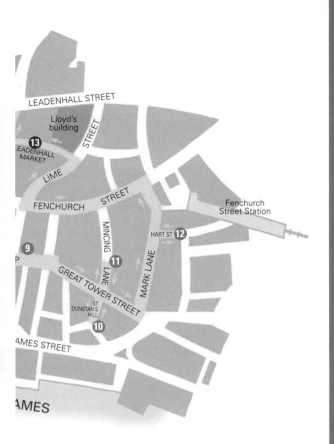

LEADENHALL STREET

Lloyd's
building

STREET

13

LEADENHALL
MARKET

LIME

STREET

FENCHURCH

STREET

Fenchurch
Street Station

MINCING

HART ST **12**

9

11

MARK LANE

GREAT TOWER STREET

LANE

ST
DUNSTAN'S
HILL

10

AMES STREET

AMES

CANNON
STREET TO
THE TOWER

CANNON STREET TO THE TOWER

Distance: 1.59mi (2.56km)
Duration: half day
Start: Cannon Street station
End: Bank tube station

Our f nal City walk takes in the south-eastern quarter of the Square Mile. It zigzags east from Cannon Street station towards the Tower of London – which is just outside the City's boundaries – before heading north to Fenchurch Street and looping back towards the Royal Exchange. This part of London has always been associated with wealth and power. A thousand years ago its authority was embodied by the Tower which was London's f rst great castle, prison, armoury and mint – and is still home to Royal treasure in the form of the Crown Jewels. By the 21st century, the power base had moved further west to the area around Lombard Street, now at the heart of the UK's f nancial district.

Trade has always been the lifeblood of the City. In the past, its residents made their money from buying and selling everything from f sh and meat to corn and lime, as many street names bear witness to. Our walk explores old market places, such as Leadenhall Market and the Royal Exchange, which are now home to smart boutiques and restaurants. In between there are some fascinating old taverns, as well as graceful churches and peaceful gardens where you can escape the hustle and bustle of City life. Along the way we discover why Lombard Street is inhabited by so many grasshoppers and what went into the puddings in Pudding Lane.

Tower of London

CANNON STREET TO THE TOWER

Start Walking...

We start this walk at Cannon Street station, pausing to admire its gleaming new façade. The station was built 1865-67 on a site in use for at least 2,000 years: the 1st-century Roman governor's palace was here and the Hanseatic League had a trading base here – called the Steelyard, after the large scales used to weigh imported items – from the 12th-16th centuries.

The station was refurbished in the last decade and is now topped by **Cannon Place** ❶, a sleek, steel and glass development completed in 2011. Cross Cannon Street, turn right and then left along Salter's Hall Court for the equally modern and arresting **Walbrook Building** ❷, named after the Walbrook River which was Roman London's starting point and main water supply.

The Walbrook Building is a striking addition to the City's growing list of innovative, creative structures – curved, metallic and sensuous. Built in 2009 by Foster and Partners, it's encased in 'solar shading' to keep it cool in summer and warm in winter. There's a small garden by the building in Salter's Hall Court, which contains a memorial sculpture dedicated to Catrin Glyndŵr and to the suffering of all women and children in war. This was formerly the churchyard of ancient St Swithin's and contains the grave of hostage Catrin Glyndŵr, the daughter of Owain Glyndŵr, a legendary 15th-century hero of Welsh independence. You can admire the other side of the building from the street called Walbrook: turn right out of Salter's Hall Court and it's the first on the right.

Walbrook Building

Cannon Street station

New Court Project

Rectory House

Back to Cannon Street, turn left past Salter's Hall Court and take the next left into St Swithin's Lane – a narrow, atmospheric street. This is the site of another eye-catching modern building, **New Court Project** ❸, the new headquarters of the bank N. M. Rothschild and Sons. It's their third building on the site and the first UK project by the Pritzker Prize-winning architect, Rem Koolhaas.

Retrace your footsteps to cross Cannon Street, turn left and take the next right down the steep Laurence Pountney Hill, a narrow passageway between the Bank of China and a branch of the Halifax at 100 Cannon Street. It's named after the church of St Laurence Pountney (lost in the Great Fire). On the right near the bottom of the hill you can enjoy the architectural delight of numbers **1 and 2 Laurence Pountney Hill** ❹. Built in 1703, these are the finest early 18th-century houses remaining in the City. Designed to mirror each other as a pair, they're notable for the rich friezes around the doors, which are reached up a flight of steps.

The hill opens into a square. On the left is the attractive **Rectory House** ❺, parts of which date to the 14th century; it also boasts a section of Roman wall in the basement. It was rebuilt in 1678 after the Great Fire and is now a Grade II listed private residence and a winner of a City Heritage Award. Opposite Rectory House is a blue plaque marking the site of Laurence Pountney Church and Corpus Christi College, both destroyed in the Great Fire.

Climb back up to Cannon Street, turn right and right again down Martin Lane, which is

Fishmongers' Hall

named after the church of St Martin Orgar, demolished in 1820 and commemorated by another blue plaque. At the bottom on the right is **The Olde Wine Shades** ❻, an atmospheric drinking establishment that's now part of the El Vino chain.

The Shades was a popular name for drinking dens in the 18th and 19th centuries, not for their shady clientele but because as they were often sited underground or protected from the sun by an arcade.

It claims to be the oldest 'wine bar' in the City; a lead cistern in the garret is dated 1663, although the attractive frontage is early Victorian.

Continue down Martin Lane as it leads into Arthur Street, then veer to the right and cross Upper Thames Street. In medieval London, Thames Street had some impressive houses, most of which were lost in the Great Fire. Go straight ahead down Swan Lane, which leads towards the river; the sleek, modern building on the corner was the site of Dyers' Hall from 1545-1681.

At the end of Swan Lane, turn left along Fishmongers' Hall Wharf, part of the Thames Path, until you reach **Fishmongers' Hall** ❼ on the left. Their first hall dated to 1310 and the next, which was on the present site, was bequeathed to the Fishmongers' Company in 1434 and was lost in the Great Fire. The current hall was built in 1834 and restored after being badly damaged during the Blitz in 1940. Fish had a religious significance in the medieval diet which made the Fishmongers' Company wealthy and influential; among its riches is a fine collection of 17th- and 18th-century silver plate, as well as the dagger with which Lord Mayor Walworth, a fishmonger, stabbed Wat Tyler to death at Smithfield in 1381.

The Fishmongers' Company is one of the few City Livery Companies that still performs its original function. It's also responsible for organising the oldest annual event in British sport, Doggett's Coat and Badge Race, which is rowed over a 4.5m (7.4km) course from London Bridge to Chelsea. It's named after Thomas Doggett, an actor who in 1715 presented a coat and silver badge as a prize to be competed for annually by six Thames watermen.

Just past the Fishmonger's Hall, take the steps up to King William Street (which is a continuation of London Bridge), turn left along it, cross the road and continue ahead, before taking the first turn on the right, Monument Street. Turn left up **Pudding Lane** 8, where the Great Fire of London started on 2nd September 1666 in Farryner's bakery, commemorated by a sign at the end of this short lane.

Pudding Lane gets its name from the 'puddings' of animals, i.e. guts and entrails, which were transported down the lane from butchers' shops on Eastcheap on their way to the Thames dung barges.

At the top of Pudding Lane, turn right into Eastcheap, which was the site of London's meat market in medieval times. **Number 33-35 Eastcheap** 9 divides opinion: it's by Victorian architect Robert Louis Roumieu and is either a remarkable Gothic brick confection or an ugly, over-the-top carbuncle, depending on your perspective. It was built in 1868 as a wine and vinegar warehouse on the site of the famous Boar's Head Tavern, where Shakespeare's Falstaff was a regular.

Directly opposite is Lovat Lane, one of the City's narrow, atmospheric alleys where it's easy to imagine times past; at the bottom is a fine view of The Shard building. Lovat Lane used to be called Love Lane, possibly because it was frequented by prostitutes. The name was changed in 1939 to avoid confusion with another Love Lane in the City (EC2 rather than EC3). Return to Eastcheap, turn right and continue into Great Tower

Pudding Lane plaque

NEAR THIS SITE STOOD THE SHOP BELONGING TO THOMAS FARYNER. THE KING'S BAKER. IN WHICH THE GREAT FIRE OF SEPTEMBER 1666 BEGAN.

PRESENTED BY THE WORSHIPFUL COMPANY OF BAKERS TO MARK THE 500th ANNIVERSARY OF THEIR CHARTER GRANTED BY KING HENRY VII IN 1486

Number 33-35 Eastcheap

Street, which leads down towards the Tower of London. Take another right down St Dunstan's Hill, with the seemingly ever-present Shard ahead, until you come to the lovely **St Dunstan-in-the-East Church Garden** ❿ (8am-7pm or dusk) on the right, the prettiest and most charming garden in the City.

St Dunstan-in-the-East church was built on the site in Saxon times, named after a Saxon Archbishop of Canterbury, as was St Dunstan-in-the-West which still stands on Fleet Street. The church here was rebuilt by Wren in 1697 but only the tower survived the Blitz, which has been occupied by a complementary medical clinic since 1990.

Heading back up to Great Tower Street, cross over to the strikingly-named Mincing Lane, so-called after the *myncheus*

(nuns) of St Helen's Bishopsgate (and nothing to do with mince pies). Head down Mincing Lane to admire the monolithic pile **Minster Court** ⓫, a blend of Gothic and Art Deco, and aptly nicknamed Dracula's Castle. Built in 1991 by the GMW Partnership, it comprises three linked office buildings surrounding a partially glazed, covered courtyard.

Return and take the next left turn off Great Tower Street into Mark Lane, possibly a corruption of Mart Lane, from the market held here in the reign of Edward I. Turn right along Hart Street – where hearths were once made – to **St Olave's Church** ⓬ (Mon-Fri, 9am-5pm). A wooden church stood here in the 11th century, replaced by a stone building in the 13th century.

St Olave's Church

Five City churches are dedicated to King Olav Haraldsson, a Norwegian monarch who was canonised for his services to Christendom (he was martyred in 1030). Olav allied himself with Ethelred the Unready in his battle against the Danes at London Bridge in 1014 and helped ensure victory by using his long-boats to topple the bridge.

The current church was built in 1450 (the 13th-century crypt remains) and restored in the '50s after Blitz damage. It isn't particularly striking externally, but the interior is, ornate in parts and an impressive survivor from medieval times; John Betjeman thought St Olave's was more like a country church than anything you would expect to find in the City. The ornate pulpit is by Grinling Gibbons.

Return to Mark Lane, turn right and head north to Fenchurch Street, where, at the junction, the distinction shape of the Gherkin looms large ahead. Fenchurch Street is an old thoroughfare, and may be named after the hay market in Gracechurch Street (*faenum* is Latin for hay). Archaeological digs here have revealed 3,000-year-old urns and Roman pavements.

Turn left and stroll west along Fenchurch Street until you reach the right-hand turn for Lime Street, another old thoroughfare where lime burners and sellers had their base. Take Lime Street Passage on the left to **Leadenhall Market** ⑬, which is built on the site of the east part of the 2nd-century Roman forum. Trade was carried out here from the 14th century, becoming a general market in the 15th century. The current elegant, ornate structure dates from 1889 and was built by Sir Horace Jones in cast-iron and

Leadenhall Market

stone; market stalls have now given way to smart shops and restaurants.

FOOD & DRINK

6 The Olde Wine Shades (☎ 020-7626 6876): A venerable wine bar serving international cuisine, with a lunchtime self-service buffet, cellar restaurant and alfresco tables. Closed weekends.

13 Leadenhall Market: A variety of cafés, pubs and restaurants.

16 George & Vulture (☎ 020-7626 9710): Georgian restaurant with a British menu of favourites such as whitebait, steak & kidney pie, roast beef and Barnsley chops. Open Mon-Fri, noon to 2.45pm only.

Take the Gracechurch Street exit from the market almost opposite Ede and Ravenscourt, London's oldest tailor and robe

St Peter's Cornhill

maker (1689). To the left of the shop, narrow St Peter's Alley leads to the church of **St Peter's Cornhill** 14. The first reference to a church here is in 1040, but legend has it that one was founded on the site in 179AD by Lucius, the first Christian king of Britain. The present church is by Sir Christopher Wren and its church garden is a peaceful spot to bide awhile in this bustling part of London. The garden's Victorian wrought-iron gates are surmounted by an attractive figure of St Peter.

Return down the alley, turn right and walk along Gracechurch Street, named after the former St Benet Grass Church, the site of medieval London's corn and hay market. Turn right along Lombard Street and look up to see the green and gold **banners and coats-of-arms** 15 on boards projecting from surrounding

banners and coats-of-arms

buildings. The Lombard merchants of northern Italy settled here from the 12th century, and it has been London's banking centre ever since.

Continue down Lombard Street past Birchin Lane on the right to number 68, where you'll see a **Gresham grasshopper** 16 above the entrance. The grasshopper is an emblem on the family crest of the influential Gresham family of merchants. According to one legend, the founder of the family in the 13th century, Roger de Gresham, was abandoned as a newborn in long grass where he was discovered by a woman whose attention was drawn to him by a grasshopper. Less

romantically, *gres* is a Middle English form of the word grass, and a heraldic rebus on the name Gresham.

Retrace your steps and turn down Birchin Lane – Old English for 'lane of the barbers' – where the remains of Roman mosaic pavements and a bakery have been found. Hidden away on the right, reached via a narrow passage called Bengal Court, is the 18th-century **George & Vulture** 17, surrounded by a maze of atmospheric alleyways. A few hundred years ago, chop houses were as common in the City as sandwich bars are today, providing food and a meeting place for merchants and traders. Although there's been a tavern on the site since 1175, the George & Vulture dates from the 1730s (Georgian panelling survives in the dining room).

George & Vulture

The George & Vulture attracted some famous – and infamous – clientele. Charles Dickens reputedly drank there and featured the tavern in *The Pickwick Papers*. In the 18th century it was a regular haunt of the Hellfire Club, whose members enjoyed such gentlemanly pursuits as wine, women and the occult.

CANNON STREET TO THE TOWER

Gresham grasshopper   Royal Exchange Building   Swan Lane Building

At the end of Birchin Lane, turn left along Cornhill and across the road is the striking **Royal Exchange Building** ⓲. Just before the actual Exchange (almost opposite Birchin Lane) is a narrow street, Royal Exchange Buildings, where you'll find a grasshopper perched on top of the bell tower, with yet another on the Royal Exchange's weathervane.

The original Royal Exchange was built by Sir Thomas Gresham (1519-79) in the 1560s. It was based on the Antwerp Bourse, as Gresham believed that London needed a similar place for people to meet and do business. The current building opened in 1844,

designed by Sir William Tite, who won the right to do so after a rather botched architectural competition. It's an imposing building although it isn't a great piece of architecture and doesn't really do this noble institution justice. The Exchange ceased to be a trading bourse in 1939 and the Guardian Royal Exchange later occupied the building, which was restored in the late 20th century. Today's 'trading' takes place in the luxury shops and restaurants which occupy the Exchange.

To reach Bank tube station, retrace your steps to Cornhill, turn right and the station is at the junction at the end.

Royal Exchange Grasshopper

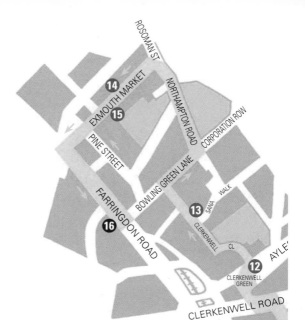

1. The Rookery
2. Cow's heads
3. Smithfield Market
4. Fox & Anchor
5. Sutton's Hospital in Charterhouse
6. Lion and monk statues
7. Florin Court
8. Museum of St John
9. 44 Britton Street
10. Jerusalem Tavern
11. St John's Path
12. Clerkenwell Green
13. Peabody Trust Clerkenwell Estate
14. Exmouth Market
15. Our Most Holy Redeemer
16. The Eagle

Places of Interest   Food & Drink

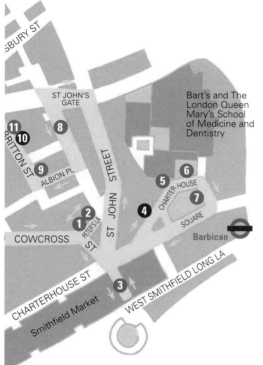

ST JOHN'S GATE

11 10
8
BRITTON ST
9
ALBION PL

ST JOHN STREET

Bart's and The London Queen Mary's School of Medicine and Dentistry

5
6
CHARTER-HOUSE
7
SQUARE
4

2
1
PETER'S LA
ST

COWCROSS

Barbican

CHARTERHOUSE ST

3

Smithfield Market

WEST SMITHFIELD LONG LA

CLERKENWELL

WALK 6

Distance: 1.33mi (2.15km)
Duration: half day
Start/end: Farringdon tube station

Tucked between the City and King's Cross, occupying the southernmost part of the London Borough of Islington, Clerkenwell is now one of the capital's trendiest corners. It's also, as our walk reveals, an area steeped in history, from the gore of Smithf eld Market to the humanity of the Knights of St John.

Clerkenwell gets its name from the Clerk's Well in Farringdon Lane, where the clerks of medieval London gathered to perform mystery plays (re-enactments of Bible stories). Clerks were persons of some importance, distinguished by their literary skills at a time when few could read and write, and many were clergyman. Clerkenwell was also the home of the Monastic Order of the Knights Hospitallers of St John of Jerusalem, medieval crusader knights whose base was the Priory of Clerkenwell (see page 81).

By the 17th century, this area was a fashionable place to live, but the Industrial Revolution changed the face of Clerkenwell and it became known for brewing, distilling alcohol, printing and, especially, the manufacture of clocks and watches. After WWII, Clerkenwell's industries declined and it became a neglected cousin of more fashionable Islington, but its fortunes have revived since the '80s, and people now f ock there to live in the spacious loft apartments converted from former industrial buildings, and to eat and drink in its buzzy bars and restaurants. Not surprisingly, it has also become a magnet for the design industry and architects.

Start Walking…

Our walk starts at Farringdon tube station, where we turn left or as posted – in 2012 the station was being redeveloped, so the exits may have changed – towards Smithfield Market. Look for the Castle pub straight ahead, then turn right to head east along Cowcross Street, an attractive, well-kept thoroughfare. The name comes from the cattle that crossed the River Fleet here on their way to Smithfield Market, until the market ceased trading in live animals in 1855.

Look up above Cowcross Street's ground-floor shops and restaurants to see the interesting detailing on the attractive red- and brown-brick buildings. Turn left down Peter's Lane, a narrow, characterful passageway and the site of **The Rookery** ❶, which dates from 1764. This one-time city slum is now a chic boutique hotel, occupying a trio of 18th-century buildings, cleverly and sensitively restored to retain many original features. Further along on the left, decorative **cow's heads** ❷ run up the front of a building.

The term 'rookery' was a nickname for the overcrowded slums where the poor lived in the 18th and 19th centuries, alongside thieves, prostitutes and other less desirable folk. The name may come from the haphazard, multi-storey design of the buildings, where people lived literally on top of one another, like rooks nesting in a tree.

Return to Cowcross Street, turn left and the main arch of **Smithfeld Market** ❸ (3am to mid-morning) looms ahead. Our route takes us along the fancifully-named Grand Avenue, which runs through the centre of the market. Much of the interest here is overhead, in the ornate, coloured iron roofing, the dragons

The Rookery

Smithfield Market — Fox & Anchor

that guard the entrances and the exotic clock in the centre of the roof. Vegetarians be warned: this is still a working market and smells of meat and blood!

Smithfield has a long and often bloody history. In the Middle Ages, a grassy space just outside the City walls called Smoothfield was the venue for a horse market where cattle, pigs and sheep were also sold. The Bartholomew Fair was also held here from 1123 until 1855. The field was also used for jousting, sports and tournaments, and was a place of public execution for over 400 years, before the gallows were moved to Tyburn in Henry IV's reign.

In 1638, the City of London Corporation formally established a cattle market on the site, but facilities were inadequate, with blood and entrails flowing through the streets. Despite this, the market wasn't moved until 1855, when the sale of live cattle and horses moved to Islington. In 1851-66, Horace Jones built the current market building which opened in 1868 as the London Central Meat Market. Today it employs around 1,500 people and sells over 150,000 tons of meat annually.

Return to the market's entrance and turn right down Charterhouse; take the left-hand fork down Charterhouse Street. On your left is an attractive, gargoyle-festooned pub, the **Fox & Anchor** ❹, designed by W. J. Neatby with an interesting Art Nouveau façade with attractive Doulton tiles. The grotesques on the pub exterior resemble the gargoyles of Notre Dame and there's some nice lettering. Inside, it's narrow and atmospheric, with an interesting selection of ales.

Soon after the pub, a set of gates leads into striking Charterhouse Square. This 'square' has a rare five-sided construction and a number of interesting buildings: Tudor, Georgian and Victorian, as well as later styles. On the left is the entrance to **Sutton's Hospital**

Sutton's Hospital, Charterhouse   Smithfield Market

in **Charterhouse** ⑤ and further along on the same side, look up to see the **lion and monk statues** ⑥ on the hospital buildings. The Charterhouse itself, a beautiful old building of mellow stone, dates back to the mid-1300s when it was a priory. It was built on a burial pit for 40,000 souls who died in the Black Death (plague). Fittingly, part of the building is now used by St Bartholomew's Hospital as a medical college.

> The Black Death lasted only two years –1348 to 1350 – but the pandemic's effect was devastating. It's thought that up to 60 per cent of Europe's population may have died as a result. It did away with such niceties as funerals and the bodies were simply disposed of in mass graves, or plague pits, upon which much of modern London has been rebuilt.

The priory closed in 1535, when the prior and three monks fell foul of Henry VIII. In 1611 it was purchased by Thomas Sutton, then England's richest man, who left funds in his will to convert it into a hospice for military pensioners and a boys' school. The school opened as Charterhouse and moved to Surrey in 1872. Today, Charterhouse is part of the campus of Queen Mary, University of London, and lodgings are still kept for gentlemen who fall on hard times.

Follow the road around the tranquil leafy square to the towering Art Deco block of **Florin Court** ⑦, the home of Hercule Poirot in a recent series of

Ceiling decoration, Sutton's Hospital, Charterhouse

Florin Court

television adaptation of Agatha Christie's stories about the moustachioed Belgian sleuth (it was called Whitehaven Mansions in the series). Florin Court was built in 1936 by Guy Morgan and Partners, and has an impressive, undulating façade. At the exit just past the Court, turn right and return along Charterhouse Square and Charterhouse Street, with Smithfield Market on your left.

Opposite Smithfield's main entrance, take the right-hand fork down St John Street, which has some attractive, elegant buildings, many of them Victorian. St John Street is first mentioned in 1170 and was originally a track for packhorses. Until 1855, it was the main street from the Angel to Smithfield – and the last leg for sheep and cattle coming from north and west London on their way to Smithfield's livestock market. It's now lined with trendy bars and restaurants, another example of the area's recent transformation, and is a good place to refuel.

There's a excellent restaurant called Pho at number 86, which is 'Vietnam in a bowl'. If Vietnamese food isn't to your taste (if you've never tried it, it's delicious), just past it is one of several intriguing courtyards and passageways that dot the area, Hat and Mitre Court, with an al fresco restaurant at the end.

From the top of St John Street, turn left into St John's Square for the area's historical highlight, which isn't on the general tourist beat: the little-known but impressive St John's Gate and the **Museum of St John** . The original gatehouse was built in 1148 but was burned down by rebel leader Wat Tyler in 1381. The present gatehouse, dating from 1504 and built of Kentish ragstone, is one of London's oldest buildings. It was part of the Priory of St John of Jerusalem, founded in the 12th century and sacked in the 1530s during the Dissolution of the Monasteries. In the 16th century it became a commercial building, including a spell as a tavern run by Richard Hogarth, father of the eminent 18th-century painter, William. It also housed the *Gentleman's Magazine*, where Dr

Samuel Johnson worked in the 1730s.

St John's Gate is the place where St John Ambulance was founded in 1877. This organisation, which has links to the Knights Hospitallers of St John of Jerusalem, was set up to provide first aid to the victims of accidents which were an unfortunate consequence of the Industrial Revolution. It was Britain's only ambulance service until the mid-20th century.

The small museum is fascinating and you can even dress up in period costume, should you so wish. It traces the history of the Order of the Knights Hospitallers of St John of Jerusalem, from the 12th century when it was founded to care for crusaders and pilgrims, to the current work of St John Ambulance. The museum has the largest collection of items about the Order outside Malta, including armour, coins, insignia, paintings, books, manuscripts, furniture, silver and jewellery.

Leaving the museum, turn left down St John's Lane and turn right into Albion Place. Take the right down Britton Street, named

Museum of St John 8
Mon-Sat, 10am-5pm, with guided tours on Tue, Fri and Sat at 10am and 2.30pm

44 Britton Street

Jerusalem Tavern

after the antiquarian John Britton who worked in one of the street's taverns for a while. Number **44 Britton Street** ⑨ is former home of long-time local resident Janet Street-Porter, the journalist and TV personality. The house was designed by Piers Gough of CZWG Architects in 1987 and uses varying shades of brick courses, blue-glazed Belgian pantiles, diamond-paned windows, and dramatic geometrical balcony and terrace screens. The result provides a stunning contrast with the area's mainly Georgian architecture.

One of the street's most interesting buildings is the **Jerusalem Tavern** ⑩, which dates back to 1720 with a shop front added in 1810, but while the interior is interestingly 'wonky', the building only become a pub in the '90s. Just past it is **St John's Path** ⑪, another of the area's many intriguing passageways in which it's easy to imagine you're exploring a much older city.

At the top of Britton Street, turn left along Clerkenwell Road – originally known as Liquorpond Street (after its breweries). Cross over and turn right for **Clerkenwell Green** ⑫. Along with much of the area, Clerkenwell Green has been smartened up since the '80s and today feels more like a European square than a London one, with fashionable bars and restaurants. But in bygone days, Clerkenwell's village green had a history of attracting malcontents. This is where rebels from the north camped during the 1387 Peasants' Revolt, and in the 19th century it was a popular site for political demonstrations. During the Chartist Agitation in 1842, Prime Minister Robert Peel banned public meetings here, but they resumed later. The world's first May Day March left from the Green in 1890. Continuing the socialist theme, the Marx Memorial Library is at 37A, in a building built in 1737 as a Welsh Charity School for the children of poor Welsh families in London.

> Clerkenwell Green was another of Charles Dickens' favourite spots. It used to host a busy street market and it's here that Oliver Twist was taught by the Artful Dodger how to 'pick a pocket or two'.

Turn left off Clerkenwell Green along Clerkenwell Close and you reach the **Peabody Trust Clerkenwell Estate** 13, a splendid example of good inner city, high-rise housing. Peabody Buildings are housing blocks for the working poor of London, named after a Trust established in 1862 by the American philanthropist George Peabody, who spent most of his later life in London. The Trust currently owns and runs some 20,000 rented homes on estates in inner London, some of which are rather austere architecturally, while others have a touch of Victorian splendour.

Continue ahead along Clerkenwell Close, turn right along Bowling Green Lane, left along Northampton Road, leading into Rosoman Street, and left into trendy **Exmouth Market** 14 (Mon-Fri, 12-3pm). This food market is pedestrianised and has a wide variety of bars, cafés, restaurants and fashion and 'lifestyle' shops; a good example of London café culture in full swing. There's also a French market three days a week.

FOOD & DRINK

4 **Fox & Anchor:** Traditional pub serving good ales and British 'posh' pub grub.

10 **Jerusalem Tavern:** Serves speciality ales from Suffolk's St Peter's Brewery and tasty food. Closed weekends.

18 **The Eagle:** Gatropub serving fine ales (Eagle IPA) with tasty Spanish & Mediterranean fare, including tapas.

Exmouth Market

Exmouth Market is named after Admiral Edward Pellew, who was made 1st Viscount Exmouth for his bombardment of Algiers in 1816 to compel it to accept a treaty abolishing Christian slavery.

While you're exploring the market, take the time to stop at number 24, **Our Most Holy Redeemer** ⑮, a beautiful, 19th-century, red-brick church built in the Italian style by the noted architect John Dando Sedding (8.30am-6.30pm). It's elegant and well-proportioned externally and internally, although often overlooked in the buzzy market environment.

At the end of Exmouth Market, turn left along Farringdon Road. A short way along on the left in a parade of shops is the arrestingly-named Meatballs, housed in a handsome Grade II listed Victorian building from the 1870s. This used to be the Quality Chop House and although it now specialises in meatballs (unsurprisingly), it remains a rare, surviving 19th-century, working-class eatery. A sign on the outside proudly declares it to be a 'Progressive Working Class Caterer' and boasts that it serves 'London's Noted Cup of Tea'.

Further down Farringdon Road, on the right, is the famous **Eagle** ⑯, one of the city's original gastropubs, where we end our walk. It's a plain space, with cream walls and bare wood, shared tables, ordering at the bar and good hearty food to enjoy with your pint.

To reach Farringdon tube station, continue south along Farringdon Road. You pass the Betsey Trotwood on the left, a classic Victorian tavern, full of atmosphere. This Shepherd Neame establishment is named after *David Copperfield*'s formidable great aunt. The station is to the left of Farringdon Road, along Cowcross Street.

The Eagle

Exmouth Market

CLERKENWELL

Our Most Holy Redeemer

Britton Street

graffiti train, Farringdon

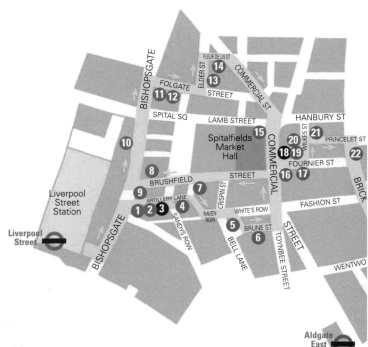

1. 56 and 58 Artillery Lane
2. Artillery Passage
3. Grapeshots
4. Sandys Row Synagogue
5. Tenter Ground
6. Soup Kitchen for the Jewish Poor
7. A. Gold
8. Sculpture of a goat
9. Bishopsgate Institute
10. Abstract modern sculpture 'Eye-I'
11. Folgate Street
12. Dennis Severs' House
13. Elder Street
14. Fleur de Lis Street
15. Spitalfields Market
16. Christ Church Spitalfields
17. Fournier Street
18. Ten Bells
19. Wilkes Street
20. Puma Court
21. Princelet Street
22. Brick Lane
23. Whitechapel Bell Foundry
24. Tower House
25. Tayyabs
26. London Muslim Centre
27. East London Mosque

⬤ Places of Interest ⬤ Food & Drink

Whitechapel ⊖

WHITECHAPEL ROAD

STREET

OSBORN ST

ᴸANE

ᵀH

23 FIELDGATE

26 **27**

24 **25**

STREET

SPITALFIELDS & WHITECHAPEL

Distance: 1.95mi (3.14km)
Duration: half day
Start: Liverpool Street station
End: Whitechapel tube station

SPITALFIELDS & WHITECHAPEL

Spitalfields and Whitechapel are where the City meets the East End of London. It's an area that's been moulded by migrants: first Huguenots, then Jews and, more recently, Bangladeshi, Bengali and Somali communities. As such its streets are full of unexpected contrasts: genteel mansions, modern mosques, smart art galleries and the pub where Jack the Ripper selected his victims.

Spitalfields is located roughly between Liverpool Street station and Brick Lane. The name is a contraction of 'hospital fields'; this was once open land next to the New Hospital of St Mary without Bishopsgate. The area has long had an association with the silk industry which began when French Protestant Huguenot refugees settled here from 1685 onwards, after the revocation of the Edict of Nantes made it impossible for them to practice their religion in France. Because Spitalfields was outside the City of London they could trade here without being bound by the rules imposed by the City's guilds.

By the Victorian era, the silk industry was declining and Spitalfields became a deprived slum district, rife with crime, although it continued to attract outsiders: Irish immigrants escaping the potato famine arrived in the mid-19th century followed by Jewish refugees from Eastern Europe, fleeing appalling conditions, growing anti-Semitism and Tsarist pogroms in Russia. In the mid- to late-20th century the Jewish community moved out and Bangladeshis and others arrived. In recent years, the area has seen much regeneration and developed a thriving arts scene.

To the immediate east of Spitalfields, Whitechapel describes the area around Whitechapel High Street and Whitechapel Road, first named for a small chapel to St Mary. Located outside the City walls, Whitechapel attracted the 'grubbier' trades such as brewing, tanning, foundries and slaughterhouses. By the 19th century it had problems with overcrowding and poverty, and its growth industry seems to have been prostitution. It's still infamous as the location of the Jack the Ripper murders in the 1880s. As in Spitalfields, it attracted Jewish settlers, although synagogues have given way to mosques as Bangladeshi immigrants have moved in.

SPITALFIELDS & WHITECHAPEL

Start Walking…

Our walk begins at Liverpool Street station, east London's busiest terminus. Leave by the exit for Bishopsgate, named after one of the original Roman city gates demolished in 1760. In Tudor and Elizabethan times, Bishopsgate was lined with the houses of the rich; it's now the workplace of City types (many of whom also make their fortunes here!). Cross Bishopsgate at the pedestrian crossing by the main exit to Liverpool Street station and walk down winding Artillery Lane.

Artillery Lane was built in the late 1600s and was previously called Artillery Yard. It was a training ground for Henry VIII's Honourable Artillery Company, which dates back to the 11th century and is now the second most senior regiment in the Territorial Army, Britain's volunteer armed forces.

Veer to the right at the end of the first section of the lane, where you can admire the 18th-century elegance of **numbers 56 and 58 ❶**, both Grade I listed, with bow windows and ornate carving. They were built in 1705, while the magnificent Georgian shop-front of number 56 dating from 1756-7. Just before you reach these houses, **Artillery Passage ❷** runs off Artillery Lane to the right; stroll down this narrow passageway for a vivid picture of what London

Artillery Lane

Artillery passage

must have been like 300 years ago. Many of its buildings now house upmarket tailors and fancy restaurants. **Grapeshots ③** at 2/3 Artillery Passage is a characterful, olde worlde Bar and Dining Room, owned by the Davy's chain of wine bars. In keeping with the streets' past, grapeshot is a type of shot made of a mass of small metal balls.

At the end of Artillery Passage turn right into Sandys Row,

another narrow, atmospheric street, which houses the Grade II listed **Sandys Row Synagogue** ④ (for tours, ☎ 020-8883 4169). The Synagogue dates from 1854 and is the oldest Ashkenazi synagogue in London – the Ashkenazi Jews once lived along the Rhine in Germany – although the building is older, built around 1766 (it was previously a Huguenot chapel). It's one of only a handful of synagogues remaining in the East End of London where there were once over 100.

Return the short distance back along Sandys Row and turn left, continuing into Raven Row. At the junction, turn right into Bell Lane, left into White's Row and right into **Tenter Ground ⑤** for more attractive Huguenot buildings. It gets its name from the tenters (wooden frames) on which woven

FOOD & DRINK

3 Grapeshots:
One of Davy's many wine bars, serving tapas and unspectacular bar-type British food such as fish goujons and bangers and mash. Closed weekends.

18 Ten Bells:
Historic, touristy pub with good selection of beers.

25 Tayyabs
(☎ 020-7247 9543): Celebrated Punjabi restaurant with an enviable reputation for great curries.

Tenter Ground

Spitalfields public art

A. Gold shop

cloth was stretched to help it dry evenly. At the end of Tenter Ground turn left down Brune Street to admire the attractive **Soup Kitchen for the Jewish Poor** 6, which still has 'Way In' and 'Way Out' signs above the doors. It dates from 1902 and was a charity funded by wealthy Jews. The building now houses expensive flats, but the fine façade has been preserved.

At the end of Brune Street, turn left down Toynbee Street, leading into Commercial Street, and turn left along Brushfield Street. On the left at number 42, is an attractive, historic shop, **A. Gold** 7, named after Amelie Gold, a Hungarian Jew who ran a French millinery shop here in the 1880s (the original shop sign remains). The four-storey, Grade

II listed building dates from 1780 and over the years has housed diamond cutters, furriers, bookmakers, drapers and bookbinders, as well as milliners.

Further along Brushfield Street, on the right, is a striking **sculpture of a goat** 8 standing atop some packing cases by Scottish sculptor Kenny Hunter. It's part of the Spitalfields Public Art Programme (SPAP) and makes an arresting introduction to Old Spitalfields Market, which lies just behind it.

Spitalfields has become a magnet for writers and artists. The author Jeanette Winterson lives in Brushfield Street, while artists Gilbert & George and Tracey Emin are based in nearby Fournier Street.

SPAP was created to provide 'an exciting array of sculptures and soundscapes in and around Spitalfields Market'. The inaugural

Spitalfields Sculpture Prize was awarded in 2010 to the above-mentioned goat. It was apparently inspired by Spitalfields' 'rich, ongoing social history': the goat is an image of persecution and sacrifice, while the crates are a nod to the market and the area's long record of human movement, with its various waves of immigration.

At the end of Brushfield Street, turn left into Bishopsgate and almost immediately on the left is the **Bishopsgate Institute** ❾. This striking Arts & Crafts building was designed by Charles Harrison Townsend, the architect responsible for the Whitechapel Gallery, which is the last stop on this walk. It opened in 1894 and houses a reference library, mainly concerned with the history of London, and a lending library. It's also a centre for adult education and cultural activities.

Proceed along Bishopsgate as if you'd turned right rather than left from Brushfield Street; an **abstract modern sculpture 'Eye-I'** ❿ by Bruce McLean rises from the pavement on the left shortly after. Constructed of multi-coloured, brightly-painted steel strips, it has the graphic quality of a French poster from the '30s. Take the second right down **Folgate Street** ⓫. This is the heart of east London's former Huguenot district and home to some of Spitalfields' best preserved Georgian houses.

At number 18 you can visit one of the area's more imaginative attractions: **Dennis Severs' House** ⓬ (tours, £7-10, ☎ 020-7247 4013). Severs was an American artist who filled his 18th-century house with period fittings and furniture, so that each of the ten rooms reflects a different era of the house's history. It's now a sort of 'performance art museum', designed to create an

Bishopsgate Institute ❾
Library, Mon-Thu and Sat, 10am-5.30pm, Fri, 10am-2pm

Dennis Severs' House

atmosphere redolent of the past and paint a picture of what life was like, including appropriate sounds and smells (tours take around 45 minutes).

Turn left into **Elder Street** 13 for more well-preserved Huguenot architecture. This narrow street dates from the 1730s and is lined with many original houses, giving it an even more authentic feel than Folgate Street. Number 32 was the home of the painter Mark Gertler, who was born in nearby Gun Street (there's a blue plaque to him). Turn right into **Fleur de Lis Street** 14, its name a reflection of the local French influence.

At the end of the road, turn right into Commercial Street. This busy main road was built through the Spitalfields slums in the mid-19th century and is the site of the first block of Peabody Buildings, opened in 1864 (see page 83). The spire of Christ Church Spitalfields looms ahead, dominating the area's skyline; we will visit it later. To the right, on Lamb Street, is **Spitalf elds Market** 15 (10am-7pm, restaurants to 11pm).

Eye-I sculpture

A vegetable market was established here in 1682, which later expanded to also sell meat and chickens. It flourished as the area grew to accommodate various waves of migrants. The market was modernised in the early 20th century and opened in 1928 as one of London's largest fruit and vegetable markets. The sales of produce were moved to Leyton in 1991 and the old Victorian market hall is now a

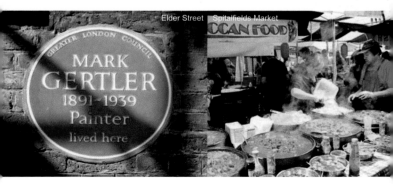
Elder Street   Spitalfields Market

touch yuppified, including arts and crafts, antiques and fashionable eateries catering to the area's new elite.

> The 'Spitalfields woman' is a Roman lady whose sarcophagus was unearthed in 1999 during work on Spitalfields Market. Her silk clothing and jet jewellery suggested she was a woman of wealth and status, and archaeologists believe she lived in the area as long ago as 400BC.

Return to Commercial Street and continue south along it to **Christ Church Spitalf elds** 16, which is on the left on the corner with Fournier Street. This imposing church was designed by Nicholas Hawksmoor (1661-1736), a noted British architect who was a pupil of Sir Christopher Wren and also

Ten Bells

worked with Sir John Vanbrugh. It was built in 1714 and has a well-proportioned interior with an impressive ceiling. The church originally served the Huguenot community and over half of the 18th-century gravestones bear French names. Some ill-judged alterations were made in the 19th century, but Christ Church has now been restored to its former glory. It's widely regarded as Hawksmoor's masterpiece and the best of his six surviving London churches; the spire is emblematic of Spitalfields, as well as being part of the inspiration for Peter Ackroyd's 1985 novel *Hawksmoor*.

On leaving the church, cross **Fournier Street** 17 to visit the **Ten Bells** 18, a pub dating back to 1755 with associations with Jack the Ripper. Victorian prostitutes socialised and picked up clients here, and two of the Ripper's 'working girl' victims were in the pub just prior to their murders.

Christ Church Spitalf elds 16
Mon-Fri, 11am-4pm and Sun, 1-4pm

19 Princelet Street

Fournier Street

Brick Lane

Fournier Street is an attractive and interesting street. It grew alongside Christ Church and has some attractive Georgian buildings which originally housed successful silk merchants, master weavers and retailers. Highlights include number 23, built 1726-28 for the minister of Christ Church and a rare example of a Hawksmoor residential building; number 37 which still sports its original fire protection badge (see box); and numbers 10 and 12, which have been the home and workplace of artists Gilbert & George since the '60s. The houses at numbers 17 to 25 have attic windows which were added to maximise the light inside for the silk weavers who worked here before the street became exclusively residential.

Court's almshouses date from 1886 and bear an inscription referring to Norton Folgate, a local area which from medieval times until 1900 was a 'liberty', meaning that it was outside the jurisdiction of the City authorities. Further along Wilkes Street turn right into **Princelet Street** ㉑ to see more attractive, beautifully panelled Huguenot buildings. Number 19 dates from 1719 and was once the home of the Huguenot Ogier family. In the 19th century it became a synagogue, while numbers 6-10 once housed a Jewish theatre.

At the end of Princelet Street, turn right into **Brick Lane** ㉒, widely considered to be the best

Fournier Street

The first fire brigades were private services which residents had to subscribe to. Houses which were insured to use their services were denoted with a fire protection badge; other properties were usually left to burn!

Return along Fournier Street and, opposite the church, turn right along **Wilkes Street** ⑲, taking a detour to the left down **Puma Court** ⑳. Puma

Whitechapel Bell Foundry ㉓
shop, Mon-Fri, 9am-5pm, tours £12
per head, ☏ 020-7247 2599

place in London to eat curry. If
you fancy something different,
number 159 is home to Brick Lane
Beigel Bake, open 24 hours and
reputedly London's oldest and
best baker of beigels (or bagels).
Brick Lane is so-called because
bricks and tiles were manufactured
nearby in the 16th century.

Since the late '40s, Brick
Lane and its surrounds have
become an East Bengali area,
sometimes dubbed Banglatown.
In 1976, the Jamia Masjid, a
mosque, replaced a synagogue
at number 59, which itself
replaced a church! Walk south
along Brick Lane, enjoying its
genial tackiness, and continue as
it becomes Osborn Street. At the
end, turn left into Whitechapel
Road, named after a 14th-
century chapel which stood in
the area. The road follows an old
highway between London and
Essex which in Roman times was
used by Queen Boadicea when
she advanced on London to burn
the city and attach its Roman
occupiers. By the 19th century it

was noted for its raucous pubs,
music halls and theatres.

Whitechapel Road is associated with
two of East London's most feared
gangsters. Ronnie and Reggie Kray
lived in Vallance Road, a left turn just
before Whitechapel tube station, in
the '30s. At the end of Whitechapel
Road stands the Blind Beggar pub
where Ronnie murdered rival gang
member George Cornell in 1966.

There are some attractive old
houses in Whitechapel Road,
including numbers 27 and 28 which
are in the same small block as
the remarkable **Whitechapel Bell
Foundry** ㉓. The foundry is listed
in the *Guinness Book of Records*
as the oldest manufacturing
company in Britain; it has been
in continuous operation since at
least 1570 and there's a link to
an Aldgate bell foundry in 1420,
suggesting it may be even older.
The present premises date back
to 1670 and are located in a

East London Mosque

former coaching inn, called The Artichoke. The foundry's business has always been, and remains, the manufacture of bells and their associated fittings. It's produced a number of famous bells, including the Liberty Bell, Big Ben and the Clock Bells of St Paul's Cathedral.

Turn right down Fieldgate Street and, keeping to the left, continue until you reach the Gothic, red-brick **Tower House** 24 . This is now a block of upmarket apartments, but used to one of the Rowton Houses, a chain of hostels built in London by Victorian philanthropist Lord Rowton to provide accommodation for working men. This one dates from 1902 and its guests have included authors Jack London and George Orwell, and Soviet leader Joseph Stalin.

Just beyond Tower House is one of the area's best restaurants, **Tayyabs** 25 . This Punjabi grill and curry house is housed in a long, green-fronted building and has become popular with curry fans, so expect a queue (no alcohol is served but you can bring your own). Retrace your steps to Whitechapel Road and turn right for more signs that this corner of London is now dominated by the Islamic faith and where we end this walk: the six-storey **London Muslim Centre** 26 and, next door, the **East London Mosque** 27 . There's been a mosque here since 1940 and the current one opened in 1985, funded by a donation from Saudi Arabia's King Fahd.

To reach Whitechapel tube station, continue ahead along Whitechapel Road and it's on the left.

Tower House

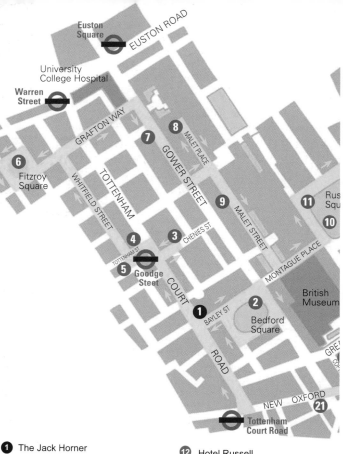

1 The Jack Horner

2 Bedford Square

3 Eisenhower Centre

4 Fitzrovia mural

5 Pollock's Toy Museum

6 Fitzroy Square

7 Grant Museum of Zoology

8 Petrie Museum

9 Royal Academy of Dramatic Art (RADA)

10 Russell Square

11 Cab shelter

12 Hotel Russell

13 Queen Square

14 The Queens Larder

15 Foundling Museum

16 Doughty Street

17 Charles Dickens Museum

18 Bea's of Bloomsbury

19 St George's Church

20 Cartoon Museum

21 James Smith and Sons

Places of Interest ● Food & Drink

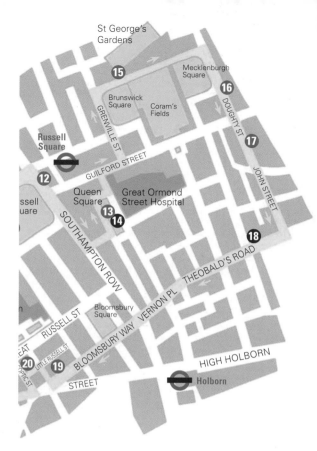

St George's
Gardens

15

Mecklenburgh
Square

16

Brunswick
Square

Coram's
Fields

GRENVILLE ST

DOUGHTY ST

**Russell
Square**

17

JOHN STREET

12

GUILFORD STREET

ssell
uare

Queen
Square

Great Ormond
Street Hospital

SOUTHAMPTON ROW

13

14

18

THEOBALD'S ROAD

VERNON PL

Bloomsbury
Square

RUSSELL ST

BLOOMSBURY WAY

HIGH HOLBORN

EAT

LITTLE RUSSELL ST

20

19

Holborn

STIC ST

STREET

WALK 8

BLOOMSBURY

Distance: 4.03mi (6.48km)

Duration: full day

Start/end: Tottenham Court Road tube station

BLOOMSBURY

Bloomsbury is the district between Euston Road and Holborn, well known for its Georgian houses and shady garden squares. It's home to numerous cultural, educational and healthcare institutions, from University College London to the British Museum, and is of particular interest for its literary connections. This was the haunt of the Bloomsbury Group, a gathering of artists, intellectuals, philosophers and writers who lived, worked and met in or near Bloomsbury in the f rst half of the 20th century, and included E. M. Forster, Lytton Strachey and Virginia Woolf.

The area's history was f rst recorded in 1201, when the land was acquired by a Norman, William de Blemond, and the name evolved from Blemondisberi – the bury or manor of Blemond. But it wasn't until the 17th and 18th centuries that Bloomsbury became a fashionable residential district under the stewardship of the Russell family, and their inf uence can be seen everywhere today.

Bloomsbury has no off cial boundaries, but can be roughly def ned as the square bounded by Tottenham Court Road to the west, Euston Road to the north, Gray's Inn Road to the east, and either High Holborn or the thoroughfare formed by New Oxford Street, Bloomsbury Way and Theobalds Road to the south. Bloomsbury merges gradually with Holborn in the south, and with St Pancras in the northeast and Clerkenwell in the southeast. The area is bisected from north to south by the main Southampton Row-Woburn Place thoroughfare, which contains several large tourist hotels and links Tavistock Square and Russell Square – the central points of Bloomsbury.

Start Walking…

Our Bloomsbury walk begins at Tottenham Court Road tube station. Head north up Tottenham Court Road, originally a market road leading from Oxford Street to Tottenham Court which was a popular place of entertainment for Londoners; in medieval times this was a route from St Giles to Hampstead. As the road became built up in the mid-18th century, it attracted furniture makers and by the 1850s there were over 100. The first branch of Heal's opened here in 1810

Although the northern section of the road is still a great place to buy furnishings, the much less attractive southern stretch is now filled with electronics outlets, many in boxy, concrete buildings which seem to be trying to outdo each other in ugliness. Matters improve markedly when you turn right down Bayley Street towards Bedford Square. The attractive Fuller's (traditional ale & pie) pub **The Jack Horner** ❶ on the corner (appropriately) is popular with theatre-goers at the nearby Dominion Theatre and media types who work locally – and also handy if you need a shot of caffeine before starting the walk.

At the end of Bailey Street, turn right into **Bedford Square** ❷. This is one of London's finest Georgian squares and a fine antidote to

Jack Horner

THOMAS WAKLEY 1795–1862 REFORMER and founder of "The Lancet" lived here

SIR JOHNSTON FORBES-ROBERTSON ACTOR LIVED HERE BORN 1853 DIED 1937

Bedford Square

the grimness of Tottenham Court Road. There are plenty of blue plaques here: reformer and founder of *The Lancet* Thomas Wakley; doctor and philanthropist Thomas Hodgkin; *The Prisoner of Zenda* author Sir Anthony Hope Hawkins; architect William Butterfield; Indian scholar and reformer Ram Mohun Roy; Lord Chancellor Lord Eldon; engineer Sir Harry Ricardo; and actor and theatre manager Sir Johnston Forbes-Robertson (who has a brown plaque). I freely admit that I hadn't heard of any of them!

Blue plaques commemorate a link between a house or location and a well-known person or event. The scheme is run by English Heritage and there are about 850 blue plaques on display in London. Pre-20th century plaques, erected by the Society of Arts, are sometimes coloured brown.

Bedford Square is Bloomsbury's one remaining complete Georgian square, a popular spot for filming period dramas. It was built 1775-80 on the Bedford Estate, and each side features a decorative central house, adorned with pilaster columns and stucco, flanked by plainer houses with wrought-iron balconies. Until 1893, the square was enclosed by gates, presumably to keep out the great unwashed public (the tree-lined garden in the middle of the square remains private). It's no longer residential and nowadays most properties are offices (until recently many were occupied by publishers).

Walk around the square anticlockwise, returning along Bayley Street to Tottenham Court Road. Turn right and take the second right down Chenies Street. On your left is the **Eisenhower Centre 3** – the squat circular buildings are the only visible part of what was the headquarters of US General Eisenhower (Ike) from 1942; the rest is hidden in tunnels deep underground. The centre was later an army transit camp, until it was closed after a fire in 1956, and it's now used for storage. Some critics regard it as pleasingly cake-like, others as rather ugly.

Returning to Tottenham Court Road, turn right and cross towards

Eisenhower Centre

Pollock's Toy Museum

Pollock's Toy Museum 5
Mon-Sat, 10am-5pm, closed Bank
Holidays, ☎ 020-7636 3452

Fitzrovia mural

Goodge Street tube station. Just
past the station, on the end of a
building set back from the road,
is the **Fitzrovia mural 4**, one of
London's best outdoor murals.
The top half was painted in 1980
by Mick Jones (son of the trades
unionist, Jack Jones – not the
guitarist in The Clash) depicting
the challenges and issues facing
the nearby area of Fitzrovia;
Simon Barber painted the
bottom half, which features local
characters who lived and worked
in the area.

Turn left along Tottenham
Street, which is also just past
Goodge Street station, and left
along Whitfield Street. On the
right, on the corner with Scala
Street, is **Pollock's Toy Museum
5**. Named after Benjamin Pollock,
the last of the Victorian toy theatre
printers, it's a quaint, little-known
delight, with many types of
toy from all over the world and
different eras. The museum is in
two houses joined together, one
18th-century, the other 19th, with
small, atmospheric rooms and
winding staircases.

On leaving the museum, retrace
your steps along Whitfield Street
and continue ahead to Grafton
Way and turn left along it. The
Grafton Arms welcomes drinkers
in with a real gas lamp outside. It's
a cosy, intimate pub, with a long,
narrow bar and a good choice of

beers, and is a tranquil alternative to the bars on Tottenham Court Road.

At the end of Grafton Way, the distinctive BT Tower rises over the buildings on your left, while the elegant **Fitzroy Square** ⑥ is on the right. The square was developed by Henry Fitzroy, 2nd Duke of Grafton, and is one of London's finest, designed by Robert and James Adam. The east and south sides were built in the 1790s (the south side was destroyed in WWII but has been restored), the west and north sides were added in 1825-9. Walking around it from right to left, you get a close-up of the splendid architecture and the flurry of blue plaques, including Prime Minister Robert Gascoyne Cecil; authors Virginia Woolf and George

Fitzroy Square plaque

Bernard Shaw, artist Roger Fry and architect Robert Adam.

The northwestern corner of Bloomsbury is also called Fitzrovia, a nod to Charles Fitzroy, Baron of Southampton; the name appeared on streets, squares and even pubs in the area. The term Fitzrovia probably wasn't coined until the '40s to describe the bohemian community then living there.

Return along Grafton Way, crossing Tottenham Court Road, and continuing east. Turn right down Gower Street, which takes its name from Lady Gertrude Leveson-Gower, wife of the 4th Duke of Bedford. Former residents include author Charles Dickens, biologist Charles Darwin and economist J. M. Keynes, although their former homes have long been demolished. The art movement known as the Pre-Raphaelite Brotherhood was founded at number 7 in 1848

Fitzroy Square

Petrie Museum

by William Holman Hunt, John Everett Millais and Dante Gabriel Rossetti.

This part of Gower Street is dominated by University College London (UCL). The gated Bloomsbury Campus is on your left and the red-brick bulk of its Cruciform Building looms on your right. In the next block you can visit the worthy **Grant Museum of Zoology** ❼ (Mon-Fri, 1-5pm), housed in UCL's Rockefeller Building. It's like stepping into a time machine; the museum has the air of a Victorian collector's rooms, with the emphasis on exhibits in glass cases rather than interactive displays and flashing lights. It's London's only remaining university zoological museum and contains around 67,000 specimens spanning the entire animal kingdom. The museum is named after Robert Grant (1793-1874), England's first Professor of Zoology and Comparative Anatomy.

After the museum, cross to the left side of Gower Street and turn left into Torrington Place and left again into Malet Place. Here you'll find the **Petrie Museum** ❽ (Tue-Sat, 1-5pm), dedicated to ancient Egypt, and also a part of UCL. The Petrie is an unsung wonder, overshadowed by the British Museum's tourist-thronged Egyptian galleries. While the latter's collection is strong on the 'big stuff', the Petrie focuses on the minutiae and gives a vivid impression of what everyday life was like in ancient Egypt.

It's named after the noted archaeologist William Flinders Petrie (1853-1942) and contains one of the earliest pieces of linen from Egypt (c 5,000BC); the earliest 'cylinder seal' found

Grant Museum of Zoology

there (c 3,500BC); a fragment from the first kinglist or calendar (c 2,900BC); and the oldest gynaecological papyrus, among other treasures.

Returning down Malet Place and into Malet Street, on the right is the arresting theatre building of the **Royal Academy of Dramatic Art (RADA)** ⑨. RADA is the country's leading dramatic school, founded in 1904 by the magnificently-named actor-manager Sir Herbert Beerbohm Tree. Malet Street also boasts some striking architecture and detail, so keep your eyes peeled; as ever in London, look up as well as all around you. At the end of Malet Street, turn left along Montague Place, which has an entrance to the British Museum on the right.

At the end turn left into **Russell Square** ⑩. This is London's second-largest square and was built on land the Parliamentarians used to construct defensive bulwarks during the English Civil War. It was designed in 1800 by

Humphry Repton and named after the ground landlords, the Russells, Dukes of Bedford. The poet T. S. Eliot lived here while working for the publisher Faber and Faber, as a brown plaque testifies on the corner with Thoroughfare Street.

> The British Museum is probably the best known building in Bloomsbury. The most popular museum in Britain, its vast collection includes some 8m permanently displayed works from all over the world. It would take many days to explore all its attractions – there's no point in just popping in as part of this walk – which range from the Rosetta Stone to the Elgin Marbles. For information and opening times, see 🖥 www.britishmuseum.org.

Just past this, to the right and next to the park in the middle of the square, is a green, wooden structure. This is a **cab shelter** ⑪, one of only 13 remaining in London. The shelters were erected by the Cabmen's Shelter Fund, established in 1875 to provide alcohol-free boltholes

Russell Square

RADA

BLOOMSBURY

for cab drivers between fares; all are now Grade II listed. Don't ignore Russell Square's park, which is large and leafy, with plenty of benches and a caféteria for when the foot slogging becomes too much.

Continue around Russell Square until you come to the magnificent, red-brick and terracotta **Hotel Russell** ⑫ on your left. It's a splendidly flamboyant example of Victorian architecture, built 1898-1900 by Charles Fitzroy Doll in French Gothic style. The hotel has colonnaded balconies, cherubs and four female figures above the main entrance, representing the four Protestant English Queens: Elizabeth, Mary II, Anne and Victoria. Follow this side of the square into Southampton Row where author Edgar Allan Poe once lived.

Turn left off Southampton Row down the narrow, pedestrianised Cosmo Place to reach **Queen Square** ⑬, a leafy oasis of calm. It was built 1708-20 and named after Queen Anne, but no

original buildings survive. Until the early 19th century this was a fashionable area – artist and designer William Morris lived at number 26 from 1865-71, with his design shop on the ground floor. The square now houses a number of medical institutions and **The Queens Larder** ⑭, a Greene King pub. It has a good choice of beers and attracts a lot of custom

Queen Charlotte Statue

Hotel Russell

from nearby Great Ormond Street Hospital.

> The Queens Larder may have royal connections. George III was reportedly treated for his 'Madness' at an address on the square and his wife, Queen Charlotte, was said to have stored his food and medicine at the pub.

Walk round the square to the pedestrianised Queen Anne's Walk, which is diagonally across from the pub. Cut through and turn right along Guilford Street, built 1793-7 and named after Prime Minister Lord North, 2nd Earl of Guilford, who was President of the Foundling Hospital 1741-92 (see below). Turn left along Grenville Street, with the Renoir Cinema on your left and Brunswick Square to the right. The Square is named after Caroline of Brunswick, wife of the Prince Regent, and was built 1795-1802, although the original buildings have long been replaced. Past residents include Bloomsbury Group stalwarts J. M. Keynes, Duncan Grant, Virginia and Leonard Woolf and E. M. Forster. Continue round to the right, following the sign for Coram's Fields until you reach the **Foundling Museum** 15.

Foundling Museum 15
Tue-Sat, 10am-5pm, Sun, 11am-5pm, £7.50 adults

FOOD & DRINK

1 **The Jack Horner:** Sophisticated Fuller's Ale & Pie pub with a great selection of pies. Open from 9am Mon-Fri (from 11am weekends).

14 **The Queens Larder:** Tiny historic Georgian pub with good beer (Greene King) and a cosy dining room serving typical British pub grub.

18 **Bea's of Bloomsbury:** Super tearoom serving a bewildering range of mouth-watering cupcakes. Weekdays 8am-7pm, weekends noon-7pm.

Doughty Street

The *Telegraph* newspaper described the Foundling Museum as 'one of London's most intriguing collections'. It tells the story of Foundling Hospital, established by the philanthropist Sir Thomas Coram as London's first home for abandoned children, from its foundation in 1739 until its closure in 1954. The museum is a fascinating blend of art, period interiors and social history. The composer Handel was a governor and benefactor of the hospital and there's a collection about his life and work. Another founding governor, the painter and cartoonist William Hogarth, designed the children's uniforms and the coat of arms. (Hogarth and his wife were childless and fostered some of the children.) Hogarth set up a permanent art exhibition here and encouraged other artists to contribute. In this way, it became Britain's first public art gallery and includes work by Gainsborough, Reynolds, Hogarth and many others.

On leaving the Foundling Museum, turn left along a narrow pathway, with football pitches to the right. At the end is pleasant, leafy Mecklenburgh Square, with some interesting buildings. The square is named after Queen Charlotte who was Princess of Mecklenburg-Strelitz before marrying George III. Veer to the right and take **Doughty Street** 16 to admire its fine Georgian townhouses in this elegant area, where number 48 on the left houses the **Charles Dickens Museum** 17 (10am-5pm, £7 adults).

The museum is spread over four floors of a typical Georgian terraced house, while the rooms have a traditional Victorian appearance. Dickens lived here from March 1837, a year after his marriage, until December 1839, and it's the only house he occupied which still survives in London. It now houses the world's most important Dickens collection, containing over 100,000 items. The most famous exhibit is the portrait of the great man known as *Dickens Dream*, showing the author surrounded by many of the characters from his books.

Dickens only lived at number 48 for a relatively short time but it was a particularly productive period for him. During this time he completed *The Pickwick Papers*, wrote *Oliver Twist* and *Nicholas Nickleby*, and worked on *Barnaby Rudge*. Two of his daughters, Mary and Kate, were born at this address.

Follow Doughty Street into John Street and at the end turn right along Theobald's Road. This was formerly part of the route used by James I to his house at Theobalds, Hertfordshire. Soon after – on the right – is the ornate teahouse **Bea's of Bloomsbury** 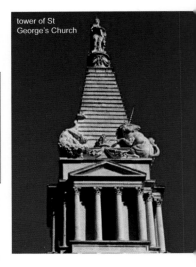, the original of a chain of four London teahouses, selling mouth-watering cakes and perfect for refuelling after a dose of Dickens.

Continue right Theobald's Road until it becomes Vernon Place. Look left for Sicilian Avenue, a nicely over-the-top, pedestrianised shopping street with colonnaded screens. It was built in 1905 by W. S. Wortley and is paved with Sicilian marble. Vernon Place leads into Bloomsbury Way, with Bloomsbury Square on the right. The square was created around 1660 by the Earl of Southampton and comprised houses for the wealthy on three sides and servants' houses on the fourth.

On the right of Bloomsbury Way is the elegant **St George's Church** (1-4pm) by Nicholas Hawksmoor, completed in 1731.

tower of St George's Church

The steeple is noteworthy, being stepped like a pyramid. Some people believe this is Hawksmoor's best church, although the more widely-held view is that Christ Church Spitalfields is his masterpiece (see page 94).

Continue a short way along Bloomsbury Way and turn right into Museum Street and then left into Little Russell Street for the **Cartoon Museum** (Tue-Sat, 10.30am to 5.30pm, Sun, noon to 5.30pm) at number 35. It has a huge collection of books, caricatures, cartoons and comics from the 18th century to the present day, and highlights Britain's important and continuing contribution to the noble art of the cartoon.

On leaving the museum, turn right and continue to the end of Little Russell Street and turn left into Coptic Street. This intriguingly-named street was originally called Duke Street, but to avoid confusion with other streets of the same name it was rechristened in 1894; the previous year a valuable collection of Coptic manuscripts had arrived at the nearby British Museum, hence the name. At number 30 is what many regard as London's best (architecturally speaking) Pizza Express outlet and one of the first, dating from 1965. It has white tiled walls with Art Deco writing on the large arc windows – and the partially open kitchen adds to its congenial, buzzy atmosphere.

At the end of Coptic Street you'll find yourself back in Bloomsbury Way, where you turn right. which after a short distance leads into New Oxford Street. At number 53 on the left, is **James Smith & Sons** ㉑. Founded in 1830, it's London's oldest umbrella and walking stick shop (admittedly, there aren't too many candidates for the title), with an attractive, original Victorian shop front and an unexpectedly interesting selection of decorative umbrellas and walking sticks.

To return to Tottenham Court Road tube station, continue along New Oxford Street and the station is around 300m ahead.

Cartoon Museum

1. Cab shelter
2. Roman Bath
3. Somerset House
4. Courtauld Gallery
5. Sewer-powered gas lamp
6. Embankment Gardens
7. York House Watergate
8. Buckingham Street
9. Gordon's Wine Bar
10. Benjamin Franklin House
11. Britain's smallest police station
12. Public art on the plinth
13. The Salisbury
14. Goodwin's Court
15. Cork & Bottle
16. Notre Dame de France
17. Waterloo Place
18. Carlton House Terrace

● Places of Interest ● Food & Drink

STRAND

② Somerset House

④ ③

① 🚇 Temple

THAMES

VICTORIA EMBANKMENT

RIVER

Waterloo Bridge

Embankment

Hungerford Bridge

WALK 9

CHARING CROSS & WEST END

Distance: 1.82mi (2.93km)
Duration: half day
Start: Temple tube station
End: Charing Cross station

Charing Cross is regarded as the geographical centre of London. Since the late 18th century, this is the point from where distances, e.g. London to Brighton, have been measured. The cross is a reference to the (wooden) Eleanor cross, erected in 1291-4 by Edward I as a memorial to his wife, Eleanor of Castile. He chose a site between the former hamlet of Charing – named after a bend (*cierring*) in the River Thames – and the entrance to the Royal Mews of the Palace of Whitehall. The cross was destroyed in 1647 during the Civil War, on the orders of Parliament.

Since 1675, the original site of the cross has been occupied by a statue of Charles I mounted on a horse. The 70ft (21m)-high stone sculpture seen today in front of Charing Cross railway station is a copy of the original cross. Erected in 1865, it's situated a few hundred yards to the east of the original cross, on the Strand. It was designed by the architect of the hotel, E. M. Barry and carved by Thomas Earp of Lambeth.

Charing Cross is just south of Trafalgar Square, at the junction of the Strand, Whitehall and Cockspur Street, but our walk also covers the eastern fringes of London's West End, taking in the Thames embankment, the tourist hotspot of Leicester Square and the imposing architecture of Pall Mall. This area of central London contains many of the city's major tourist attractions, shops, businesses, government buildings, and entertainment venues, including the commercial West End theatres.

CHARING CROSS & WEST END

Start Walking…

Our circuit of the 'heart' of London's begins at Temple tube station. Leaving the station, turn left up a short flight of steps and left again along Temple Place. The green, wooden structure, a sort of glorified garden shed, is one of London's 13 **cab shelters** ❶ where weary taxi drivers can put their feet up between fares and enjoy an alcohol-free drink.

Turn right up Surrey Street and on the left is the entrance to the National Trust-managed **Roman Bath** ❷; a sign directs you down a set of steps to a pedestrianised passageway, Strand Lane, which unfortunately smells like a latrine. The bath is a stone-lined hole in the ground and is viewed through glass, although a sign declares that 'parties may visit the interior by prior arrangement' (☎ 020-7641 2000). It's a plunge bath measuring 4.7m x 2m (15x6ft),

which is probably fed by water from the adjacent holy well (located near St Clement Danes church). The age of the bath is uncertain. Its brick design appears Roman but there's no record of it until 1784, after which it's referred to as the 'old Roman bath'; Charles Dickens mentions it in *David Copperf eld*.

Return down Strand Lane to Temple Place and turn right along Victoria Embankment, with the Thames on your left. The first building of note is **Somerset House** ❸ (10am-6pm), with its many and varied attractions. Among them is the terrace overlooking the river, which is self-confidently described as 'London's best al fresco venue'. To reach it, enter the building, take a lift to the 'ground' floor and follow the signs; there's also direct access from Waterloo Bridge. The terrace is a large, airy space with panoramic views of the tree-lined

Somerset House in winter

river, with The Shard to the left and the London Eye to the right. It's a good place to admire the impressive façade of Somerset House and there's a café from early May to the end of October.

Somerset House is on the site of England's first Renaissance palace, built in 1547-50 for Lord Protector Somerset; the current building dates from the 18th and 19th centuries. Over the years many notable institutions have made their home in Somerset House (see box) and it's currently the home of HM Revenue and Customs.

Courtauld Gallery ❹
10am-6pm, £6 adults, free Mon, 10am-2pm

> Somerset House has a long association with the arts and learning. The Royal Academy was sited there from 1771 to 1836, the Royal Society (1780-1857) and the Society of Antiquaries (1781-1873). Many people associate the address with the offices of the General Registry of Births, Deaths and Marriages, which occupied the north wing until 1973.

Many people visit Somerset House for the Courtauld Institute of Art which moved into the north wing of Somerset House in 1990. In 1998 the **Courtauld Gallery** ❹ took over the Fine Rooms, once home to the Royal Academy, and it's an essential pit stop for art lovers.

To reach the Courtauld, cross the impressive, fountain-festooned courtyard in the centre of Somerset House and climb some flights of steep stairs. The gallery has some many truly world class paintings, but is sometimes overlooked in a city with so many

fine galleries. The Impressionist and Post-impressionist paintings alone justify the effort; there are also Old Masters, prints, drawings and sculpture. The name Courtauld comes from Samuel Courtauld who had a vast personal collection of art. He gave part of it to London University at the time of the Courtauld Institute's foundation and bequeathed the remainder after his death in 1947; further bequests have boosted the collection.

Leaving Somerset House by its exit onto the Embankment, turn right and pass under Waterloo Bridge. Turn right up Savoy Place; first on your right is the Institution of Electrical Engineers, with a statue of Michael Faraday (1791-1867) in front, and then it's the Savoy Hotel. The BBC moved to 2 Savoy Place in 1923, a year after it was founded, and stayed for nine years. Turn right up Carting Lane to see the **sewer-powered gas lamp** ❺, which is alight 24 hours a day (no, it doesn't smell). It's a Webb Patent Sewer Gas Lamp, invented in the 19th century to draw smells from the sewers.

York House Watergate

sewer-powered gas lamp

Embankment Gardens

This is London's only remaining example, which operated on human 'gas' until the '50s, but (alas) now runs on the standard fossil version.

Return down Carting Lane, go right and straight ahead into **Embankment Gardens** ❻ (8am-8pm). It's part of a series of gardens on the north side of the river between Blackfriars Bridge and Westminster Bridge, and is a tranquil spot with plenty of benches and some attractive plants, including banana palms, which survive in the mild microclimate generated by the river's proximity. The garden also has a number of statues and monuments; on the river bank next to it is Cleopatra's Needle (for more information, see page 255).

Head to the right in Embankment Gardens, through the outdoor café

at the western end, which leads to a large, ornate gateway, the **York House Watergate** ❼, dating to 1626. It's the last surviving part of York House, which was built prior to 1237 for the Bishops of Norwich; later, Francis Bacon lived here. The house was demolished in 1670, leaving just the gateway as a reminder of the great mansions that once lined The Strand. Built by James I's favourite, George Villiers, Duke of Buckingham, the Watergate marks the position of the north bank of the Thames and led from the garden to the river steps, but is now set back from the river by

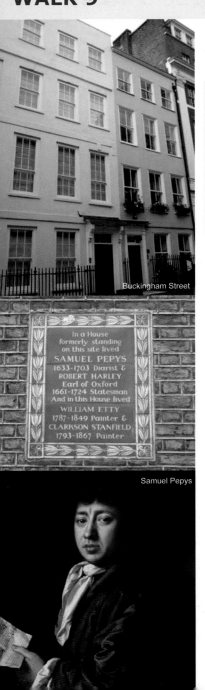

Buckingham Street

In a House
formerly standing
on this site lived
SAMUEL PEPYS
1633-1703 Diarist &
ROBERT HARLEY
Earl of Oxford
1661-1724 Statesman
And in this House lived
WILLIAM ETTY
1787-1849 Painter &
CLARKSON STANFIELD
1793-1867 Painter

Samuel Pepys

land reclaimed during the building of Victoria Embankment (see box).

Victoria Embankment was built by Sir Joseph Bazalgatte (1819-91), the engineer who also provided London with a modern sewer system. His series of massive embankments, which run for 3.5mi (5.6km) along the Thames, is an enduring monument to Victorian enterprise. Begun in 1865 and completed in 1870, they involved moving huge amounts of mud, brick, concrete and masonry, and reclaiming 32 acres (13ha) of 'land' in the process.

Leave the garden at the exit near the Watergate and turn right into Villiers Street, built in the 1670s on the site of York House. Very soon, turn right along Watergate Walk, which runs along the side of Gordon's Wine Bar (and which is lined by the wine bar's outdoor tables – see below), to view the rear of York House Watergate. Opposite the Watergate, turn left up a flight of steps into **Buckingham Street** ❽, a short thoroughfare of handsome late 17th- and early 18th-century houses. The street was built around 1675 and proudly claims to having housed more celebrities than any other comparable street in London.

Diarist and MP Samuel Pepys has two blue plaques here, a round one at number 12, where he lived 1679-88, and a rectangular one at number 14, where he lived from 1688. Politician Robert Harley and painters William Etty and Clarkson Stanfield also lived at number 12 – or, more accurately, in a house on the site – as it was rebuilt in 1791. Philosophers David Hume and Jean-Jacques Rousseau lived at number 10 in 1766, while poet Samuel Taylor Coleridge lived at number 21 in 1799. Russian leader Peter the Great stayed at number 15 in 1698; writer Henry Fielding also lived here in 1735 and, in 1833 Dickens occupied the top floor.

Return the short distance to Villiers Street and turn right into it. The street was pedestrianised in the '80s and is the site of **Gordon's Wine Bar** ❾ which dates back to 1890 and is reached down a narrow, creaky flight of steps. Number 43 Villiers Street is the former home (1889-91) of Rudyard Kipling, as evidenced by a blue plaque and the name Kipling House, although the building is much older and was home to Samuel Pepys in the 1680s.

Turn left along The Arches Shopping or Craven Passage, as a sign at the other end states. Turn right into Craven Street, called Spur Alley until it was redeveloped around 1730, when the Craven family owned the land. The noted wood carver Grinling Gibbons lived here for a while; German poet Heinrich Heine lived at number 32 in 1827; and Benjamin Franklin rented lodgings at number 36 from 1757-75, now a museum dedicated to the great man.

Benjamin Franklin House ❿ is a Grade I listed, architecturally-important building dating from around 1730, housing an intriguing, well-conceived exhibit.

Benjamin Franklin House ❿
pre-booked Historical Experience,
Wed-Sun, £7 adults,
☎ 020-7839 2006

The 'Experience' is based on Franklin's life in London, which takes an interactive 'museum as theatre' approach: you're 'accompanied' by an actress who plays Polly Hewson, Franklin's landlady's daughter, who became like a daughter to him. This live performance, along with lighting, sound and visual projections, successfully evokes 18th-century life.

Benjamin Franklin's pioneering work in electricity is enough to secure his reputation, but he was also a key founder of the United States of America and the only statesman to sign all four documents that created the new nation.

Turn right when you leave Franklin House, then left into the Strand and right up Charing Cross Road, noting the golden antelope

9 Gordon's Wine Bar: The oldest wine bar in London, serving traditional English food, including superb homemade pies, mature cheeses and other favourites.

13 The Salisbury: Traditional Victorian pub with stunning art nouveau details, serving great cask ales and tasty pub grub.

15 Cork & Bottle (☎ 020-7734 7807): Wine bar with a 'proper' restaurant, serving excellent bistro food, famous for its pies (try their raised ham & cheese pie).

to the right on the front of Africa House. Almost immediately, cross the road for Trafalgar Square, built in 1827-35 to John Nash's design, and now sometimes dubbed 'London's meeting place'. **Britain's smallest police station 11** is to the left, in the southeast corner of the square, contained in the base of an ornate lamp.

At the opposite end of the square, near the National Gallery, is **public art on the plinth 12**. Over the past six years, the empty Fourth Plinth in Trafalgar Square's northwest corner has been home to 'innovative' artworks. The plinth was designed in 1841 for an equestrian statue, but lack of funds meant the statue was never finished. In 2012 it was occupied by 'Powerless Structures, Fig. 101' (a giant child on a rocking horse) by artist duo Elmgreen & Dragset. A website (🖥 www.london.gov.uk/fourthplinth) keeps you up to date on what's happening there.

With the National Portrait Gallery on your left, cross Charing Cross Road and take a right-hand diagonal up St Martin's Lane. This was an open drain in medieval times but became a fashionable place to live after the Great Fire devastated the City and the population began to move 'up west'. St Martin's Lane Academy – London's first art school – was founded here in the 1720s (William Hogarth was an early student).

Number 90 on the left houses a glitzy pub, **The Salisbury 13**, promising 'no football here'. It was rebuilt in its current form in 1892 and is decorated with bronze nymphs, etched glass and mahogany. It's popular with theatre-goers and gets crowded before and after shows.

Opposite the pub is a passageway leading to narrow, pedestrianised **Goodwin's Court 14**, a visual treat from centuries ago. On its south side is a row of glorious, late 18th-century houses with bowed windows,

Goodwin's Court

offers tasty food and interesting wines, an antidote to the surrounding area's uninspiring chain restaurants and bars. It's a subterranean affair, reached via a spiral staircase. It can become very busy after 6.30pm, when you may have to wait for a table.

Leaving the cosy embrace of the Cork & Bottle, turn left and carry on into tourist-clogged Leicester Square. It's named after Robert Sidney, 2nd Earl of Leicester, who acquired the land in the 1630s. The square was designed in the 1670s and has had some famous residents over the years, including painters William Hogarth and Sir Joshua Reynolds.

which hint at the buildings' previous incarnation as a row of shops. It's more of an alley than a court and is lit by functioning gas lamps, which cast an atmospheric glow at night.

While the atmosphere is Dickensian, Goodwin's Court is much older: the current buildings first appear in local rate books in 1690 as a row of tailors' shops. Look for the 'fire marks' on the front of some of the buildings, an interesting throwback to the time before an organised fire brigade (see page 95).

Return to St Martin's Lane and turn right; at the junction, turn left along Cranbourn Street and continue along it after the junction with Charing Cross Road for the **Cork & Bottle** 15. It's marked by a doorway with an awning that sits, unpromisingly, between a discount theatre booth and a tattoo parlour. Established in 1972 by New Zealander Don Hewitson, the Cork & Bottle

Leicester Square is now best known as the heart of the UK's cinema industry and is where the biggest film premieres take place. There are five cinemas on the square, plus another three nearby. The Odeon Leicester Square is the largest single-screen cinema in Britain with 1,683 seats.

Turn right into Leicester Place, which was created in the 1790s on part of the site once occupied by Leicester House and its garden. There's a small Catholic church

Cork & Bottle   Waterloo Place

on the right, **Notre Dame de France** (generally 12.15-6pm), with some impressive murals in the Lady Chapel by Jean Cocteau (1889-1963), the French poet, novelist, artist, designer, playwright, filmmaker and all-round over-achiever. The church was designed by the exotically-named Hector O. Corfiato in the late '40s in a style known as beaux arts modern, replacing a church destroyed during WWII.

Return along Leicester Place, turn right along Leicester Square, which becomes Swiss Court and Coventry Street, and left down Whitcomb Street to Pall Mall, which is noted for its gentlemen's clubs, including the Athenaeum (see below), Royal Automobile Club, Reform, Travellers', United Oxford & Cambridge University Club, and the Army & Navy Club. Pall Mall was a game similar to croquet which originated in Italy as *pallo a maglio* (ball to mallet) and became popular in London during the reign of Charles II.

Turn right along Pall Mall and cross the road to turn left along **Waterloo Place** , which is lined with magnificent, imposing buildings, and continue to **Carlton House Terrace** at the end. Waterloo Place was begun in 1816 and the 38m (125ft) Duke of York Column was installed at the south end in 1833. There are a number of statues here, including the mounted Duke of Wellington outside the veritable Athenaeum club; its front is on Pall Mall, the side along Waterloo Place. The club was founded in 1824 and is the most intellectual of London's

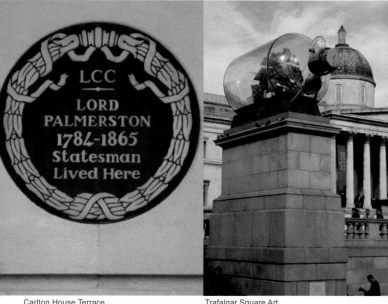

Carlton House Terrace

Trafalgar Square Art

clubs, named after the Athenaeum in Rome, a university founded by Hadrian. The Institute of Directors has been here since 1978 in a building that used to house the United Services Club. Founded in 1903, it's the world's largest body representing individual business leaders.

Our walk ends with some splendid architecture. Built by John Nash in 1827-32 on the site of Carlton House, Carlton House Terrace comprises two lovely terraces, east and west of Waterloo Place. Two Prime Ministers have lived here: William Gladstone at numbers 4 (in 1856) and 11 (from 1857-75), and Lord Palmerston at number 5 from 1840-6; Foreign Secretary Lord Curzon also lived at number 1 from 1905-25. The noted architectural expert Nikolaus Pevsner said of Carlton House Terrace that it 'may rank as the greatest terrace of houses ever built in Britain' – praise indeed!

To reach Charing Cross station, return to Pall Mall and turn right along it, leading to Trafalgar Square and the Strand.

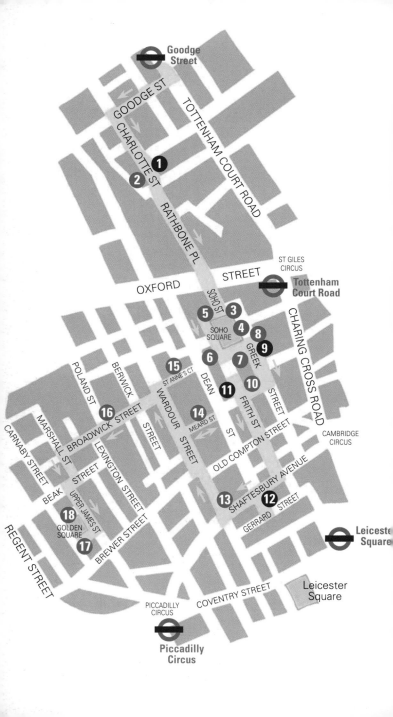

WALK 10

SOHO & FITZROVIA

Distance: 1.28mi (2.07km)
Duration: half day
Start: Goodge Street tube station
End: Piccadilly Circus tube station

SOHO & FITZROVIA

Soho is a tiny district with a huge reputation. Although it covers only around a square mile of Westminster in London's West End, its name has because synonymous with entertainment and, more especially, the sex trade. Soho is bounded by Oxford Street to the north, Leicester Square to the south, Charing Cross Road to the east and Regent Street to the west. French Huguenots settled in and around Soho Square from the late 17th century and it became known as London's French quarter. But by the mid-19th century, the respectable families had moved elsewhere, to be replaced by music halls, theatres and brothels. Between the '30s and '60s, the area's many bars and pubs were the haunt of bohemian artists, poets and writers, which, along with Soho's red light status, gave the area its racy reputation.

Since the '80s, Soho has been transformed – some would say over-sanitised – and only a small remnant of the former sex industry remains. It's now home to a plethora of media off ces, trendy bars, clubs and restaurants, plus the odd sex shop and Italian café from earlier years; there are also some churches.

North of Soho and sandwiched between Marylebone and Bloomsbury, Fitzrovia (also called Noho) strives to be as trendy and cutting edge as its southern neighbour. It doesn't offer the history and variety of Soho but is still an attractive part of London. Full of delicatessens, restaurants and shops, it has an Italian feel. Its name is thought to be linked to the Fitzroy Tavern (see below). The term was only adopted in the inter-war years, f rst by and then in recognition of the pub's arty clientele. The pub itself was named after Charles Fitzroy who developed the northern part of the area in the 18th century.

The name Soho first appears in the 17th century and many claim that it was originally a hunting cry, 'So-ho!', as the area used to be a royal park.

Start Walking…

This walk begins on the outskirts of Fitzrovia. Leave Goodge Street tube station, turn right and right again down Goodge Street. Take a left turn at Charlotte Street and note pretty Colville Place on the left, which is a fine example of the mews which are tucked away all over central London. Formerly stables and carriage houses now converted into attractive homes, these are often overlooked by all but those lucky enough to inhabit them.

Charlotte Street itself dates back to 1789 and is named after Charlotte of Mecklenburg-Strelitz, wife of George III. It became popular with artists and developed a nonconformist character, which continued into the 20th century. Nowadays it's part of media-land, with advertising agencies and upmarket restaurants; painter John Constable lived at number 76 from 1822 to 1837.

A little way down Charlotte Street after Colville Place, **Elena's L'Etoile** ❶ is on the left at number 30. It's a French bistro which has been feeding those in the know since 1896, serving Gallic classics to a mixed business and artistic crowd. The restaurant is unashamedly old-school in atmosphere and menu,

and is decorated with celebrity photographs. A few doors along from Elena's, at number 16, is another Fitzrovia stalwart, the above-mentioned Fitzroy Tavern. Built in 1897 with ornate *fin de siècle* flourishes, it became a favourite with the area's arty types and other free spirits from the 1920s. Regulars included poet Dylan Thomas, Satanist Aleister Crowley, who invented a cocktail for the pub (I wouldn't like to speculate what went into it), hangman Albert Pierrepoint, artist Augustus John and writer George Orwell.

Opposite the pub is the five-star, boutique **Charlotte Street Hotel** ❷, stylish and reassuringly expensive. The hotel has some exceptional art on its walls, including works by the Bloomsbury

Charlotte Street Hotel

Group's Duncan Grant and Vanessa Bell. It also has a popular restaurant and bar (The Oscar), which opens onto the street in summer.

FOOD & DRINK

1 Elena's L'Etoile (☎ 020-7636 7189): Legendary French bistro famous for its high quality food and warm hospitality. Closed Sun and Bank Holidays.

9 The Gay Hussar (☎ 020-7437 0973): Traditional historic Hungarian restaurant serving authentic Hungarian dishes and wines.

At the end of Charlotte Street, turn right along Percy Street, where Hitler's half brother Alois lived at number 4 in the years before the Great War and Adolf himself visited in 1912. A sharp left takes you along Rathbone Street, which has an impressively ugly Royal Mail building running along its right side. The street was built in the 1720s by Captain Thomas Rathbone; writer and literary critic William Hazlitt lived at number 12 from 1802-5 (more on him later) and artist John Constable

at number 50 in 1802. At the end of the street, look left for a view of the Centre Point building, one of the West End's more hideous icons, before crossing Oxford Street, and continuing south into Soho Street.

Number 18 Percy Street has an interesting literary connection. It was once the home of George Orwell's second wife and he reputedly used a room here as the model for the one in which Winston and Julia conduct their ill-fated affair in his novel *1984*.

The frenetic and sometimes tawdry retail Mecca of Oxford Street has ancient roots: it sits on part of a Roman road that ran from Hampshire to Suffolk. As a route west across London, it's had many names, including the King's Highway, the Road to Oxford, the Acton Way and the Tyburn Way, as the River Tyburn once flowed across it. (The notorious Tyburn gallows were situated at its western end, near Marble Arch.) It became Oxford Street in the 18th century when the land on its north side was acquired by Edward Harley, 2nd Earl of Oxford. In the late 19th century, it began to develop into the shopping street we see today.

On Soho Street don't be surprised to see men with shaved heads and saffron robes: on the right is the Radha Krishna Temple and next to it, Gorinda's Pure Vegetarian Restaurant and Take-away. The temple is run by The International Society

Soho Square

for Krishna Consciousness, commonly called the Hare Krishnas, whose belief system is a form of Hinduism. Gorinda's is run by the temple, so there's no caffeine or alcohol, but the food is excellent and it's a friendly place, if sometimes hectic and crowded.

At the end of Soho Street is attractive, leafy **Soho Square** ❸, created in the 1680s on land formerly known as Soho Fields. The square was a fashionable place to live and several noble families had grand homes here, although only two survive: number 10, which is an amalgamation of two houses from the late 17th century, and number 15. The rest were rebuilt in the 18th and 19th centuries, some becoming hotels and offices. Doctors, lawyers, dentists and architects moved here in the late 18th and early 19th centuries, as the remaining noble families moved on to Mayfair and Piccadilly. These days, the square is popular with publishers, film and music companies, including Bloomsbury, Paul McCartney's MPL Communications and 20th Century Fox.

On the left as you enter the Square, just past Sutton Row at 21A Soho Square, is an unexpected surprise in this lusty, hedonistic part of London: **St Patrick's Church** ❹ (for opening hours, ☎ 020-7437 2010). It's a notably large Roman Catholic church, with extensive catacombs which run under the Square and beyond. There's been a church here since 1792, with the current one built in 1891-3 in Italianate style by John Kelly. It's a long and narrow building, owing to the restrictions of the plot of land. Originally built to serve the local area's Irish community, the church is now a focus for helping Soho's burgeoning population of homeless people.

On the right as you enter the Square is another worthy, sometimes-overlooked spiritual site: the elegant, red-brick **French Protestant Church of London** ❺ (for opening hours, ☎ 020-7437 5311). It was built in 1893 by Sir Aston Webb, most famous for the Victoria and Albert Museum, on land formerly occupied by houses at numbers 8 and 9. The building is four storeys high, in the Flemish Gothic style, with an attractive tiled façade; services are still held in French.

20th Century Fox building

detail of French Protestant Church

There's a bench commemorating the late singer Kirsty MacColl in the garden of Soho Square, bought by her fans after her death in 2000. It's a fitting tribute as MacColl wrote a song called *Soho Square*.

Continue round the Square from the French Protestant Church to **20th Century Fox Film Co Ltd** ❻ at numbers 31-32, with the name distinctively displayed at the top of the building. Further along at number 30 is **The Hospital for Women** ❼, which has been here since 1852; the house at number 29 was demolished in 1867 to extend the hospital, which is now a general health centre.

Don't neglect the garden in the middle of Soho Square, a favourite with office workers, itinerants seeking somewhere to rest and the gay community who like to see and be seen here. It remains largely as it was in the 19th century, and features include Caius Gabriel Cibber's statue of Charles II and a mock Tudor hut that used to house an electrical transformer and is now the gardener's tool shed.

Turn right off Soho Square down 17th-century Greek Street. This road takes its name from a Greek church that stood in Hogs

Lane – the street's original name – or from the Greeks who settled here in the mid-18th century. Some early 18th-century buildings remain but the façades of most are more recent; number 17 has an interesting 19th-century shop front. Infamous lothario Casanova stayed in Greek Street when he visited London in 1764.

Immediately on the left as you enter Greek Street is **The House of St Barnabas-in-Soho** 8, another spiritual stop in sinful Soho (tours Tue and Thu, 9-11am, ☎ 020-7437 1894). It's in a standard Georgian mansion built in the 1740s which, since 1852, has been a hostel for homeless women run by the House of Charity. This is one of Soho's oldest properties and has managed to retain many original fittings. The interior has an abundance of rich carving and plasterwork, and is one of London's best examples of the

English rococo style. It retains a cantilevered 'crinoline' staircase over five floors, so-called because the railings were shaped to accommodate the ladies' wide skirts fashionable at the time. Charles Dickens is reputed to have used the house and garden as the setting for the London lodgings of Dr Manette and Lucy in *A Tale of Two Cities*.

> The Gay Hussar's Hungarian connections are tenuous at best. It was opened in 1953 by a Briton of Italian heritage who'd studied catering in Hungary!

Next door is **The Gay Hussar** 9, a Hungarian restaurant that's long been a favourite haunt of left-wing politicians and intellectuals. Regular diners have included Tony Benn, Barbara Castle, Michael Foot, Tom Driberg and Roy Hattersley. It was sold to

Hospital for Women

The Gay Hussar

Pillars of Hercules

Hazlitt's Hotel

the Wheeler's restaurant company in the '80s, but is still frequented by journalists, media figures and other middle class lefties.

Further down the street, also on the left, is an excellent pub, The Pillars of Hercules. There's been a pub here since 1733, which is mentioned in Charles Dickens's *A Tale of Two Cities*, but while the current building looks suitably ancient, it only dates back to 1935. In the '70s, rising stars Martin Amis, Julian Barnes and Ian McEwan were regulars.

Turn right down Bateman Street – the Viscounts Bateman lived in Monmouth House, a large mansion on nearby Soho Square – and at the end, turn right a short distance along Frith Street, for **Hazlitt's Hotel** ⑩.

Frith Street was laid out from the 1670s and is named after

Richard Frith, a wealthy builder. The only remaining original late 17th-century house is number 60; most of the other early houses have later frontages. Hazlitt's is one of London's better hotels, occupying three Georgian houses dating from 1718, which have largely original interiors. It's named after William Hazlitt (1778-1830), who's regarded as England's second-greatest literary critic (after Samuel Johnson). He lived here in his final year and his last words, apparently, were the rather splendid "Well, I've had a happy life"; he merits a hotel named after him for that alone!

Turn and walk back along Frith Street, heading south. On the right at number 18 is Soho's oldest pub, the **Dog and Duck** ⑪. There's been an inn on this site since 1734 and

Dog & Duck

De Hems

this one is cosy and atmospheric, with a splendid tiled interior. One of George Orwell's regular haunts, it's small and can become very crowded, with customers spilling onto the pavement.

> Frith Street has had some famous residents. Mozart stayed at number 20 when he was aged eight (in 1764-5) and is commemorated by a blue plaque opposite Ronnie Scott's (another Soho stalwart). Poet Samuel Taylor Coleridge stayed at number 10 in 1810 and, more recently, John Logie Baird transmitted the first television pictures from number 22 in 1925 (look for the plaque above Bar Italia).

At the bottom of Frith Street, turn right down Shaftesbury Avenue – the heart of London's theatre land. This thoroughfare

was built in 1886, much more recently than much of Soho, and acknowledges the 9th Earl of Shaftesbury for his charitable work for the local poor. Cross the avenue and turn right, then take the next left down Macclesfield Street for **De Hems** ⑫ at number 11. De Hems is a Dutch pub which became a meeting place for the Resistance in WWII. It's named after a Dutch seaman who bought the pub in 1890 (though it dates back to the 17th century) and offers an extensive range of Dutch and Belgian beers.

Macclesfield Street dates from 1685 and is named after Charles Gerard, 1st Earl of Macclesfield; Friedrich Engels lodged at number 2 in 1850. More recent residents are almost exclusively Chinese, for this is the northern border of

FOOD & DRINK 🍴

11 Dog and Duck:
Tiny Nicholson's pub
serving an eclectic
range of real ales,
including Sharp's
Doom Bar, London
Pride and Timothy
Taylor Landlord,
and quality pub
grub.

12 De Hems:
Unusual Dutch café
bar serving
traditional English
food plus a range
of Dutch beers and
'bar bites' such as
bitterballen,
frikandellen and
uitsmitjer.

London's Chinatown where even the street signs feature Chinese script.

Cross back across Shaftesbury Avenue, turn left and head north up Wardour Street.

Almost immediately on the right is **St Anne's Church 13**; or rather, the frontage of the church, as this is all that survived the Blitz. The building dates from 1677-86 (possibly designed by Wren or William Talman, perhaps by both of them) and that loyal friend of

old buildings Sir John Betjeman campaigned successfully to save what remains from demolition in the '70s. The former churchyard is now a small garden, its level raised by the 10,000 burials underneath.

Further along Wardour Street on the right is attractive **Meard Street 14**. Built between 1722 and 1732, this is Soho's most authentic and complete original street, although often overlooked; it feels more like Bloomsbury or Belgravia than Soho. Meard Street was built by carpenter John Meard, who also erected the spire of nearby St Anne's church.

Wardour Street has a long association with rock music. The famous Marquee Club once stood at number 90 and was one of London's most important rock venues from 1964 to 1988. Famous bands that played residencies at the Marquee include Led Zeppelin, Pink Floyd, The Who (there's a blue plaque to drummer Keith Moon), The Jam (who immortalised the venue in their song *A-Bomb in Wardour Street*) and Iron Maiden. Sadly it's now just another of Soho's many bar/restaurants.

Head north along Wardour Street until you reach St Anne's Court which is on the right, just

Trident Studios

respectful of its rich history, with tours of the site possible (☎ 020-7734 6198).

Return the short distance to Broadwick Street and follow the street as it doglegs till you reach Poland Street, built from the 1680s and named for the King of Poland tavern which once stood here. A few 18th-century houses remain; writer and artist William Blake lived at number 28 from 1785-91.

At the junction with Poland Street is John Snow's **Cholera Pump** ⑯. It isn't much to look at but has an interesting history. Cholera spread to Europe along trade routes in the early 19th century and quickly took hold. There was no cure and it had a 50 per cent mortality rate; in 1849 alone, over 50,000 Londoners died of the disease. Dr John Snow (1813-58, vice-president of the Westminster Medical Society and

past Broadwick Street on the left. **Trident Studios** ⑮ is at 17 St Anne's Court and will be of interest to rock music lovers. This recording studio was built in 1967 by the Sheffield brothers and its superior equipment and facilities soon attracted many notable musicians. Lou Reed's *Transformer* was recorded at Trident and was produced by David Bowie, who also used the studios for some of his own albums, including *The Rise and Fall of Ziggy Stardust*. Parts of The Beatles *White Album* were recorded here and in the '70s a distinguished selection of musicians used Trident, including Black Sabbath, Elton John, Marc Bolan and T Rex, Frank Zappa, Free, The Rolling Stones and Rod Stewart. The original business was sold in 1981 but it's still a studio and the current owners are

cholera pump

WALK 10

Beak Street

pump nearby and a blue plaque to Dr Snow at 53 Frith Street, his former home.

Continue along Broadwick Street and turn left down Marshall Street, which was built in the 1730s. Turn right down Beak Street, which dates from the late 17th and early 18th centuries (when it was Silver Street). It was renamed for Thomas Beake, one of Queen Anne's messengers. Polpo restaurant is on the right, serving an Italian version of tapas. It has a blue plaque for the Italian painter Canaletto, who leased a studio here.

Turn left down Upper James Street, which leads to **Golden Square** ⑰, Soho's second and lesser-known square begun in 1675, where this walk terminates. The square is spacious if unremarkable, with benches and banana palms, and a number of attractive houses such as **numbers 23 and 24** ⑱. The name could be a corruption of gelding, as the land had been used for grazing horses and was once known as Gelding's Close. It quickly became a fashionable place to live and later a number of embassies moved here.

The square was much less attractive by Charles Dickens's time. In *Nicholas Nickleby*, Dickens chose it as the location for Ralph Nickleby's gloomy home and described it as a place where single gentlemen take lodgings. By the early 20th century, it housed businesses associated with the wool trade, some of which are still here, alongside the inevitable film company offices.

Queen Victoria's obstetrician) disagreed with the majority view that cholera was an air-borne poison produced by rotting vegetables or bodies. He thought it was water-borne and was ultimately proved right, despite initial opposition.

Snow realised during a cholera outbreak that many of the victims had used the water pump on Broad Street (now Broadwick Street). The handle of the pump was therefore removed to render it useless and almost at once, the outbreak stopped. Today, the original site of the pump is indicated by a kerbstone on Broadwick Street, outside the John Snow pub, named in the good doctor's honour (even though he was teetotal). There's a replica

To reach Piccadilly Circus tube station, head south from Golden Square, cross Brewer Street and head along Sherwood Street. The station is across the junction at the end.

Golden Square

1. Institut Français
2. Statue of Bartok
3. St Luke Chelsea
4. Godfrey Street
5. Cadogan Square
6. Belgrave Square
7. The Grenadier
8. Victoria Square
9. Chester Square
10. Royal Hospital Chelsea
11. National Army Museum
12. Tite Street
13. Japanese Peace Pagoda
14. Chelsea Physic Garden
15. Thomas Carlyle's House
16. Cheyne Walk Brasserie
17. Sir Thomas More
18. Crosby Hall

V & A Museum

CROMWELL RD

South Kensington

HARRINGTON RD

SYDNEY PL

SYDNEY ROAD

FULHAM

SYDNEY ST

CALE ST

WHITEHEAD

BRITTEN ST

KING'S

DERESON

Chelsea FC (Stamford Bridge)

FULHAM ROAD

GUNTER GR

Fulham Broadway

HARWOOD RD

KING'S ROAD

CHEYNE WALK

RIVER

Battersea Bridge

Places of Interest   Food & Drink

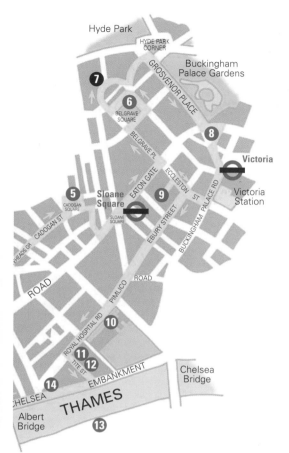

Hyde Park

HYDE PARK CORNER

Buckingham Palace Gardens

7

GROSVENOR PLACE

6
BELGRAVE SQUARE

BELGRAVE PL

8

EATON GATE

5
CADOGAN SQUARE

Sloane Square

ECCLESTON ST

Victoria

9

SLOANE SQUARE

EBURY STREET

Victoria Station

CADOGAN ST

EHEADS GR

BUCKINGHAM PALACE RD

CADOGAN ST

ROAD

ROAD

PIMLICO

ROYAL HOSPITAL RD

10

TITE ST

11 **12**

EMBANKMENT

Chelsea Bridge

14

CHELSEA

THAMES

Albert Bridge

13

BELGRAVIA & CHELSEA

Distance: 4.76mi (7.66km)

Duration: full day

Start: South Kensington tube station

End: Fulham Broadway tube station

These exclusive corners of London are best known for their millionaire inhabitants and eye-wateringly expensive real estate. Belgravia and Chelsea are the haunts of titled landlords, Sloane rangers and, more recently, Russian oligarchs. As you walk these streets you're following the footsteps of some very well-shod feet.

Belgravia is a district in the City of Westminster and the Royal Borough of Kensington and Chelsea. It lies mainly to the southwest of Buckingham Palace and its approximate boundaries are Knightsbridge to the north, Pimlico Road to the south, Buckingham Palace Road and Grosvenor Place to the east, and Sloane Street to the west. It's the wealthiest area in the UK and, quite possibly, in the world. The name Belgravia comes from one of the subsidiary titles of the Duke of Westminster: Viscount Belgrave, after a village in Cheshire near the family's main country seat. As London's largest landowner, the duke is the landlord of many properties here.

Chelsea is an equally desirable, though rather more fashionable part of London, which is bounded to the south by the Thames, to the east by Chelsea Bridge Road and Sloane Street, and to the north and northwest by Knightsbridge and South Kensington. Chelsea has an ancient heritage. The f rst record of the Manor of Chelsea precedes the Domesday Book of 1086 and its name in Old English meant 'landing place (on the river) for chalk or limestone'. A partly rural area until the 1800s, it began to attract the rich and famous in the 19th century and has been doing so ever since. Artists, writers and musicians moved in f rst, followed by f lm stars, models and fashion designers. Chelsea played a prominent role in the Swinging Sixties (1960s).

BELGRAVIA & CHELSEA

Swinging London was a term coined by *Time* magazine in 1966 to describe the blossoming music, fashion and cultural scene happening in the capital. It was led by such icons as the Beatles, designer Mary Quant and fashion model Twiggy and centred on smart shopping areas, including King's Road, Chelsea.

Institut Français

Start Walking…

Our walk around London's most exclusive quarter begins at South Kensington tube station. Leave by the main exit and walk west up Harrington Road, named for the estate once owned by the Stanhopes, Viscounts Petersham and Earls of Harrington. Turn right into Queensbury Place for the **Institut Français** ❶, which is on the right at number 17; you run the gauntlet of hordes of French-speaking children from the French Lycée around the corner. The Institut is housed in a striking Art Deco building and has been here since 1939. It was founded in 1910 by a private benefactor to introduce London to French artists and writers, and is now the official centre for French language and culture in Britain.

Return to the tube station and continue to the right, passing Pelham Street to Onslow Square, where there's an elegant **statue of Bartok** ❷ on the corner. Bela Bartok (1881-1945) was a Hungarian pianist and one of the 20th century's most important composers. Continue straight ahead rather than going around the square; on the left, as Onslow

statue of Bartok

Square becomes Sydney Place, is a blue plaque marking Bartok's home. Onslow Square is named after the Earl of Onslow, and the elegant, stuccoed houses were built by C. J. Freake in 1846. Architect Edward Lutyens was born at number 16 in 1896 and author William Thackeray lived at number 36 from 1854 to 1862.

St Luke's

FOOD & DRINK

7 The Grenadier: Small historic (allegedly haunted) pub with an excellent range of ales and good traditional pub grub. Closed Sun.

16 Cheyne Walk Brasserie (☎ 020-7376 8787): Chic French brasserie and salon with a Provençal menu including specialities such as Pyrenean lamb and grilled sea bream. Mon dinner only; Sun lunch only.

At the end of Sydney Place, turn right along Fulham Road. Fulham's history dates back to the 7th century or earlier. Its name may be derived from a former inhabitant and roughly translates as 'Fulla's settlement on a low-lying bend of the river'. It's been an important route since the 15th century, known as King's Highway and London Road, and is one of the area's longest thoroughfares at almost 3mi/5km.

Turn left down Sydney Street. After crossing Cale Street you come to the elegant, sandstone-coloured parish church of **St Luke Chelsea 3** (Mon-Fri, 9am-4.30pm). St Luke's was built in 1820-4 by James Savage and is almost the size of a cathedral, with seating for 2,500 worshippers; Charles Dickens was married here in 1836. Next to the church, leafy, bench-endowed St Luke's Gardens is a welcome retreat and the second-largest private gardens in central London after Buckingham Palace.

From Sydney Street turn left down Britten Street; at the end, turn right and then left down Burnsall Street and left again along **Godfrey Street 4** for the pretty artisans' cottages, which now form part of a desirable and expensive residential area. This is one of London's most attractive streets, but a glance at house prices in a local estate agent's window will almost certainly shatter any dreams of living here.

At the end of Godfrey Street, turn right into Cale Street, named for an 18th-century benefactress Judith Cale, who made a bequest to 'six poor widows of Chelsea'. The '60s boutique Hung on You was located at number 22 and was the first shop to have the front of a car stuck (deliberately)

According to the property website Zoopla (🖳 www.zoopla.co.uk), the average value of a property in Godfrey Street in March 2012 was £1.8m. In the wider SW3 area, the average asking price was over £2.5m.

Cadogan Square

ahead and follow Whiteheads Grove as it becomes Cadogan Street. On the right of Cadogan Street are the attractive St Joseph's Cottages, dating from 1850 and later restored.

At Cadogan Gardens, turn left into **Cadogan Square** ⑤, which is lined with magnificent red-brick buildings with some attractive mews running off it. It was one of the first 19th-century developments in London to use red brick rather than stucco, along

in its window! The Beatles shopped there and it later moved to King's Road. Swing left down Whiteheads Grove, which has interesting, red-brick buildings on its right-hand side. At the junction with Sloane Avenue, go straight

Belgrave Square

with Lennox Gardens and Pont Street. The square is so-called because it was built on land belonging to the Cadogan Estate and Smith's Charity Estate. A number of different architects designed the houses, hence the interesting variety of styles with, for example, a Gothic-style home sitting next to a Queen Anne residence.

Return along Cadogan Gardens and turn left along King's Road. This is Chelsea's main thoroughfare, originally a private road that Charles II used to get to Hampton Court and George III used on the way to Kew. It only became a public highway in 1830 and is now one of London's most glamorous roads.

At the Sloane Square junction, turn left and cross Sloane Square, which leads into Eaton Gate via Cliveden Place. Sloane Square was designed in 1771 and is named after Sir Hans Sloane, Lord of the Manor of Chelsea. It's a popular meeting place and an unofficial boundary between Chelsea and Belgravia. It's also the spiritual home of the Sloane Ranger: well-bred young women (and men) about town, of whom the late Princess Diana was an prime example. Eaton Gate becomes Eaton Square, named for Eaton Hall in Cheshire, the country seat of the Grosvenors; it was built in 1826-55 by Thomas Cubitt. Eaton Square has been home to many famous residents, including politicians Stanley Baldwin and Neville Chamberlain, author Raymond Chandler and philanthropist George Peabody.

At the second junction, turn left down Belgrave Place to **Belgrave Square** ❻, one of London's grandest Victorian squares, covering 10 acres (4ha). The architect was George Basevi, a pupil of Sir John Soane, and Benjamin Disraeli's cousin. The houses are sizeable and stuccoed, with detached properties at its four corners. Belgrave Square is no longer residential and the houses are mainly embassies or offices. Take care when crossing the road

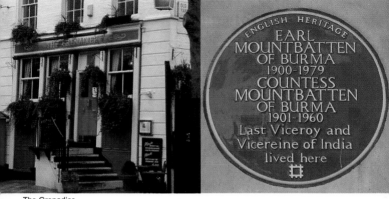

The Grenadier

here as taxi drivers seem to use the Square as a Formula One circuit!

Current 'occupants' of Belgrave Square include Simon Bolivar, Christopher Columbus and Leonardo Da Vinci's Vitruvian Man, all of whom are immortalised by statues in the square.

Turn right down Wilton Terrace, which leads into Wilton Crescent; there's a blue plaque to Earl Mountbatten at number two. Wilton Terrace, Crescent and Row are named after the 1st Earl of Wilton, father-in-law of the 1st Marquess of Westminster, who owned the land. The crescent was built in 1827 by W. H. Seth-Smith and Thomas Cubitt; proceed around it and on the left is Wilton Row, a mews originally called Crescent Mews and built in 1828-30. Take it for the attractive pub at the end, **The Grenadier** ❼, one of London's prettiest pubs and (allegedly) the most haunted. It was originally called the Guardsman and, according to some sources, was once a mess for the Duke of Wellington's officers. It's certainly full of Wellington mementoes, military prints and old weapons, and is supposedly haunted by a guardsman who was beaten to death for cheating at cards.

Return along Wilton Row and Wilton Crescent, then turn left along Grosvenor Crescent. Keep left and at the end turn right into Grosvenor Place; Hyde Park is on your left, with impressive mansion blocks to the right. Development began here in 1746 and Prime Minister Henry

145

WALK 11

Victoria Square

Campbell-Bannerman lived at number 6 from 1877-1904. Turn left down Lower Grosvenor Place, right down Beeston Place and left into attractive, tranquil **Victoria Square** 8. It's much quieter than the surrounding traffic-choked area and has a small central garden with a statue of Queen Victoria. The square was built in 1838-9, designed by Matthew Wyatt, and has around two dozen houses, all Grade II* listed. These five-storey, stucco-fronted properties were built to celebrate the start of Queen Victoria's reign. Former residents include author Ian Fleming and politician Michael Portillo.

At the far end of the square turn right down Buckingham Palace Road, the least attractive part of this walk and home to some of Victoria's transport termini; it was called Chelsea Road in the 18th century. The scenery improves markedly when you turn right along upmarket Eccleston Street, with its stylish cafés and shops; it's named after the Duke of Westminster's estate at Eccleston, Cheshire. More upmarket still is **Chester Square** 9, reached by turning left, which was created in 1840 by Thomas Cubitt. A smaller version of Eaton Square, this pretty garden square is one of London's most prestigious addresses and has long attracted the good and the great.

There's a blue plaque at number 24 commemorating the former home of Mary Shelley, the author of *Frankenstein* (and wife of the romantic poet Percy Shelley), who died here in 1851. Poet and cultural critic Matthew Arnold lived at number 2 from 1839-67, and Prime Minister Harold Macmillan at number 14. More recent residents have included musician Sir Yehudi Menuhin, composer Lord Lloyd Webber, and Sir Denis and Baroness Margaret Thatcher at number 73.

> In the early 21st century, Chester Square was reported to be one of Europe's richest streets, if not *the* richest, based on the combined wealth of its residents.

Return to Eccleston Street and turn right, before taking another right down attractive Ebury Street. Built in 1820 on land belonging to Ebury Farm, a 430-acre (174ha) estate once owned by Elizabeth I, it later became part of the Grosvenor Estate. There's a blue plaque to Mozart at number 180, where the eight-year-old musical prodigy wrote his first symphony

Royal Hospital

Chelsea Pensioner

in 1764-5, and one for writers and nonconformists the Sackville-Wests at number 182. Actress Dame Edith Evans lived at number 109, and author Ian Fleming at number 22. Continue along Ebury Street as it becomes Pimlico and then Royal Hospital Road, once known as Queen's Road.

On the left of Royal Hospital Road is the **Royal Hospital Chelsea** ⑩, home of the Chelsea Pensioners and the site of the Chelsea Flower show in May (grounds, Mon-Sat, 10am-noon and 2-4pm; Great Hall, Mon-Sat, 11am-noon and 2-4pm). It was founded by Charles II for the 'succour and relief of veterans broken by age and war', a purpose it still serves. It has been suggested that Charles II was persuaded to build a hospital for veterans by his mistress Nell

Gwynn, whose father had been made destitute by the Civil War.

It's a beautiful, red-brick, Grade I listed building, regarded as having London's second-loveliest façade on the Thames, after Greenwich. It was designed by Sir Christopher Wren and completed in 1692, with minor alterations by Robert Adam between 1765 and 1782; the stables were added by Sir John Soane in 1814. Thus, the hospital you see today is the work of three of Britain's finest architects.

Shortly after the Royal Hospital, also on the left, is the **National Army Museum** ⑪ (10am-5.30pm). It tends to be ignored in favour of the Imperial War Museum, which is a pity as it's excellent. The museum's covers the period from 1066 to the present day, with exhibitions

Tite Street

Oscar Wilde lived at number 44 in 1881 and at number 34 from 1884-95. He wrote at a desk that had belonged to author Thomas Carlyle, a Chelsea resident himself (see below). Wilde's mother lived nearby, in Oakley Street, while, coincidentally, the judge who convicted Wilde of gross indecency in 1895 lived only a few doors away.

At the end of Tite Street, look to the left for a view of the monolithic Battersea Power Station and ahead across the river for the **Japanese Peace Pagoda** ⑬, which overlooks the Thames in Battersea Park. It was a gift to London from the Nipponzan Myohoji Buddhist Order and is made of Portland Stone and wood. It's 33.5m (110ft) high and features four gilded statues of the Buddha, facing north, south, east and west. They show him making various *mudras*

divided into different eras. Especially interesting and poignant are some of the personal accounts by soldiers, their families and the citizens of war-torn countries. It also asks poignant questions about the consequences of both military intervention and inaction.

On leaving the museum, turn left and soon after take another left down **Tite Street** ⑫, which has a number of attractive buildings. On the right side are mainly red-brick mansion blocks, while on the left there's a variety of building styles, including The River House at the end overlooking the Thames. The street is named after Sir William Tite MP, who was on the Metropolitan Board of Works and responsible for building Chelsea Embankment in the 1870s. At the end of the 19th century, Tite Street was as fashionable an address as nearby Cheyne Walk, and was popular with artists and writers. Writer

Japanese Peace Pagoda

(hand gestures), which have different symbolic meanings.

> The Japanese Peace Pagoda was built to mark the now-defunct Greater London Council's Peace Year in 1984. Permission to build the pagoda was the GLC's last legislative act before it was abolished by Margaret Thatcher.

From Tite Street turn right along Chelsea Embankment, which soon becomes exclusive Cheyne Walk, with the river to the left and some attractive properties to the right, many set back behind gardens. The road is named for the Cheyne family, Lords of the Manor of Chelsea from 1660-1712, and is noted for its Queen Anne houses and interesting later properties. Famous residents comprise a who's who of London's glitterati from the last few centuries, and include author George Eliot at number 4, Prime Minister David Lloyd-George at number 10, painter Dante Gabriel Rossetti, writer and critic Algernon Swinburne and author George Meredith (jointly) at number 16, while writer Henry James lived (and died) at Carlyle Mansions. Painter James Whistler lived at numbers 96 and 101, and engineer Sir Marc Brunel and his son Isambard lived at number 98. Hilaire Beloc lived at number 104 and painter J. M. W. Turner at number 119. More recent residents have included poet T. S. Eliot, rock stars Mick Jagger and Keith Richards, actress Jane Asher, footballer George Best and author Ian Fleming, who was

fortunate to live in a number of London's most desirable streets.

Also along Chelsea Embankment is the renowned **Chelsea Physic Garden** . This living museum and haven of beauty was founded in 1673 by the splendidly-named Worshipful Society of Apothecaries of London, so that its apprentices could study the medicinal properties of plants. It's London's oldest garden – and

Chelsea Physic Garden 14
April to October, Tue-Fri noon-5pm,
Sun and Bank Holiday Mondays,
noon-6pm, £8 adults

Britain's second-oldest, after the University of Oxford's which was founded in 1621. The word 'physic' refers to the science of healing.

The garden's proximity to the Thames is deliberate, as the river tempers the climate, giving it a relatively warm microclimate which helps the survival of non-native plants, including Britain's largest outdoor fruiting olive tree (30ft/9m high). The garden contains around 5,000 types of plant, concentrating on medicinal plants and rare and endangered species. It also has England's first greenhouse and stove, built in 1681, and a well-regarded café for light lunches (plus dinner on Wed, July-August).

Continue along Chelsea Embankment – which soon becomes Cheyne Walk – and turn right up Cheyne Row, one

of London's best-preserved early 18th-century streets, for **Thomas Carlyle's House** ⑮ (Wed-Sun 11am-5pm, £5.10 adults). Thomas and Jane Carlyle were a celebrated literary couple of their day; historian, philosopher and satirist, Thomas was one of the Victorian era's greatest writers, said to have inspired Charles Dickens – although he's little read today – while his wife was a woman of letters and renowned hostess. Their house, which dates to 1708, is a beautiful Queen Anne property and provides a fascinating insight into what life was like in a middle class, creative Victorian home.

Return to Cheyne Walk and turn right, with the popular **Cheyne Walk Brasserie** ⑯ at 50 Cheyne Walk. As you may expect in this notably upmarket part of London, it isn't cheap to enjoy this brasserie's superb Provencal-style cooking, but neither is it prohibitively expensive. On leaving the restaurant, continue right along Cheyne Walk almost as far as Battersea Bridge, to the statue of **Sir Thomas More** ⑰ on the right, in front of Chelsea Old Church. It's a seated bronze by L. Cubitt Bevis (1969), with black robes and golden face and hands.

Thomas More

Sir Thomas More was a philosopher, theologian and statesman, who served under Henry VIII – a risky business! He opposed Henry's Reformation and paid the price by losing his head.

Further along Cheyne Walk, there's another link with More: the impressive, red-brick

Crosby Hall , where we end the walk. It stands on a site that was once part of Sir Thomas More's garden at Beaufort House, built around 1521 and demolished in 1740; Sir Walter Raleigh lodged here in 1601. The hall is the surviving part of the Bishopsgate mansion built for Sir John Crosby, a wealthy wool merchant, in 1466-75. The building was moved stone-by-stone from Bishopsgate to Chelsea in 1910 to rescue it from demolition, where it was incorporated into the buildings of the British Federation of University Women (used as a dining hall); it's now a private residence.

To reach Fulham Broadway tube station, continue along Cheyne Walk as it becomes Gunter Grove and turn left along Fulham Road; the station is along it on the right.

Crosby Hall detail

1. Ely Place
2. St Etheldreda's
3. Ye Olde Mitre
4. Holborn Bars
5. Staple Inn
6. Cittie of Yorke
7. Chancery Court Hotel
8. Fleet River Bakery
9. Lincoln's Inn Fields
10. Sir John Soane's Museum
11. Lincoln's Inn
12. Land Registry
13. Old Curiosity Shop
14. St Mary le Strand

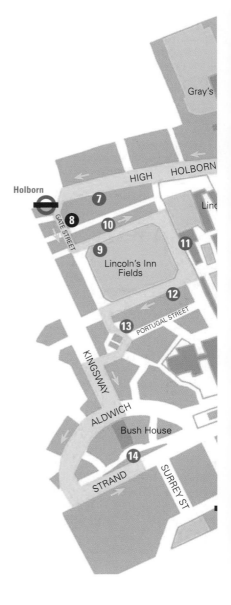

Places of Interest ● Food & Drink

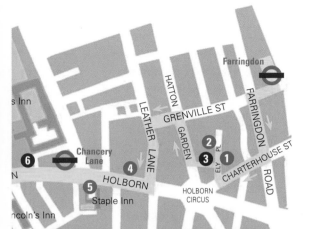

Farringdon

HATTON GARDEN

LEATHER LANE

GRENVILLE ST

FARRINGDON ROAD

CHARTERHOUSE ST

Chancery Lane

2
3
1

ELY PL

6

HOLBORN

4

5

HOLBORN CIRCUS

Staple Inn

Lincoln's Inn

Royal Courts of Justice

STRAND

Temple

HOLBORN

WALK 12

> **Distance:** 1.79mi (2.87km)
> **Duration:** half day
> **Start:** Farringdon tube station
> **End:** Temple tube station

Holborn is a largely commercial area, but with some f ne Georgian and Victorian architecture, and some welcome green spaces, such as Lincoln's Inn Fields. Holborn used to be associated with entertainment, especially inns and taverns, of which a number of f ne examples survive.

In the 18th century, Holborn was the location of the infamous Mother Clap's molly house – an inn or tavern primarily frequented by homosexual men – but in the modern era it has become a centre for entertainment venues to suit more general tastes: 22 inns or taverns were recorded in the 1860s and the Holborn Empire, originally Weston's Music Hall, stood between 1857 and 1960, when it was demolished after sustaining structural damage in the Blitz in WWII. Nowadays, it's home to the legal profession and the centre of the UK's jewellery trade in Hatton Garden, and has also become the site of new off ces and hotels.

The name Holborn – which can be pronounced with or without the 'l' – refers to both the area, bound by Bloomsbury to the north and the Thames to the south, and to High Holborn, the main street which bisects it from east to west. Holborn is one of oldest districts in London and f rst gets a mention in 959 in a charter of Westminster Abbey. The name probably comes from the Middle English *hol* (hollow) and *bourne* (brook), a reference to the River Fleet as it ran through a steep valley to the east; the Fleet was sometimes called the Hole Bourn.

Start Walking…

Our walk takes in some of Holborn's hidden gems, including some exquisite churches and a very unusual museum. It starts at Farringdon tube station. Leave the station and head west along Cowcross Street, turn left along Farringdon Road, right along Charterhouse Street and right up **Ely Place** ❶, an attractive Georgian cul-de-sac. This was the site of the Bishops of Ely's London residence from the end of the 13th century until 1772. The grounds included orchards and vineyards, and the bishops' strawberries were reputedly the finest in London (mentioned by Shakespeare in *Richard III*). The dilapidated Bishop's residence was demolished in the late 18th century, replaced by the brick terraces that now line the street, although the adjoining ancient church was preserved.

St Etheldreda's ❷
Mon-Sat, 8am-5pm, Sun, 8am-12.30pm

Ely Place

Standing to the left of Ely Place, between the end of one of the Georgian terraces and Audrey House, **St Etheldreda's** ❷ is Britain's oldest Catholic church. It was built in 1250-90 as the Chapel of the Bishops of Ely on the site of an earlier structure. St Etheldreda was a 7th-century Abbess of Ely and part of her hand is a venerated relic stored by the high altar. The church has an unusual layout, partly subterranean, and conveys a real sense of age and mystery. The crypt dates to around 1250 and incorporates much older walls, possibly part of a Roman basilica.

> Ely Place is Crown property, which means it officially belongs to the Queen. As such it isn't a part of the City of London and is exempt from the authority of the Lord Mayor. It remains a private road and is protected by a small gatehouse, guarded by a ceremonial officer called a beadle.

Stroll back down Ely Place, turning right along a narrow passageway just before reaching the gatehouse. This leads to **Ye Olde Mitre** ❸ tavern, one of London's oldest traditional pubs and the first of a number of historic pubs mentioned on this walk – it isn't compulsory to have a pint in every one! It used to have a reputation as being the most difficult to find, but there are now signs at both ends of the passageway.

Ye Old Mitre is a tiny pub with an oak front and opaque leaded windows, which dates from 1547, although the current building is from the early 1770s, erected shortly after the demolition of the nearby Palace of the Bishops of Ely. Ely is in Cambridgeshire,

FOOD & DRINK

❸ **Ye Olde Mitre:** Picturesque historic tavern with small selection of well-kept real ales and tasty snacks and bar food. Closed weekends.

❻ **Cittie of Yorke:** Another ancient pub with a great atmosphere, superb Sam Smith's ales and good pub grub. Closed Sun.

❽ **Fleet River Bakery** (☎ 020-7691 1457): Celebrated café serving homemade quiches, frittatas, soup and salads, plus great cakes, biscuits and pastries. Closed Sun.

Ye Olde Mitre

and though this quaint old pub sits at the geographical heart of London, until recently it was also considered to be a part of Cambridgeshire (see below). As a result, criminals would hide here and in the surrounding alleyways which were beyond the reach of London's law officers!

Turn left out of the pub, follow the passage to the end and turn right along Hatton Garden, into the heart of London's jewellery district, which goes by the same name. It's named after Hatton House, which was built around 1576 by Sir Christopher Hatton, Elizabeth I's Chancellor. Jewellers began arriving here in the 1830s and it's now the centre of the UK's diamond trade.

Turn left into Greville Street, which also houses a wealth of jewellers. This is where Sir Fulke Greville, Elizabethan poet, writer and 1st Baron Brooke, made his home. Unfortunately Sir Fulke, friend and biographer of Sir Philip Sidney, met a sticky end in Brooke House where he was murdered in 1628 by one of his servants. The murder scene has long been demolished.

Continue left into Leather Lane, passing the rear of Holborn Bars (see below), with attractive, red-brick road signs on its walls. Leather Lane has a shabby bohemian feel, home to a regular clothes market, plus cafés selling vaguely 'right-on' food and drink – in complete contrast to the surrounding streets selling gold and precious stones. It was once the preserve of leather traders although its name could also come from an inn which stood here, called the Greyhound – *leveroun* in old French.

At the end of Leather Lane, turn right into Holborn, which was originally a Roman road, and soon on the right is the impressive, red-brick **Holborn Bars** ❹ (formerly

Holborn Bars

Staple Inn

the Prudential Building and still often called this) at numbers 138-142. It's built partly on the site of Furnival's Inn (a former Inn of Chancery), which was demolished in 1897, as a blue plaque attests. Holborn Bars is one of London's Victorian Gothic landmarks. The original red-brick and terracotta building (1879) was designed by Alfred Waterhouse and subsequent extensions and redevelopments have followed the original style; the Prudential sold the building in 1999, which is now an event's venue.

Continue along Holborn as it becomes High Holborn and soon, across the road on the left, is **Staple Inn** 5. This is a large, impressive building that dates from 1585 and was once a wool staple: a place where wool was weighed and taxed. The Inn survived the Great Fire in 1666 only to be badly damaged by bombing in 1944, but has subsequently been restored. It's a black and white half-timbered building, with a cruck roof (one supported by curved timbers) and

internal courtyard; it's a fine and enduring example of what much of London looked like before the Great Fire. An archway in the front of the Inn leads to a tranquil courtyard, which has benches and four trees, and is a haven in this busy, traffic-choked part of London. Writer Samuel Johnson had lodgings at Staple Inn in 1759; today much of it's occupied by the Institute of Actuaries, resident since 1887.

Further along, on the right, at 22-3 High Holborn, is the **Cittie of Yorke** 6 public house. There's been a hostelry here since 1430 and the current one was rebuilt in 1923 using some of the original materials, when the previous structure became unsafe. The ground floor bar is one of Britain's longest and has a high arched ceiling – it's sometimes known as the Cathedral Pub. One wall has cubicles with swing doors, which date from the early 20th century and were installed so that lawyers could speak privately with clients over a drink or meal.

Chancery Court Hotel

Leaving the pub, turn right and continue west. There's not much of interest until you reach number 252 on the left and the nicely blowsy **Chancery Court Hotel** ❼. It's a five star hotel in an Edwardian heritage building (1914), designed by H. Percy Monckton, which was the headquarters of the Pearl Assurance Company from 1914-89. It's worth having a peek to see the Renaissance-style Grand Staircase, an architectural tour de force in marble.

Cross High Holborn and turn down Little Turnstile, a short way along on the left. This narrow, atmospheric passageway leads to the historic Ship Tavern, on the corner with Gate Street. Established in 1549, during the Tudor period Catholics would sneak in to attend masses conducted by outlawed priests. Past the pub, turn left down Gate Street, and at 71 Lincoln's Inn Fields – which is on the corner of Gate Street and Twyford Place, almost opposite Whetstone Park – is the **Fleet River Bakery** ❽, serving breakfasts, sandwiches, quiches, frittatas, salads, soups, cakes, wine and beer, all freshly made on site (except the alcohol).

From here, proceed to **Lincoln's Inn Fields** ❾ itself. This classic garden square is London's largest, covering 12 acres – which (coincidentally?) is the same area as the base of Giza's Great Pyramid. When this area was still fields, it was a popular venue for duels and public executions. The square was designed by Inigo Jones in the early 17th century; beneath it is a network of tunnels used during WWII.

Lincoln's Inn Fields

Lincoln's Inn Fields has housed some notable residents over the years. Number 59/60, dating to around 1640, is probably by Inigo Jones and was home to Spencer Perceval, the only British Prime Minister to have been assassinated. Other residents included Nell Gwynne, Charles II's best-known mistress, Prime Ministers William Pitt and Ramsay Macdonald, and architect Sir John Soane.

Turn left into Lincoln's Inn Fields and almost immediately on the left is **Sir John Soane's Museum** ⑩ (Tue-Sat, 10am-5pm), which offers candlelit viewings on the first Tuesday of the month from 6-9pm – arrive early as there are long queues. This is one of London's most interesting museums but it isn't as widely known as it deserves to be. Sir John Soane (1753-1837) was a bricklayer's son who became one of Britain's greatest architects. The museum is housed in his former home, which he designed both as a residence and a place to display his antiquities and works of art. The building has a distinctive façade, with a projecting first-floor loggia, Coade Stone statues and Gothic pedestals. Internally, Soane used top-lighting, sometimes with coloured glass, and lots of mirrors to produce an atmospheric environment.

Sir John Soane was an avid collector and at one stage he and his family were forced to live in just two rooms. His paintings alone include works by Canaletto, Piranesi, Reynolds, Turner and Hogarth, including all eight of Hogarth's noted *Rake's Progress* series.

Sir John used some creative devices to cram in his bewildering collection, including having panels hung with paintings lining the walls that can be pulled out like leaves or which unfold from the walls. As well as art, he also amassed furniture, timepieces, jewellery and more. Some of the more unusual items include Roman cremation

Sir John Soane's Museum

urns, a human skeleton, the sarcophagus of Egyptian Pharaoh Seti I, and the marble tomb of Sir John's favourite dog.

Leaving the museum, turn left and enjoy the square's elegant buildings, which are in a variety of architectural styles. Turn right along Newmans Row and on the left are the magnificent buildings of **Lincoln's Inn** ⑪. It's one of the four Inns of Court, founded in the middle of the 14th century, named either for Thomas de Lyncoln, the King's Serjeant of Holborn, or Henry de Lacy, 3rd Earl of Lincoln and a close advisor of Edward I. The Inn moved to its present site between 1412 and 1422 and the buildings we see today span the period from 1489-1845.

Soon after Lincoln's Inn, turn right along the south side of Lincoln's Inn Fields. On the left at number 32 is the impressive, former **Land Registry** ⑫ building. This was the headquarters of the UK's Land Registry from 1913-2011 and has recently been sold to the London School of

Old Curiosity Shop

Economics and Political Science; the building dates from 1903 and is Grade II listed. Take a sharp left down Portsmouth Street and on the left at number 13/14 is the **Old Curiosity Shop** ⑬ (Mon-Sat, 10.30am-7pm). It was built in the 1560s, making it a rare example of a London Elizabethan building, and perhaps the capital's oldest shop. Despite the name,

Land Registry building

it's uncertain whether it was the inspiration for Charles Dickens's eponymous book. Today it sells antiques, gifts and mementoes, and has an attractively higgledy-piggledy feel to it.

> The stocks were a form of punishment that relied on public humiliation and were erected in the busiest places. Offenders were locked into place by their head, hands or feet and passers-by were encouraged to add their own chastisement by throwing rubbish at the offender or tickling their bare feet!

Turn right along Portugal Street, which has the distinction of being the last London site where stocks were erected (until 1820). Turn down the narrow, cobbled St Clement's Lane, which used to be a long country lane leading to the parish church of St Clement Danes.

Today it's the site of another refined watering hole Ye Olde White Horse, at number 2. There's been a pub here for over 200 years and the cellar dates back to the 1600s. Return the short distance to Portugal Street and continue ahead into Kingsway, one of the last and largest of the Victorian London building schemes, along with Aldwych. Costing £5m (a huge fortune in those days), it was opened in 1905 by Edward VII and named in his honour.

Head south along Kingsway until you reach Aldwych, the crescent-shaped street which links Kingsway to The Strand. The name first appears in 1398 and is derived from Aldwic, meaning old settlement, a term which dates back to King Alfred's time (9th century). Turn right to pass the Waldorf Hilton and the Novello Theatre – there's a blue plaque to songwriter Ivor Novello – and at the end of Aldwych turn sharp left, with Somerset House on your right.

In the middle of the road is the church of **St Mary le Strand** ⑭, where we end this walk with some spiritual sustenance (Tue-Thu, 11am-4pm, Sun, 10am-1pm). It's small and elegant with an exotically jewelled interior in the Italianate style, including an amazing decorated ceiling. There's been a church here from at least 1147. It was demolished in 1549 to make room for Somerset House, and wasn't replaced until 1714-17, when the current baroque church was built, designed by James Gibbs; Charles Dickens's parents were married here in 1809. From the church, it's a short walk down Surrey Street towards the river and Temple tube station.

Ye Old White Horse

YE OLD WHITE HORSE

St Mary le Strand

1. Royal Courts of Justice
2. Twinings
3. Thai Square
4. Temple Bar
5. Child and Co.
6. Law Society
7. The Maughan Library
8. Ede & Ravenscroft
9. Cross-eyed statue of John Wilkes
10. Gough Square
11. Dr Johnson's House
12. Statue of Hodge
13. Ye Olde Cheshire Cheese
14. Peterborough Court
15. 128 Fleet Street
16. Punch Tavern
17. Whitefriars Crypt
18. El Vino
19. Hoare's
20. St Dunstan-in-the-West
21. Prince Henry's Room
22. Temple Church
23. Master's House
24. King's Bench Walk
25. Inner Temple Gardens
26. Middle Temple Hall
27. Fountain Court
28. Middle Temple Gardens
29. The Devereux

Places of Interest   Food & Drink

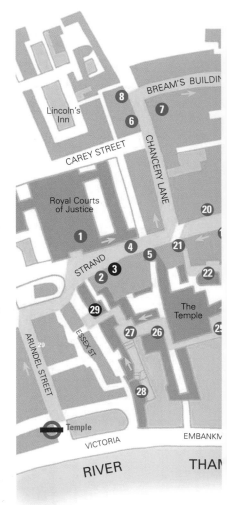

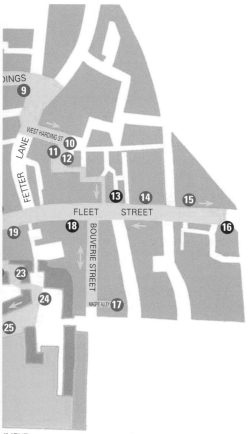

INNS OF COURT & FLEET STREET

Distance: 1.79mi (2.88km)
Duration: half day
Start/End: Temple tube station

Walk along the lanes and alleyways to the north and south of Fleet Street and you'll encounter some fascinating ghosts, from literary genius Dr Johnson to the mysterious Knights Templar. This area is at the heart of the legal profession, ancient and modern – but don't let that put you off! As you take in the fascinating Law Courts, and the tranquil oases of Inner and Middle Temples, you may envy the lawyers who congregate here.

The Inns of Court are the professional associations for barristers in England and Wales, to which all barristers must belong, with supervisory and disciplinary functions over their members. The Inns also provide libraries, dining facilities and professional accommodation. Each also has a church or chapel attached to it and is a self-contained precinct where barristers traditionally train and practise, although growth in the legal profession, together with a desire to practise from more modern accommodation, caused many barristers' chambers to move outside the precincts of the Inns of Court in the late 20th century.

Fleet Street – named after the River Fleet, London's largest underground river – is closely associated with the newspaper industry and was the origin and home of most British newspapers until the 1980s, when most moved to the Docklands. Even though the last major British news off ce, Reuters, left in 2005, the term *Fleet Street* continues to be used as a metonym for the British national press. Step into one of the street's older watering holes and you may hear the echo of inebriated gossip or the headlines of yesteryear.

INNS OF COURT & FLEET STREET

Start Walking…

Start your investigation of Fleet Street and the Inns of Court at Temple tube station, turning left up a short flight of steps and crossing the road. Walk up Arundel Street, named for the Earl of Arundel who built the street in 1678 in the hope of raising funds to have a house designed and built by Sir Christopher Wren. Turn right along the Strand, which links Trafalgar Square with the City. This road earned the name Strandway in the 11th century because it ran along the strand, or edge, of the river.

The first major building on the left is the impressive **Royal Courts of Justice ①** (Mon-Fri, 9.30am-5pm) or Law Courts. They were constructed in the 19th century as a hub for all the country's superior courts concerned with civil cases – criminal cases are tried at the Old Bailey to the east of Fleet Street. Work began in 1874 but the project was beset by bad weather, labour problems and lack of finance, and wasn't completed until 1882.

The Law Courts were designed by George Edmund Street and are built to a massive scale. There are over 1,000 rooms and 3.5 miles (5.6km) of corridors and the building features 35 million bricks faced with slabs of Portland stone. Many notable people and companies have fought cases here, including such diverse players as Satanist Aleister Crowley, novelist and politician Jeffrey Archer, and fast-food restaurant chain McDonald's.

On the right of the Strand opposite the Courts building is the small, ornately-decorated entrance to **Twinings ②** shop and museum. Twinings was founded in the early 18th century by Thomas Twining (1675-1741) who saw there was money to be made from selling tea, which was then an exotic drink, enjoyed mainly by the wealthy. He bought the old Tom's Coffee House at the back of the site in 1706, introduced tea and in 1717 opened the Golden Lyon to sell both tea and coffee.

Twinings ②
Mon-Fri, 8.30am-7.30pm, Sat, 10am-5pm, Sun, 10am-4pm

Twinings is the oldest shop in the City of Westminster, and is thought to be the oldest company to have traded continuously on the same site with the same family since its foundation.

The handsome doorway to Twinings was added to the shop in 1787 by Thomas' grandson Richard Twining (1749-1824). It incorporates his grandfather's Golden Lyon symbol and two

WALK 13

Chinese figures to acknowledge that tea drinking began in China. The Twining's logo also dates to 1787 and is one of the world's oldest in continuous use. There's an interesting museum at the back of the shop, where you can taste a selection of different teas.

Soon after Twinings, also on the right, is the restaurant **Thai Square** 3, occupying a building dating from 1625. It was allegedly once the home of the Gatekeeper of Temple Bar (see below), and was the only building on the Strand to survive the Great Fire of 1666. Nearby, in the middle of the road, is the former site of **Temple Bar** 4 which since 1293 has marked the western boundary of the City; it features a statue of a dragon, the City's symbol. The Temple Bar evolved from a chain slung between two posts in medieval times to a magnificent gateway built by Wren in 1672. It was removed from this spot

FOOD & DRINK

3 Thai Square (☎ 020-7497 0904): Good value authentic Thai food in attractive Thai-inspired surroundings. Closed Sun.

13 Ye Olde Cheshire Cheese: Atmospheric old Sam Smith's pub with a traditional chophouse and restaurant on the ground floor.

16 Punch Tavern: Lovely old pub serving superb cask ales and good value award-winning British food, including steak pies, chicken pie, fish & chips and Sunday roasts. Closes at 7pm weekends.

Child & Co. BANKERS

in 1878 when traffic began to increase on Fleet Street and now stands near St Paul's Cathedral (see page 56).

At 1 Fleet Street, next to the former site of Temple Bar, is **Child and Co.** 5, Britain's oldest bank. Francis Child began banking

Law Society

Maughan Library

'at the sign of the Marygold (or marigold)' here in 1673 and when it was dismantled in 1878, the company built the present elegant, Grade II listed premises on the site. The bank is now owned by the Royal Bank of Scotland but retains its own identity.

Cross the road and turn left up Chancery Lane. Once called New Street, it became Chancellors Lane in 1377 when Edward III took over the House for Converted Jews for the use of the Master of the Rolls (the second most senior judge in England and Wales after the Lord Chief Justice). At number 113 on the left is the **Law Society** 6 building, a classic temple-like structure designed by Lewis Vulliamy in 1831, with small golden lions topping the railings in front of it. The Law Society – which represents and regulates solicitors in England and Wales – dates from 1825 and has been known by its current name since 1903.

Opposite is **The Maughan Library** 7, an impressive, neo-Gothic, Grade II* listed building which houses the main library of King's College London. Built between 1851 and 1858, it was designed by Sir James Pennethorne and is named after Sir Deryck Maughan, who made a large donation towards its cost. Further along Chancery Lane, at number 97, is a branch of **Ede & Ravenscroft** 8, London's oldest tailor established in 1689. It specialises in legal and ceremonial attire, and is where barristers and judges buy their gowns and distinctive wigs.

The wigs worn by the legal professional used to be made from human hair but are now made from horse hair, a technique which was pioneered by Humphrey Ravenscroft in the 1830s. A wig costs several hundred pounds.

cross-eyed statue of John Wilkes

Turn right down Bream's Buildings and right again along Fetter Lane, with London's only **cross-eyed statue** ❾ in front of you. It's a 1988 bronze by James Butler of the political commentator, campaigner and Lord Mayor John Wilkes (1725-97) – and yes, he was cross-eyed. As befits its location, Fetter Lane may derive its name from the Old French *faitor* meaning lawyer. Past residents include poet John Dryden, philosopher Thomas Hobbes, writer Tom Paine and Lemuel Gulliver, Swift's fictional hero.

Cross Fetter Lane and turn left down West Harding Street – named after Agas Hardinge, who in 1513 left a bequest for poor goldsmiths' widows – which becomes Pemberton Street. Sir James Pemberton, Lord Mayor and a member of the Goldsmiths' Company, owned much of the land in the area. On the right is **Gough Square** ❿, the site of **Dr Johnson's House** ⓫. The square was built by Richard Gough, a wool merchant, and isn't actually a square, being L-shaped (court is a

more accurate term). Dr Johnson's House is the only original building.

Samuel Johnson (1709-84) was a biographer, editor, essayist, lexicographer, literary critic, moralist, poet and, obviously, a splendid time manager. He's regarded by some as the most distinguished man of letters in English history and was also the subject of perhaps the world's most famous biography, by his friend James Boswell. The house at 17 Gough Square was built around 1700, one of the few residential properties of its vintage surviving in the City of London. Johnson lived here from 1748-59, during which period he compiled the first comprehensive English dictionary. It's an elegant building, restored to its original condition, and the exhibits provide a fascinating insight into this all-round genius.

Dr Johnson's House ⓫
Mon-Sat, 11am-5.30pm from May-September, 11am-5pm from October to April, £4.50 adults

FOOD & DRINK

18 El Vino:
Famous Victorian wine bar with over 200 wines (plus a wine shop) and traditional home cooked English food and tapas. Closed weekends.

29 The Devereux:
Traditional, cosy pub serving a good selection of well-kept ales and tasty pub grub. Closed weekends.

Hodge

Gough Square itself is attractive and boasts a small **statue of Hodge** 12, one of Dr Johnson's cats, immortalised in a whimsical passage in Boswell's *Life of Johnson*. The bronze was unveiled in 1997 and shows the cat sitting next to a pair of empty oyster shells on top of a copy of Johnson's famous dictionary, with the inscription 'a very fine cat indeed'.

At the far end of Gough Square from Dr Johnson's House, turn right, then right again down a narrow passageway to the right of 11 Gough Square. Turn left down Bolt Court, which leads to Fleet Street, and is probably named

after the Bolt-in-Ten, an inn which once stood on this spot. Fleet Street is named after the river; in medieval times Fleet Street was a major thoroughfare and later had a long-standing association with printing and publishing, although much of the newspaper industry moved east to Wapping and Canary Wharf in the '80s.

Turn left along Fleet Street, soon reaching **Ye Olde Cheshire Cheese** 13 pub on the left and, soon after, **Peterborough Court** 14. The pub's entrance is in Wine Office Court, a left turn off Fleet Street. The 'Cheese' is one of London's oldest pubs and was the first new building to be constructed locally after the Great Fire, in 1667. It's little changed since the 17th century; a sign outside lists the 15 monarchs who have reigned throughout its existence, while another details its famous patrons, including Charles Dickens, who was a regular. The name comes from the cheese that

Peterborough Court Fleet Street

ousted Suffolk as London's most popular at the time.

Although national newspapers are no longer published in Fleet Street, it's still connected to some eminent publications: *The Beano* and *The Dandy* are published by DC Thomson & Co, which has its London base in Fleet Street.

The striking Art Deco Peterborough Court is so-called because the site was owned by the Bishops of Peterborough from the 14th century. It belonged to the *Daily Telegraph* from 1863-1987 and is currently the London HQ of Goldman Sachs bank. A little further along Fleet Street is a historic pub in which to end this walk,

Suitably refreshed, you can retrace your steps back down Fleet and New Bridge Streets to Blackfriars.

Continue east along Fleet Street and soon you come to

number 128 **15**, a Grade II* listed Art Deco delight. This was the home of the *Daily Express* from 1931 till 1989 when it moved to Blackfriars Road – 'Express' is still written on either side of the entrance. The building was designed by Sir Owen Williams and has rounded corners, covered in clear glass and black vitrolite with chromium strips. The *Express* had similar eye-pleasing offices in Manchester and Glasgow.

The lobby of the Daily Express building is as flamboyant as its exterior, featuring silver and gilt decorations, a recessed ceiling and sweeping oval staircase. Unfortunately, it isn't open to the public, except on rare occasions, so the only people who can enjoy it are employees and guests of the current occupants, Goldman Sachs.

Continue to the end of Fleet Street, cross the road and ahead,

Punch Tavern | Whitefriars Crypt

at number 99, is the **Punch Tavern** . A large, attractive, Grade II listed Victorian pub, its name derives from the fact that the now-defunct *Punch* magazine was conceived here in 1841. The current pub was rebuilt 1894-5 and retains many original features, including a glazed tiled entrance hall with etched glass doors, barrel-vaulted ceiling, six-foot mirrors, marble bar, dark oak panelling and an ornate fireplace.

Return along Fleet Street – the heart of the UK's newspaper industry from the 18th century until the '80s – and take a left turn down Bouverie Street, where there's a blue plaque to literary critic William Hazlitt. The street was built around 1799 on the site of Whitefriars Priory and named after the ground landlords, the Pleydell-Bouveries, Earls of Radnor. Turn left along Magpie Alley for **Whitefriars Crypt** , which is down some stairs at the end. It's an

intriguing, imaginatively-displayed section of medieval crypt, which is situated behind a glass wall with a modern commercial building constructed around it. It's a remnant of a priory that belonged to a Carmelite order known as the White Friars, who wore white mantles over their brown habits on formal occasions. The crypt is thought to date from the 14th century, part of a much larger development, and is now the only visible remains of the priory.

Return to Fleet Street and turn left for the legendary journalists' watering hole **El Vino** at number 47. Since the newspaper industry moved away from the area, it has become a favourite with lawyers, who enjoy its discreet, old-school atmosphere. Established in 1879, El Vino has a vast selection of fine wines and also has a wine shop.

Further along at number 37 is **Hoare's** , Britain's only

WALK 13

St Dunstan-in-the-West

St Dunstan-in-the-West is noted for its clock, which dates from 1671, and was the first in London to be marked on the dial with minutes; it incorporates two figures, Gog and Magog, in delightfully camp poses. In 1825, the clock was acquired by the Marquess of Hertford for his Regent's Park villa for £210, but in 1935 newspaper magnate Lord Rothermere purchased it and returned it to the church.

remaining independent bank. The business was founded in 1672 by goldsmith Richard Hoare; it later became a bank and has been based at this address since 1690, although the current building dates from 1829. Customers have included politician and diarist Samuel Pepys, writer John Evelyn and poet John Dryden.

Opposite the bank is **St Dunstan-in-the-West** 20 (Mon-Fri, 11am-2pm), which boasts the only statue (of Elizabeth I) with its own income, the result of a bequest in 1929! Founded in around 1185 as St Dunstan's Over Against the Temple, from 1278 it became known as St Dunstan-in-the-West, to distinguish it from St Dunstan-in-the-East in Stepney. The current church, which is octagonal, was built in 1831-3 and is an early London example of Gothic revival.

Further along Fleet Street on the left is **Prince Henry's Room** 21. It's one of the few buildings in the area to survive the Great Fire and the attractive façade gives an idea of how London must have looked before the conflagration, with its original 17th-century, half-timbered front. One large room on the first floor is open to the public, notable for its elegant, rare, highly decorated Jacobean plaster ceiling, with Prince of Wales feathers and the initials PH in the centre. It's suggested that Prince Henry (1594-1612), son of James I, used it as an office, hence the name. It was an inn for a while and from 1795-1816 the front of the building was occupied by a well-known exhibition, Mrs Solomon's Waxworks.

Pass through the narrow doorway beneath Prince Henry's

Temple Church 22
11am-1pm and 2-4 pm, £3 adults

the south window depicts that of the Inner Temple (Pegasus, the winged horse). A door in the northwest corner of the choir leads to the Penitential Cell, where knights who'd broken Temple rules were imprisoned and sometimes starved to death.

When the Knights Templar were discredited in the 14th century, their property was given to the Knights Hospitallers who leased the Temple to lawyers. They continued as tenants until Henry VIII appropriated the property. In 1608, James I presented the freehold of the church to the lawyers, giving the southern half to the Inner Temple and the northern half to the Middle Temple. The legal professional has occupied the location ever since.

Room, which leads into the lovely Inns of Court. Ahead is the impressive, 12th-century **Temple Church** 22, the first Gothic church built in London (1160-85). Styled on Jerusalem's Church of the Sepulchre, it was consecrated in 1185 by Heraclius, the Patriarch of Jerusalem. In the 13th century the Temple Church is where newcomers were initiated into the order of the Knights Templar, the warrior monks who were formed in 1118 to protect pilgrims in the Holy Land; their name was taken from the church.

The church escaped the Great Fire but was refurbished by Wren in the late 17th century, with further restoration in the 19th century; it suffered severe damage in the Blitz but was once again restored. The north window bears the crest of the Middle Temple (the Holy Lamb and Flag), while

The Temple Church features in Dan Brown's popular novel *The Da Vinci Code* and provided one of the locations for the Tom Hanks film of the same name.

Continue with the church on your left and turn left at a sign for

Temple Church

Farrar's Building, which leads into a spacious courtyard. At the end, a short flight of steps leads up to the elegant **Master's House** ㉓; built of red brick and Portland stone, it's a 1955 replica of the 1667 building destroyed in WWII.

Keeping this building on your left, go through the passageway ahead and into **King's Bench Walk** ㉔, a wide, elegant street that's part of the Inner Temple. Most of the buildings here are of red brick and date from 1677-8, designed by Wren, although numbers 9-11 are in yellow brick and much later (1814). Tony and Cherie Blair worked at 11 King's Bench, while number 4 was the home of writers Sir Harold Nicolson and his wife Vita Sackville-West from 1930-45, and author H. Rider Haggard lived at number 13.

Turn right by the Pegasus restaurant and on the left is the impressively-gated and lovely **Inner Temple Gardens** ㉕ (Mon-Fri, noon-3pm). The gardens cover 3 acres (1.2ha) and lead right down to the Embankment and River Thames. Inner Temple Gardens form one of the City's most attractive green spaces, praised in Charles Dickens's *Barnaby Rudge*. The gates date from 1730 and are embellished with a griffin and Pegasus from, respectively, the coats of arms of Gray's Inn and Inner Temple. From 1888 to1913, the Royal Horticultural Society held its Great Spring Show here, before moving to Chelsea where it became the Chelsea Flower Show.

Middle Temple Hall ㉖
pre-booked meals and functions,
☎ 020-7427 4820

As you walk past the gardens, pass under an archway and turn right for an important Elizabethan building, **Middle Temple Hall** ㉖. The original Hall dates to around 1320, although this one was built in 1563-73. It's one of the finest surviving Elizabethan halls in Britain with a double hammer beam roof and was the venue for the first performance of Shakespeare's *Twelfth Night*. A notable feature is the 29ft (9m) Bench Table, allegedly a gift from Elizabeth I and cut from a single oak tree on her Windsor estate; the Benchers who run the Middle Temple still dine off it. In front of the Bench is a small table traditionally known as the Cupboard, supposedly made of wood from the hatch of Sir Francis Drake's ship *The Golden Hind*.

Next to the Hall is **Fountain Court** ㉗; its fountain dates to 1681 and is reputedly London's first permanent water feature. Fountain Court also has an ancient mulberry tree and is where John Westlock met Ruth Pinch in Charles Dickens's *Martin Chuzzlewit*. Down two flights of steps by the fountain is the pretty Garden Court. The larger **Middle Temple Gardens** 28 (12-3pm, in May, June, July and September) are on the south side of Middle Temple Hall, and provide another peaceful haven overlooking the Thames.

Middle Temple Gardens have feature borders of red and white roses. In Shakespeare's *Henry VI, Part 1*, this is where the red rose of Lancaster and white rose of York were first plucked, marking the start of the English War of the Roses (1455-85).

The Deveraux

named for Robert Devereux, Earl of Essex, whose mansion (Essex House) occupied part of the site. The pub was formerly the Grecian Coffee House and was re-modelled in 1843; on the façade is a bust of Essex.

To reach Temple tube station, turn left out of the pub, left along the Strand and left again down Arundel Street – the station is at the end, across Temple Place.

Returning to the fountain, continue up another small flight of steps and turn left for Essex Street, built in 1680, and **The Devereux** 29 pub, where we end this walk. The public house and the adjoining chambers were

1. Geo. F. Trumper
2. The Red Lion
3. Harvie & Hudson
4. Paxton & Whitfield
5. Floris
6. John Lobb
7. Hackett
8. Pink
9. Fortnum & Mason
10. Beau Brummel
11. Turnbull & Asser
12. The Royal Academy
13. Albany Court
14. Boodle's
15. Economist Plaza
16. Justerini & Brooks
17. Blue Ball Yard
18. John Lobb
19. Lock & Co.
20. Pickering Place
21. Berry Brothers & Rudd
22. Oxford and Cambridge Club
23. RAC Club
24. St James's Square
25. The London Library
26. Chatham House
27. Memorial to Yvonne Fletcher
28. Naval & Military Club
29. Norfolk House

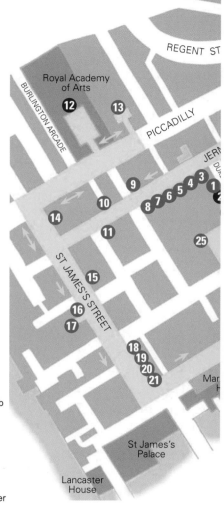

Places of Interest ● Food & Drink

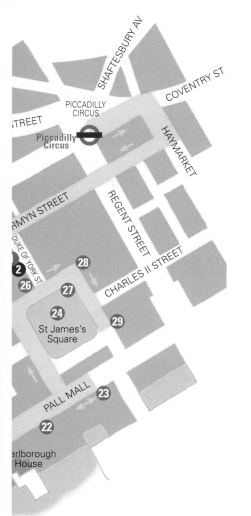

SHAFTESBURY AV

COVENTRY ST

PICCADILLY
CIRCUS

**Piccadilly
Circus**

HAYMARKET

STREET

RMYN STREET

REGENT STREET

DUKE OF YORK ST

2

28

26

27

CHARLES II STREET

24
St James's
Square

29

PALL MALL

23

22

arlborough
House

ST JAMES'S

Distance: 1.36mi (2.20km)
Duration: half day
Start: Piccadilly tube station
End: Charing Cross station

A small but exclusive corner of London, St James's has long been popular with the aristocracy – as a place to live, shop and seek entertainment. It was once part of a vast royal park that's now represented by Green Park and St James's Park. In the 17th century, Henry Jermyn, 1st Earl of St Albans, was given the right to develop some of this parkland. He created a fashionable residential district for the upper classes, and St James's remained one of London's most exclusive places to live until WWII.

Famous residences in St James's include St James's Palace, Clarence House (London home of Prince Charles), Marlborough House, Lancaster House, Spencer House, Schomberg House and Bridgwater House. It's now a predominantly commercial area with some of the highest rents in London and, consequently, the world; corporate off ces include the global headquarters of BP. The auction house Christie's is based in King Street, and the surrounding streets contain a great many upmarket art and antique dealers. It also features some of London's most luxurious shops (it's as well to leave your credit card at home on this excursion) and is home to many of the capital's best known gentlemen's clubs.

St James's is bounded to the north by Piccadilly, to the south by the Mall, to the east by Haymarket and to the west by Green Park.

St James's Hotel & Club

ST JAMES'S

Start Walking…

Our walk begins in the less salubrious surroundings of Piccadilly Circus, one of London's brashest and busiest junctions. Leave the tube station and turn sharp left, with the Criterion to your right and the statue of Eros behind you. Turn right along Haymarket, passing Rudy Weller's striking bronze of four horses leaping from a fountain. This is where hay, straw and animal fodder was bought and sold in the mid-17th century; the name Haymarket was first recorded in 1657. The market was moved to near Regent's Park in 1830 and today the street is best known for its theatres.

Turn right along Jermyn Street, renowned for its upmarket men's retailers and equally upmarket customers. The street was built in the 1680s on part of the Crown land granted to Henry Jermyn. A relief on number 73 shows Charles II handing the deeds to Jermyn, but none of the original buildings remain. Jermyn Street became a popular address for those aspiring to live near the royal palaces, and by the 19th century there were a large number of hotels, although only The Cavendish remains.

Despite its high-class credentials, St James's has more humble beginnings. Some sources say that its appellation comes from a leper hospital, which was established in the name of one of the Twelve Disciples, St James the Less.

The first section of Jermyn Street is undistinguished but improves after you cross Regent Street, itself one of London's most elegant boulevards. Regent Street was built by John Nash in the early 19th century for the Prince Regent, later George IV. As you cross it, look left for views of the statue of Frederick, Duke of York, in Waterloo Place and, in the distance, Nelson's Column and the Houses of Parliament.

The second section of Jermyn Street becomes more interesting the further west you travel, with many ornately decorated shops. It's particularly known for its shirt-makers, such as New & Lingwood and Turnbull & Asser, while other smart retailers include shoemakers Church's, John Lobb and Russell & Bromley, and men's toiletry specialists, Czech & Speake.

Down Duke of York Street on the left you'll find **Geo. F. Trumper** ❶ at number 1, which styles itself a 'gentlemen's hairdresser and perfumer'. **The Red Lion** ❷ is next door, at number 2, a Fullers pub serving tasty pub fare in a small but spectacular space, adorned with ornate, cut-glass mirrors. On leaving the pub, turn left and left

Paxton & Whitfield

The red coats worn by fox hunters are referred to as 'hunting pinks' although they're actually bright scarlet. It's been claimed that this is because they were first designed and made by a tailor called Pink.

Fortnum & Mason

again along Jermyn Street and immediately you reach shirt-maker **Harvie & Hudson** ❸, which is at 96-7 Jermyn Street, with another branch at number 77. There's attractive detailing on Harvie & Hudson's façade, which is one of London's finest mid-Victorian shop fronts. Further along, at number 93, is Britain's oldest cheese shop, **Paxton & Whitfeld** ❹, founded by a Suffolk cheesemonger around 1740.

At number 89 is the splendid perfumer **Floris** ❺, established in 1730 by Juan Famenias Floris, from the Spanish island of Minorca. Its neighbour at number 88 is the stylishly understated, venerable outlet of **John Lobb** ❻, makers of expensive hand-made shoes (founded 1849), while next door is fogey retailer **Hackett** ❼ with a blue plaque to Isaac Newton at number 87, marking the site of a house once occupied by the great man. Next door is shirt-maker **Pink** ❽, one of the street's few newcomers, founded in 1984. Its logo is a fox in a pink jacket.

Backing onto Jermyn Street on the right is legendary retailer **Fortnum & Mason** ❾. Charles Fortnum was a footman in the household of George III; on retiring, he opened a grocery shop in the 1770s close to the present site with his friend John Mason. They began to specialise in exotic and esoteric foods, and opened a specialist department to attend to the needs of gentlemen's clubs. The shop was rebuilt in 1923-5 and now also sells furniture and clothes. It's worth a quick detour for the food hall alone!

Nearby, next to New & Lingwood and Burlington Arcade, there's a statue of **Beau Brummel** ❿ by Irena Sidiecka (2002), which is highly appropriate on a street dedicated to dandyism. Brummel (1778-1840) was the arbiter of men's fashion in Regency England and a friend of the Prince Regent, the future George IV.

Burlington Arcade was designed in 1819 by Samuel Ware for Lord George Cavendish of Burlington House to prevent passers-by throwing oyster shells and other rubbish into his garden; another storey was added in 1911. It's full of small, exclusive shops and its rules (regarding dress and behaviour) are enforced by beadles (ceremonial officers) wearing traditional uniforms, including top hats and frockcoats. Further along Jermyn Street, at numbers 71-2, is shirt-maker **Turnbull & Asser** ⑪, with its ornamental premises dating from 1902-3.

At the end of Jermyn Street, turn right along St James's Street and right again along Piccadilly, one of the two main roads which once led west out of London; the other is Oxford Street. Building here began in the early 17th century and the street is named after the picadil, a stiff collar made by a local tailor, Robert Baker. Piccadilly used to be lined with aristocratic mansions, though only Albany Court and Burlington House (see below) remain.

FOOD & DRINK

2 Red Lion:
Attractive traditional pub with a great atmosphere serving excellent Fuller's ales and tasty bar food. Closed Sun.

12 The Royal Academy restaurant/cafés:
Choice of courtyard/ gallery cafés and restaurant (bookings ☎ 020-7300 5608); the latter offers small plates and terrines in addition to two-three course meals. Dinner (evening) Fri and Sat only.

Cross Piccadilly and keep walking east, past Burlington Arcade and to **The Royal Academy** ⑫, which is a useful pitstop, as it has a restaurant and two cafés. Leave the Royal Academy by the Piccadilly exit and turn left and left again along

Turnbull & Asser

WALK 14

the short Albany Court Yard for **Albany Court** ⑬, once a mansion, and later converted into exclusive bachelors' apartments.

The house was built in 1770-4 for the 1st Viscount Melbourne, designed by Sir William Chambers. In 1802 it was sold and converted into around 70 chambers, sometimes called sets, for bachelors who weren't involved in 'trade' and who had good social connections; women weren't allowed until later! It became one of London's most fashionable addresses; famous residents have included Prime Ministers Lord Palmerston, William Gladstone and Edward Heath; poet Lord Byron; authors Aldous Huxley, Graham Greene and J. B. Priestley; dramatist Terence Rattigan; photographer and royal consort Anthony Armstrong-Jones; journalist and broadcaster Malcolm Muggeridge; philosopher Sir Isaiah Berlin; and actors Terence Stamp and Dame Edith Evans.

> Albany Court was the 'home' of A. J. Raffles, the fictional gentleman thief created by Sir Arthur Conan Doyle's brother-in-law E. W. Hornung in the 1890s. It was the base from which he planned his ingenious burglaries.

Return to Piccadilly, turn right, cross the road and retrace your steps back down St James's Street. Built at the beginning of the 17th century and the main route between Piccadilly and Pall Mall, notable residents have included architect Sir Christopher Wren, who's thought to have died here in 1723, and poet Alexander Pope. In the 18th century, St James's Street contained many of London's most celebrated coffee houses, which later developed into gentlemen's clubs.

Some of the street's most elegant buildings still house gentlemen's clubs, although many are far too discreet to put up a sign. Number 28 on the left is **Boodle's** ⑭ (no sign), founded in 1762 by Edward Boodle, which was originally in Pall Mall but moved here in 1783. Past members include politicians Pitt the Elder and Younger, historian Edward Gibbon, politician and slavery abolitionist William Wilberforce, dandy Beau Brummell and military commander and Prime Minister, the Duke of Wellington. Today, members are mainly country gentry, who stay at their clubs when visiting London.

Just along from Boodle's, also on the left, is the small **Economist Plaza** ⑮, which is reached up a short flight of steps and has some

Boodles

Economist Plaza Sculpture

Justerini. It later received a royal warrant from George III, which has been renewed by every subsequent monarch, reflected by the gold seal on the front of the premises. In 1831, the company was sold to Alfred Brooks.

Soon after, also on the right, is a narrow passageway, **Blue Ball Yard** 17. Pop in here to admire this traditional mews, which dates from 1741-2; the houses were originally coach houses, later used as garages. Their doors display the names of famous racehorses and are now luxury suites belonging to the Stafford Hotel.

Return to Jermyn Street, turn right and cross the road. On the left is shoemaker **John Lobb** 18, proudly displaying two royal warrants, from Prince Charles and the Duke of Edinburgh, while a short way along (at number 6) is long-established hatter, **Lock & Co.** 19. James Lock inherited his father-in-law's hatter's business in 1759 and it moved here in 1764, providing headwear to the wealthy.

outdoor sculptures of human figures in the style of Anthony Gormley. The *Economist* building, where the magazine is published, is at numbers 25-7, designed by Alison and Peter Smithson and the first '60s building to be listed.

At 61 St James's Street, on the right, is upmarket wine merchant **Justerini & Brooks** 16. It has only been at this address since 1968 but was established in 1749 by George Johnson and Giacomo

Justerini & Brooks

Blue Ball Yard

John Lobb

> Lock & Co customers included Lord Nelson, who had a hat made with a built-in eyeshade, and the Duke of Wellington – they made the plumed hat he wore at the Battle of Waterloo.

Pickering Place

A few doors down, a narrow passageway, **Pickering Place** 20, leads into a small courtyard. This is Britain's smallest public square. A Georgian delight – it's still lit by the original gaslights – it used to be a popular and suitably private venue for duels. The houses in the courtyard date from the 1730s when it was known as Pickering Court. It's named after William Pickering, whose mother-in-law founded the grocer's shop that became Berry Brothers & Rudd, the retail premises next door (see below). A plaque on the wall of the passageway marks the fact that from 1842-5 a building here housed the Legation from the Republic of Texas to the Court of St James's.

Next to Pickering Place, at number 3, is the noted wine merchant **Berry Brothers & Rudd** 21, majestically decorated in green and gold, Britain's oldest wine and spirit merchant which has traded from here for over 300 years. It was officially established in 1698 by a certain Widow Bourne, and the company evolved from selling coffee, tea, spices and other provisions to fine wines and spirits. The premises are redolent of a bygone age, little changed over the years, with crooked floors and wood-panelled walls.

The modestly-sized shop is renowned for being able to supply huge quantities of wine, almost at the drop of a hat. This is thanks to its vast cellars – previously part of Henry VIII's residence – covering 8,000ft² (745m² or the equivalent to three tennis courts), which extend under the courtyard outside and as far as Pall Mall, with a capacity of around 100,000 bottles.

Turn left out of Berry Brothers and at the end of St James's Street, turn left along Pall Mall. It was once a fashionable street and has had a number of famous residents, including authors Jonathan Swift and Laurence Stern, and historian Edward Gibbon. Look out, too, for blue plaques to painter Thomas Gainsborough and courtesan Nell Gwynne. It's now the location of several famous gentlemen's clubs.

Soon on the right is Marlborough House, which was built in 1709-11 for the Duchess of Marlborough, and extended in the 1770s. The Crown purchased the building in

1817 and in 1959 it was donated to the government, and now houses The Commonwealth Secretariat and The Commonwealth Foundation. To the rear of

Oxford and Cambridge Club

RAC Club

Marlborough House is the Mall, the pink-paved royal road.

Most of Pall Mall's clubs are anonymous (as we saw on St James's Street), including the **Oxford and Cambridge Club** ㉒ at number 71 on the right, an elegant neoclassical building dating from 1836. It's now the United Oxford and Cambridge University Club, formed in 1971 by the amalgamation of the Oxford and Cambridge University Club, founded 1830, and the United University Club (1921). Members must have attended either of the two universities.

Slightly more ostentatious and in an impressive building also on the right of Pall Mall is the **RAC Club** ㉓ at number 89, with a flag flying outside. It was founded in 1897 'for the protection, encouragement and development of automobilism' and the current building has been its headquarters since 1911. The club has over 13,000 members and is probably the least exclusive of London's gentlemen's clubs.

After the RAC Club, retrace your steps a short distance and turn right off Pall Mall along **St James's Square** ㉔. It's the area's centrepiece, although often overlooked, a large garden square graced by elegant buildings in a variety of architectural styles; the central garden boasts a mounted

St James's Square

WALK 14

statue of William III. The square was built in 1667-77 by Henry Jermyn, Earl of St Albans, with some fine Georgian townhouses added later. St James's Square is no longer residential, housing mostly businesses and various institutions.

The **London Library**  is at number 14, a private library founded in 1841 by Thomas Carlyle, and situated here since 1845. A little further around the square, at number 10, is **Chatham House** 26, with its blue plaques to many former residents. Built in 1736, it's been home to three Prime Ministers: William Pitt the Elder, the Earl of Derby and William Gladstone. It's now the headquarters of the Royal Institute of International Affairs.

Number 5 is the former Libyan People's Bureau in the '80s. On April 17th 1984, policewoman Yvonne Fletcher was killed by shots fired from within the building during a disturbance involving dissidents opposed to Colonel Gaddafi. Subsequently, around 60 embassy staff were deported for refusing to cooperate in identifying the culprit. A **memorial to Yvonne Fletcher** 27 stands opposite number 5, by the garden.

Number 4, the **Naval & Military Club** 28, has a blue plaque to Nancy Astor (1879-1964), the first woman MP in Britain and a famously scathing wit, while at number 31 is the monumental **Norfolk House** 29, with plaques detailing its American ties, where we end this walk. It was rebuilt in 1938 and was the headquarters of Anglo-American intelligence in WWII, when General Eisenhower directed the D-Day landings.

Yvonne Fletcher was the first officer to be commemorated by the Police Memorial Trust, a charity set up to honour police officers killed in the line of duty. The Trust grew out of a campaign, spearheaded by film director Michael Winner and supported by public donations.

Just after Norfolk House, continue ahead and down to Pall Mall, which is signposted in front. Turn left along it, leading back to Trafalgar Square and Charing Cross station.

Norfolk House

1. St Christopher's Place
2. Ukrainian Catholic Church
3. Brown Hart Gardens
4. Grosvenor Square
5. US Embassy
6. Ronald Reagan statue
7. South Audley Street
8. James Purdey & Sons
9. Mount Street
10. Mount Street Gardens
11. T. Goode & Co
12. The Punch Bowl
13. Church of the Immaculate Conception
14. Crewe House
15. Shepherd Market
16. Ye Grapes
17. 37 Dover Street
18. Brown's
19. 45/46 Albermarl Street
20. Salvatore Ferragamo's
21. The Allies sculpture
22. Henry Moore abstracts
23. Statuette of Sekhmet
24. Bruton Place
25. Handel House Museum
26. Apostrophe

Places of Interest ● Food & Drink

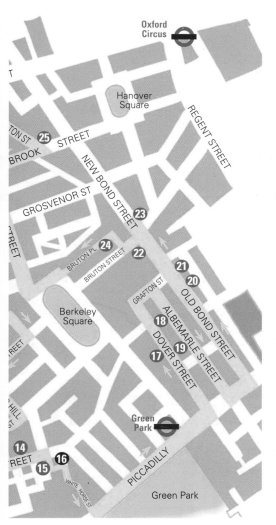

Oxford
Circus

Hanover
Square

REGENT STREET

25

...TON ST
BROOK STREET

NEW BOND STREET

GROSVENOR ST

23

STREET

BRUTON PL **24**

BRUTON STREET

22

21

20

OLD BOND STREET

GRAFTON ST

Berkeley
Square

18

ALBEMARLE STREET

19

DOVER STREET

17

...REET

...HILL
...ST

14

...REET

15

16

Green
Park

WHITE HORSE ST

PICCADILLY

Green Park

MAYFAIR

WALK 15

Distance: 2.71mi (4.37km)

Duration: half to full day

Start/End: Bond Street tube station

MAYFAIR

Named after the May Fair, a rowdy fortnight-long annual celebration that took place from 1686 on the site that is now Shepherd Market, until being banned for 'lowering the tone of the neighbourhood' in 1764 (when it moved to Fair Field in Bow, East London).

Mayfair is the area north of St James's and south of Marylebone, with Soho to the east and Hyde Park to the west. It's been one of London's most prestigious districts for over 300 years and became the place to live for the upper and would-be upper classes from the mid-18th century to the present day. Mayfair is now mainly commercial – an attractive location away from the City of London for private banks, hedge funds and wealth managers – as few individuals can afford to live there. However, it retains much of historical and aesthetic interest and is still home to some of London's most desirable shops – from Fortnum and Mason to exclusive Bond Street boutiques – as well as luxurious hotels and exclusive clubs.

This circuit of Mayfair takes in its prime shopping streets and most interesting buildings, plus Madonna's pub and the house where Handel lived and composed. It also includes the unique charm of Shepherd Market, a village square tucked away among Mayfair's smartest streets.

St Christopher's Place

Start Walking...

This walk begins in the heart of the West End's retail district, at Bond Street tube station. Leave by the Oxford Street exit. Cross to the opposite (north) side of Oxford Street and turn right down **St Christopher's Place** ❶, a narrow passage tucked away behind Selfridges. Look for the sign on the face of the upright clock outside clothing outlet H & M.

This is one of London's lesser known but more attractive shopping areas, a cluster of upmarket cafés, restaurants and retailers. St Christopher's Place dates from the 18th century and the streets leading off it are worth exploring, e.g. Barrett Street, which provides a peaceful oasis with a touch of café culture, a world away from the nearby bustle of Oxford Street.

> Oxford Street's largest shopping emporium, Selfridges, was opened in 1909 by an American, Harry Gordon Selfridge, and is the UK's second-largest department store after Harrods).

Return to Oxford Street, turn right, cross over and take a left down Duke Street. Building here began in the 1720s and parts of Duke Street were rebuilt in 1886-96. On the left, opposite the right turn for Brown Hart Gardens, is the impressive **Ukrainian Catholic Church** ❷, which is little known despite its proximity to London's major shopping street (for opening times, ☎ 020-7629

icon, Ukrainian Catholic Church

1534). It used to house a Free Chapel congregation founded in 1148 by Queen Matilda near the Tower of London, which moved here in the late 19th century. The building was designed by Alfred Waterhouse, who is most famous as the architect of the Natural History Museum. The Ukrainian Catholic Church took over the building in the '60s.

Turn right along **Brown Hart Gardens** ❸ to admire its walled Italianate garden (11am-6pm from May to September, 11am-3pm from October to April). Strangely, the garden stands above an electricity substation, both designed in 1903 by Stanley Peach. The garden reopened in 2007 after being closed for two decades; managed by the Grosvenor Estate, it hosts musical and theatrical productions.

At the end of Brown Hart Gardens turn left along Balderton Street, left again along George Yard and right down Duke Street, until you come to **Grosvenor Square** ❹ on the right. One of London's largest squares, it was created in 1725-31 and used to

Volare, Brown Hart Gardens

Street ⑦, entering an area of confident, understated wealth. Part of South Audley Street is on the Grosvenor Estate, named after Hugh Audley, from whose heirs the estate was acquired by the marriage of Sir Thomas Grosvenor in 1677. The street was built from 1720 and several buildings from the 1730s survive, including numbers 71-75. Thomas Goode's china and glass shop at numbers 17-22 (see below) is one of several buildings reconstructed from 1875 to 1900 in the Queen Anne style.

be a fashionable residential area. Little of the square's Georgian past remains, although it retains some interesting architecture.

Walk anti-clockwise around the square, passing a blue plaque to Eisenhower on the right. Grosvenor Square's major occupant soon looms large: the heavily fortified bulk of the **US Embassy** ⑤. The embassy was built in the '60s by Eero Saarinen and to most people is an unattractive pile. There are a couple of interesting statues nearby, however, including a rather good one of **Ronald Reagan** ⑥.

Turn left into Mount Street and as you do, have a look at **James Purdey & Sons** ⑧, gun and rifle manufacturer to the wealthy. The shop is diagonally opposite at 57-8 South Audley Street, where it joins Mount Street. The business was founded in 1814 by James Purdey and the current premises date from 1881.

Mount Street ⑨ has elegant, pink-and-red-brick buildings, housing a variety of upmarket galleries, restaurants and shops.

The noted architectural critic Nikolaus Pevsner described the US Embassy in Grosvenor Square as 'an impressive but decidedly embarrassing building'. The embassy is due to move to a new building south of the Thames some time after 2015.

Once past the embassy, continue ahead into **South Audley**

Ronald Reagan statue

It's named after Mount Field, which used to have an earthwork called Oliver's Mount, said to have been part of London's defences built during the Civil War. The street was built in 1720-40 and rebuilt in 1880-1900, mainly in pink terracotta Queen Anne style. Continuing down Mount Street, look to the right between Wetherell Estate Agents and a branch of Jordan International Bank to spy a passageway leading to the charming **Mount Street Gardens** ⑩ (8am–dusk). This former burial ground was transformed into elegant, tranquil gardens in 1899, and is surrounded by some of the area's most attractive buildings. The gardens feature a number of London plane trees and the sheltered, relatively warm location allows exotic species to survive, including a Canary Islands Date Palm and an Australian Silver Wattle. It's a popular retreat for locals but little visited otherwise, so you may have it all to yourself.

Leave the gardens by the South Audley Street exit, which is to the right of the entrance where you came in, and turn left. Turn left along South Street, which was built in the 1730s, although many of the original houses have long been replaced. Famous residents have included nursing pioneer Florence Nightingale and Prime Minister Alec Douglas-Home. There's attractive tiled decoration on the side of the premises of **T. Goode & Co** ⑪ – purveyors of porcelain and china – which was established in 1827 and relocated here in 1876; the rich and famous include its wares on their wedding lists.

Continue into Farm Street – the area was known as Hay Hill Farm in the 17th century. Building began in the 1740s, mostly of coach houses and stables, and today much of the street is given over to garages with mews flats above. On the left of Farm Street at number 41 is the Georgian, Grade II listed pub, **The Punch**

South Audley Street

Mount Street Gardens

WALK 15

Bowl ⑫, a popular drinking spot for celebrities.

> The Punch Bowl was famous for being Madonna's 'local'. In March 2008, she and then husband, film director Guy Ritchie, bought the pub (reportedly for £2.5m). The couple divorced later the same year and Ritchie is now the pub's sole landlord.

Soon after, also on the left, is the elegant, neo-Gothic **Church of the Immaculate Conception** ⑬ (8am-6pm most days) – more commonly known as Farm Street Church. It's one of London's most attractive and atmospheric churches, host to fashionable weddings and christenings. Be sure to have a look inside at its beautiful ornate interior. The ceiling is imaginatively decorated, while the altar was designed by Augustus Pugin (famous for the Palace of Westminster), a pioneer of the Gothic Revival style. The church was commissioned by the Jesuits and opened in 1849. The writer Evelyn Waugh reportedly converted to Catholicism here in 1939.

When you leave the church, turn left along Farm Street, right at the end and right along Hill Street. Turn left along Chesterfield Hill, right along Charles Street and left along Chester Street. At the end of the last, turn left along busy, winding Curzon Street. Built in the 1720s, it's named after Nathaniel Curzon, an early 18th-century Derbyshire aristocrat who owned the land. Curzon Street retains some fine mid-18th-century

terraced houses and there's a blue plaque to Prime Minister Benjamin Disraeli, who died at number 19 in 1881.

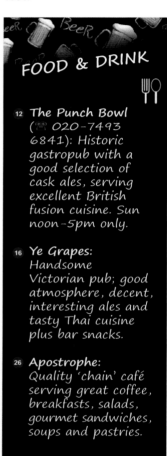

FOOD & DRINK

⑫ **The Punch Bowl** (☎ 020-7493 6841): Historic gastropub with a good selection of cask ales, serving excellent British fusion cuisine. Sun noon-5pm only.

⑯ **Ye Grapes:** Handsome Victorian pub; good atmosphere, decent, interesting ales and tasty Thai cuisine plus bar snacks.

㉖ **Apostrophe:** Quality 'chain' café serving great coffee, breakfasts, salads, gourmet sandwiches, soups and pastries.

Shortly, on the left, is **Crewe House** ⑭, currently the Saudi Arabian embassy. It's a large, elegant building with an attractive stone façade, generally regarded as the best of Mayfair's few

Church of the Immaculate Conception

enclave is described (modestly) by its own website as 'London's best kept secret' and consists of a series of closely packed streets just south of Curzon Street. They were built in 1735–46 by Edward Shepherd to house shopkeepers to serve the large houses on nearby Piccadilly. Shepherd Market has managed to retain its modest 18th-century feel. Not long ago the area was infamous as the haunt of prostitutes but nowadays is home to intimate restaurants, boutiques and some excellent Victorian pubs.

To reach the Market, turn right off Curzon Street down Trebeck Street. There's a blue plaque on the right, declaring this to be the original site of the May Fair, a 15-day festivity that took place from 1686 onwards. The fair continued until 1764, when it was banished to Bow in the East End. It had become too boisterous, attracting troublemakers who disturbed the residents, and building the market was seen as the best way to deter the fair from returning.

Edward Shepherd's market included paved walkways, a duck pond and even a theatre, all of which were designed to attract a more desirable clientele than attended the May Fair.

remaining Regency houses. It has a garden and carriageway in front, with decorated gates. The house was built in 1730 by Edward Shepherd, an architect who gave his name to the nearby Shepherd Market (see below), and was originally called Wharncliffe House. The Marquess of Crewe bought it in 1899 and the Saudi government acquired it in the '70s.

This is one of the best areas of London for Middle Eastern restaurants and exotic aromas may tempt you as you approach nearby **Shepherd Market** 15. This hidden

Shepherd Market

Trebeck Street is atmospheric, narrow and car-free, lined with Middle Eastern restaurants; at the end on the left is a well-known pub, **Ye Grapes** 16 . Built in 1882, it's cosy and atmospheric, packed with old world memorabilia, including stuffed animals. The small square in front of the pub is the heart of buzzy Shepherd Market.

Leaving the Market, take White Horse Street, and turn left along Piccadilly, then continue for around 200m until you reach Dover Street on your left. It's dotted with expensive art galleries and retains a number of mid-Georgian houses, the best of which is **number 37** 17 , with a bishop's mitre above the window on the first floor. It indicates that the building was constructed in 1772 for the Bishops of Ely by Bishop Edmund Keene, as his town residence. Designed by Sir Robert Taylor, it's a fine example of the Palladian style, with a three-bay,

stone-faced front. Dover Street is named after Henry Jermyn, Baron Dover, and past residents have included poet Alexander Pope, architect John Nash and composer Frederic Chopin.

Turn right along Grafton Street then right again along Albemarle Street. On the left at number 20-21 is the long, cream-coloured building of the Royal Institution of Great Britain. Look up at the first floor windows and you can see the white busts of some erstwhile VIPs. It was founded in 1799 and some of the country's most significant scientists have worked here, including Sir Humphrey Davy, Sir Lawrence Bragg and Michael Faraday. In fact, 14 of its resident scientists have been Nobel Prize winners. The building's classical façade was added in 1838 by Lewis Vulliamy, based on Rome's Temple of Antonius; the basement houses the Faraday Museum.

On the right of Albemarle Street at number 33-4 (and also on Dover Street) is elegant, understated **Brown's** 18 , London's oldest hotel. In 1837 James Brown, a former manservant, opened a hotel at 23 Dover Street. It did well and expanded into other buildings, eventually becoming the establishment we see today. Famous guests have included inventor Alexander Graham Bell, US Presidents Theodore and Franklin Roosevelt, mining magnate Cecil Rhodes and author Rudyard Kipling.

By way of architectural contrast, further along on the right at numbers **45 and 46** 19 are two offices by the noted Hungarian-born architect Erno Goldfinger, a leading member of the architectural Modern Movement. This example of his work is from 1955-7 and has been praised for its sensitivity to the surrounding Georgian architecture. While it's true that the proportions are in keeping with the buildings around it, Goldfinger's creation is stark and ugly to many eyes.

At the end of the street, turn left along Piccadilly, one of two old thoroughfares leading west out of London. Then take a second left into Old Bond Street, noted for its designer clothes shops and recently named the most expensive retail street in Europe. Famous former residents include historian Edward Gibbon, Admiral Lord Nelson, spy Guy Burgess, authors Jonathan Swift, Laurence Stern and James Boswell, and Prime Minister William Pitt the Elder.

Just before Old Bond Street becomes New Bond Street,

Salvatore Ferragamo's outlet at number 24 is housed in one of the area's more interesting and imaginative buildings. It has gilded decoration, including a rather fine grasshopper which recalls the Gresham grasshoppers found in the City (see page 72); the building is from 1926 by Emmanuel Vincent Harris.

Although you'll hear references to 'Bond Street', it doesn't technically exist! The road linking Piccadilly to Oxford Street is, in fact, two streets: Old Bond Street, built in the 1680s by Sir Thomas Bond, and New Bond Street, the section further north, which was created around 40 years later.

As you continue into New Bond Street, smart jewellers replace the designer clothing outlets in this notably posh shopping district. Aspreys is on the left and just past it, on the right and

Browns Hotel

outside a couple of Swiss watch shops, is a fine modern sculpture, **The Allies** . It was made by US sculptor Lawrence Holofcener and shows Roosevelt and Churchill sitting on a bench and chatting amiably. The sculpture was financed by the Bond Street Association to mark 50 years of peace and unveiled in 1995. Interestingly, Churchill's mother was American and he and Roosevelt were actually distant cousins.

Further along, on the left, is the Time & Life Building at number 153 New Bond Street, adorned with four **Henry Moore abstracts** and a decorated entrance. The entrance is actually at 1 Bruton Street, which is left off New Bond Street. Bruton Street was built from 1738; Queen Elizabeth II was born here in 1926 and famous residents include dramatist Richard Brinsley Sheridan and Prime Minister George Canning. There's also a bronze by Moore, *Draped Reclining Figure*, inside the Time & Life Building. The four external pieces are in a cubist style, carved from Portland

stone and installed in 1953; Moore subsequently tried to buy them back as he thought their position on the third floor was too high for people to get a good view of them.

Near the top of New Bond Street, at numbers 34-5 on the right, is Sotheby's. The entrance to this famous auction house is topped with London's second-oldest work of public art: **the statuette of Sekhmet** . It's an ancient Egyptian black basalt effigy of the warrior goddess of Upper Egypt, dating back to between 1600BC and 1320BC. It's been Sotheby's mascot since the 1880s, when it was sold at auction for £40 but never collected by the buyer.

After admiring Sekhmet, turn around and retrace your steps a short distance to Bruton Street; turn right and right again to enter **Bruton Place** , an attractive mews in a tranquil area of narrow streets and smart restaurants; even the garages here are well-designed and expensive-looking. It's named after the Bruton estate in Somerset, the property of the

The Allies

land owner, 1st Lord Berkeley of Stratton. Bruton Place provided coach houses and stables for the mansions of Berkeley Square and Bruton Street (it connects the two). Numbers 36 and 38 date from 1890 and still have the hoists used to lift grain sacks into the lofts.

Berkeley Square, where the nightingale sang, reputedly has one of London's most haunted houses. Legend has it that number 50, once the home of Prime Minister George Canning, is haunted by the ghost of a young women who committed suicide in the attic and people have allegedly died of fright when staying there!

At the end of Bruton Place, continue into Berkeley Square and turn right along Davies Street. Turn right along Brook Street (the River Tyburn flowed under here) for number 25, the **Handel House Museum** 25, denoted by blue plaques to two musical greats: George Frederic Handel and, more recently, Jimi Hendrix.

This Grade I listed building has finely restored Georgian interiors; it was home to the noted baroque composer Handel from 1723 until his death in 1759, and is now a museum dedicated to the man and his work. There must be something musical in the air around here, as ground-breaking American rock guitarist Jimi Hendrix lived for a while next door in the top floor flat of 23 Brook Street, which is now the Handel House Museum's administration office. It's said that Hendrix was delighted to discover that he lived next door to Handel's old home,

and he purchased a lot of the composer's music. Some people even claim to hear Handel's influence in some of Hendrix's later compositions!

Handel House Museum 25
Tue-Sat 10am-6pm, Thu until 8pm,
Sun noon-6pm, £6 adults

When you leave the Handel House Museum, proceed ahead along South Molton Street, cross Oxford Street at the end, turn left along it and right down St Christopher's Place again for **Apostrophe** 26 at 23 Barrett Street, a left turn off St Christophers Place. It serves breakfasts, salads, gourmet sandwiches, soups and pastries, and is part of a small chain; but it's 'un-chain-like', stylish rather than formulaic, a civilised place to end this walk.

To reach Bond Street tube station, return along St Christophers Place and the station is almost in front of you, on the other side of Oxford Street.

1 Rudolf Steiner House

2 Clarence Terrace

3 Sussex Place

4 Park Square West

5 Park Square East

6 Cambridge Gate

7 Chester Terrace

8 Chester Place

9 Regent's Park Barracks

10 Park Village West

11 Dublin Castle Tavern

12 St Pancras Old Church

13 Camley Street Natural Park

14 British Library

15 Sculpture of Sir Isaac Newton

16 St Pancras Station and Hotel

17 Camino

⬤ Places of Interest ⬤ Food & Drink

REGENT'S PARK
TO ST PANCRAS

REGENT'S PARK TO ST PANCRAS

Distance: 3.69mi (5.94km)
Duration: half to full day
Start: Baker Street tube station
End: King's Cross St Pancras station

This walk is for lovers of green space and architecture, from the semi-rural space of Regent's Park with its classic Georgian terraces, to the Victorian splendour of St Pancras. The park is bordered by Marylebone to the south and west and Primrose Hill to the north, with three mainline stations, Euston, King's Cross and St Pancras (the latter two share a tube station, King's Cross St Pancras) to the east. Back in the Middle Ages, it was owned by Barking Abbey but Henry VIII seized it in the late 1530s and it's been owned by the Crown, more or less, ever since.

Its current splendour is down to George IV. When he was still Prince Regent in 1822 he commissioned architect John Nash to design a palace and grand houses for himself and his friends; the idea was dropped but Nash went ahead with a series of terraces and houses, and today Regent's Park is one of the capital's most exclusive and expensive residential areas.

St Pancras was a large parish in medieval times, and covered most of what is now the London Borough of Camden. It's a largely shabby and industrial area but one which is shedding its unsavoury reputation thanks to a major regeneration project around King's Cross, and there are some unexpected pleasures, like St Pancras' ancient church and the magnif cent station hotel.

Regent's Park

REGENT'S PARK TO ST PANCRAS

Start Walking…

Our starting point is Baker Street tube station; leave by the Baker Street North exit and turn right, following the signs for Lords Cricket Ground. Baker Street was created from 1755 onwards by builder William Baker, and its most famous resident is fictional: Sir Arthur Conan Doyle's detective Sherlock Holmes who lived at number 221B. The house is on the left as you walk towards Regent's Park, and is now a museum.

At the top of Baker Street, go left along Park Road which, unsurprisingly, runs along the boundary of nearby Regent's Park. On the left is the impressive, Grade II listed **Rudolf Steiner House ❶** (for opening times, ☎ 020-7723 4400), the British HQ of the Anthroposophical Society. The building is a unique example of Germanic Expressionist architecture with a hint of Modernista, reminiscent of the buildings of Barcelona (particularly Gaudí) and Palma. It was designed by architect Montague Wheeler and built in two phases, in 1924 and 1931. The house has curves, cleverly placed asymmetrical windows with stone frames, a coved hood at the entrance and bookshop front, a free-form twisting concrete staircase and other details that make it unique. The rounded door and window frames have something of a Hobbit house style about them, an interesting contrast with the building's Art Nouveau leanings.

Rudolf Steiner (1861-1925) was an Austrian who founded a spiritual movement called Anthroposophy, a philosophy which sprang from transcendentalism and attempts to reconcile the scientific with the spiritual.

Rudolf Steiner House

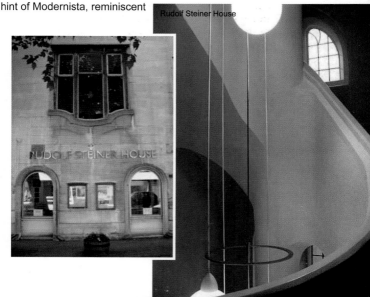

Returning to Baker Street, turn left towards the green of Regent's Park. Immediately on the left is **Clarence Terrace** , one of the graceful terraces which sit on the Outer Circle of the park. Named after William IV's earlier title, Duke of Clarence, it's the smallest of the terraces designed by Decimus Burton and was praised for its elegance, gaining the young architect recognition and other work.

Just beyond it is the glorious curving sweep of **Sussex Place** ❸, a striking, cream-coloured terrace, adorned with Corinthian columns and enjoying one of the best views over Regent's Park. Completed in 1822, Sussex Place comprises 26 townhouses and is one of John Nash's most ambitious projects; nearly 200m (656ft) long with 77 bays. It's named for George IV's younger brother Augustus, Duke of Sussex, and now houses the London Graduate School of Business Studies.

Retrace your steps back towards Baker Street, keeping left to follow the Outer Circle.

This famous road encircles 487 acres (197ha) of parkland which surrounds a boating lake, several colleges and London Zoo – and the smaller Inner Circle which forms the heart of Regent's Park. You pass more desirable cream-coloured terraces to the right, lining the park and along the side streets, including **Park Square West** ❹, from where there's a good view of the BT Tower.

At the opposite end of Park Square West, turn right for a detour down **Park Square East** ❺, which sits at the far south-eastern tip of Regent's Park. It's another of the area's majestic terraces, home to sophisticated Grade I listed Nash properties, built in 1823-4. Here, as all around Regent's Park, the visual combination of verdant parkland and elegant architecture is truly uplifting.

Back on the Outer Circle, continue with the park on your left. On the right, the boxy, modernist Royal College of Physicians building (a rare Grade I listed modern building) provides an

Sussex Place

architectural contrast with another magnificent terrace. **Cambridge Gate** 6 is more ornate than most in the area, with nicely over-the-top statues at the entrances. It also stands out for its colour as it's faced with Bath stone rather than stucco. It was built later, in 1876-80, by Archer and Green, and is named after another of George IV's brothers, Adolphus, Duke of Cambridge.

Next on the right is the impressive Chester Gate and, just off it, handsome **Chester Terrace** 7, named for one of George IV's former titles, Earl of Chester. Built in 1825 by James Burton, to John Nash's designs, and restored after WWII, this is the longest continuous Nash terrace at 919ft (280m); numbers 22 and 23 are fronted with classical columns and particularly striking. Look for the huge street signs that announce 'Chester Terrace' on the arches at either end.

At the end, turn right towards **Chester Place** 8, left along Cumberland Place and right

again at the end. Go through the archway in the wall ahead and turn left on to Albany Street, which runs parallel to the east side of Regent's Park. On your right are **Regent's Park Barracks** 9, also known as Albany Street Barracks. Built in the 19th century, they're currently the base of a number of army units, including the Queen's Royal Hussars.

Chester Terrace is one of the few Regent's Park terraces that's residential; most house businesses and organisations. It has had some famous/infamous residents over the years, including Tory politician John Profumo, who lived here with his wife in 1963 at the time of the Profumo Affair.

Further along on the right take a loop around pretty **Park Village West** 10, a semi-circular street of characterful, detached properties, designed by Nash and his pupil James Pennethorne, which seem to have been transplanted from a Jane Austen novel.

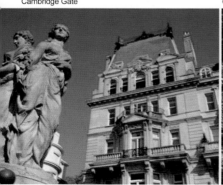

Cambridge Gate

Chester Terrace

WALK 16

On rejoining Albany Street, turn right and then right again down traffic-choked Camden Parkway. At number 94, the **Dublin Castle Tavern** ⑪ is noted for its live music and has launched many a career, as attested to by photographs of Madness, Blur and the late Amy Winehouse, among others.

FOOD & DRINK

⑪ **Dublin Castle Tavern:** A legendary music venue, the Dublin is also a good pub serving a selection of real ales and tasty pub grub.

⑰ **Camino** (☎ 020-7841 7331): Award-winning Spanish bar and restaurant serving authentic regional Spanish cuisine, tapas and wines.

At the bottom of Parkway, turn right into lively Camden High Street, cross over and take a left along the unfortunately-named Pratt Street. At the end, turn right down St Pancras Way, passing the Canal Side Studios on the left. St Pancras Way used to be called Longwich Lane, then King's Road, and follows the route of an ancient track that ran along the Fleet River. In 1809, the St Pancras Workhouse opened here, and much of the area is now occupied by factories and warehouses.

Turn left along Granary Street and as it bends to the right, a gated entrance gives a glimpse of a canal. At the end is Camley Street; turn right and look for a gate on your right where a flight of steps leads up to the attractive gardens and graveyard of **St Pancras Old Church** ⑫ (gardens, 7am-dusk). The leafy graveyard has some benches and doubles as a park, while the church is built on one of England's most ancient sites of Christian worship, possibly dating back to 314AD. The church is small, with a quirky interior; a Saxon altar from 600 has been found here, while the chancel was rebuilt in around 1350 and the church was restored in 1847-8. St Pancras

St Pancras Old Church

was a 14-year-old Christian martyr killed in Rome in AD304, and it's the church which gives the surrounding area its name.

Leaving the church, turn left along Pancras Road, left again along Goods Way and then left into Camley Street for the impressive gated entrance to **Camley Street Natural Park**  on the right, which is run by the London Wildlife Trust. This small urban nature reserve opened in 1985 and is a sanctuary for wildlife and an educational centre. It covers 2 acres (0.8ha) on the banks of the Regent's Canal on the site of a former coal-yard, and has a variety of habitats including meadow, wetlands and woodland.

British Library 14
exhibition galleries and shop, Mon and Wed-Fri, 9.30am-6pm, Tue 9.30am-8pm, Sat, 9.30am-5pm, Sun, 11am-5pm

by Eduardo Paolozzi, a Scottish sculptor of Italian parentage. *Newton* is modelled on William Blake's 1795 print of the same name and was commissioned for the British Library; a controversial decision, as Blake is often regarded as being anti-scientific.

Camley Street Natural Park 13
Mon-Fri and Sun, 10am-4.30pm in spring and autumn, 10am-5.30pm in summer

Opened in 1999, long overdue and hundreds of millions of pounds over budget, the library complex gives the British Library the facilities its world class collection merits. It wouldn't claim to be London's prettiest structure, but internally it's perfectly designed for its purpose, with a total of 112,000m² (1,205,558ft²) spread over 14 floors, five of which are below ground.

Return along Camley Street and turn right into Pancras Road and left along Midland Road. After the underpass, turn left and as you walk south along Midland Road, the imposing red-brick silhouette of the **British Library** 14 appears on the right. The courtyard is a large open space with benches and some fine outdoor art, notably a large **sculpture of Sir Isaac Newton** 15

St Isaac Newton

Returning to the courtyard's entrance, turn right along Midland Road, with the striking, red-brick **St Pancras Station and Hotel**  complex to the left; turn left to admire its façade from Euston Road. It's fronted by the former Midland Grand Hotel, now the St Pancras Renaissance London Hotel, a majestic building with a vast Gothic façade. John Betjeman famously remarked that it was "too beautiful and too romantic to survive in a world of tower blocks and concrete".

St Pancras Station was built in 1867, with Sir George Gilbert Scott's red-brick extravaganza of a hotel added in 1873. It was the result of a design competition between 11 architects, which Scott only entered under duress, having declined a number of times. On completion, the hotel was described as 'the most sumptuous and best conducted hotel in the Empire'.

The hotel was converted to offices in 1935 and served as such until the '80s, after which it was derelict for some years. From 2003 to 2007 the St Pancras Station complex was redeveloped and is now one of Europe's largest termini, serving Eurostar routes alongside domestic destinations. The hotel reopened in 2011 and is one of London's most monumental and impressive buildings. It's 172m (564ft) in width and fronted by an 82m (269ft) clock tower – a truly great example of Victorian architecture.

We end this walk at **Camino** , a vibrant Spanish restaurant and bar specialising in tapas,

steaks and grilled meats. With the St Pancras Hotel on the left, continue along Euston Road, cross the junction into Pentonville Road ahead and turn left into Varnishers Yard – Camino is at number 3. To get to King's Cross St Pancras station, turn right on Pentonville Road and it's 100m ahead.

The Lovers, St Pancras Station

St Pancras Station and Hotel

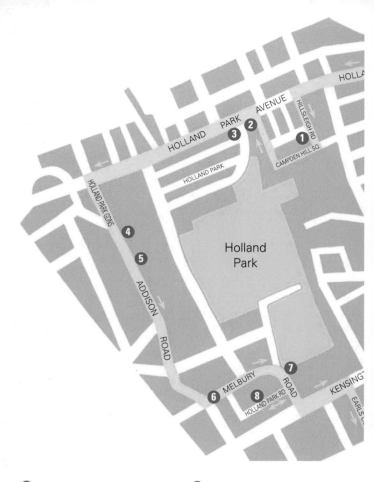

1. Campden Hill Square
2. Statue of St Volodymyr
3. Holland Park
4. Addison Road
5. Debenham House
6. Melbury Road
7. Tower House
8. Leighton House
9. Iverna Gardens
10. St Sarkis Armenian Church
11. Iverna Court
12. Observatory Gardens
13. Churchill Arms
14. Ottolenghi
15. Kensington Church Walk
16. St Mary Abbots
17. Kensington Palace Gardens

● Places of Interest ● Food & Drink

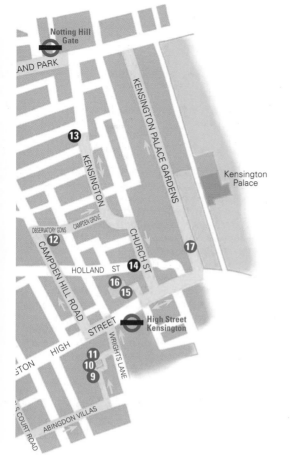

HOLLAND PARK TO KENSINGTON

Distance: 4.15mi (6.69km)

Duration: full day

Start/End: Notting Hill Gate tube station

From millionaires' mansions to celebrities' cribs, this walk focuses on some of the most desirable residential streets in London, all crammed into a few square miles between Hyde Park and Hammersmith. It's only the rich and famous who can afford to set up home in these sought-after districts, and our walk takes in the homes of characters as diverse as middle-aged boy band leader Gary Barlow, self-regarding film director and restaurant critic Michael Winner and Led Zeppelin OAP guitarist Jimmy Page.

Holland Park is, unofficially, the area bounded by Holland Park Avenue to the north, Kensington High Street to the south, Kensington Church Street to the east and Holland Road to the west. It was mainly rural until the 19th century, much of it formerly the estate of Holland House, a Jacobean mansion. The owners gradually sold off land for development and it's now a showpiece of large, desirable Victorian houses – some of which sell for over £10m – surrounding a tranquil and semi-wild city park.

Kensington is the affluent and aspirational district, densely-populated even by London standards – many of its houses now divided into flats – and a magnet for shoppers. It's bordered by Notting Hill to the north, Chelsea and Earls Court to the south, Knightsbridge to the east and Hammersmith to the (slightly shabby) west. Kensington gets its first mention in the Domesday Book as Chenesitone but it most likely dates back to Saxon times when it was probably called Kenesignetun, meaning Kenesigne's land.

Between these two quarters is small, exclusive Campden Hill – from the Campden House Estate – which is the name of both a road and the area surrounding it.

Start Walking...

We begin this walk by leaving Notting Hill tube station via exit two and walking ahead at the top of the steps, going west along Notting Hill Gate. This is the main east-west road in the southern part of Notting Hill, named after a tollgate that was at Pembridge Road corner from 1769 to 1864. It isn't a particularly attractive road and provides no clue to the gorgeous houses tucked away in the surrounding streets. But take a peek down one of the side streets, such as Farmer Street on your left, and you'll see some attractive, ice cream-coloured houses that make it such a pleasing place to live.

> Look out for the green plaque (on the left) outside 1 Holland Park Avenue, which marks it as a one-time home of Scottish-born painter and etcher James McBey (1883-1959).

As you continue, Notting Hill Gate becomes Holland Park Avenue and the vista improves. Large, elegant, four-storey houses line the right side of the avenue, which is part of the old west road connecting London with Oxford. Its present design dates to the 19th century and it's shaded by well-established plane trees.

Turn left up steep Hillsleigh Road and right along **Campden Hill Square** ❶, a charming, residential garden square built on the slope of Campden Hill, commanding sweeping views of the surrounding area. The artist J. M. W. Turner (1775-1851) painted sunsets from here, commemorated by a plaque on a tree in the garden. Built in 1827-38 by J. F. Hanson, Campden Hill Square was called Notting Hill Square until 1893, when residents successfully campaigned for a name change. It's quiet and prosperous, with quirky, old-fashioned lampposts and a number of blue plaques. There's one at number 23 for Siegfried

Campden Hill Square

Sassoon (1886-1967), one of the leading poets of WWI and later a successful novelist; other notable residents have included the philosopher Evelyn Underhill at number 50 and explorer John McDougall Stuart at number 9.

Continue down either side of the garden and turn left along Holland Park Avenue. Soon, on the left, is a **statue of St Volodymyr** ❷ (c958-1015), ruler of Ukraine 980-1015. It was erected by Ukrainians in Britain in 1988 to celebrate the establishment of Christianity in Ukraine by the saint in 988. Further along, **Holland Park** ❸ runs left off Holland Park Avenue and has a number of grand, majestic properties. This area is also home to many embassies, representing countries as diverse as Cameroon and Uzbekistan.

Turn left down Holland Park Gardens, which links up with **Addison Road** ❹, constructed in

FOOD & DRINK

13 Churchill Arms: Traditional, award-winning, flower-bedecked pub serving great ales and reasonably-priced Thai cuisine.

14 Ottolenghi: Renowned chain of gourmet food shops offering great coffee and take-away food, including mouth-watering pastries, salads, lasagna, fish pie, cherry trifle, etc.

statue of St Volodymyr

the 1820s. Apart from some bland, modern, red-brick terraces on the left, Addison Road is lined with interesting, stately villas in what is one of London's most desirable residential thoroughfares. It's named after essayist and statesman Joseph Addison, who lived at Holland House, a local mansion built around 1606 – it was bombed out in the Blitz and only a small part remains. Former Addison Road residents include Prime Minister David Lloyd-George (number 2, 1928-36), Chaim Weizmann, a founding father and first President of Israel (number 67, 1916-19), and John

Debenham House

Melbury Road

Galsworthy, author of *The Forsyte Saga* (number 14, 1905-13).

Number 8, on the left, is perhaps the most high-profile and eye-catching property on Addison Road, designed by Halsey Ricardo in 1905-6 for Sir Ernest Debenham, the founder of the eponymous store. Officially called **Debenham House** , it's also known as the Peacock House due to its ostentatious design. It's been called London's most extravagantly showy 20th-century private property and looks more like a museum than a house. The design is a mix of classical, Byzantine and Arts and Crafts styles, with blue and green glazed bricks, turquoise tiles and Doulton ware.

By way of contrast, numbers 16 and 17, also on the left of the road, are stately and understated, while number 69 on the right is a large detached villa that costs around £20m in this much sought-after part of the world; it's

said to be owned by Gary Barlow of (ageing) boy band Take That. This is very much a rich man's enclave and the collections of cars parked in the gated drives of many Addison Road properties are worth more than many people's houses!

> One of the richest residents in this minted neighbourhood is television guru Simon Cowell, who's rumoured to have paid a cool £40m for his home on nearby Addison Crescent.

Turn left along **Melbury Road** ⑥, where the houses, though often smaller, are quirkier and more interesting; this is one of west London's most visually enticing streets. Melbury Road is on the Ilchester Estate, named after the Dorset home of the Earls of Ilchester, where many of the properties were built for artists in the mid-19th century.

217

Tower House, Melbury Road

While the buildings on nearby Addison Road are usually white or cream, red brick dominates on Melbury Road. Interesting houses include number 2, with its blue plaque to sculptor Sir Hamo Thorneycroft (1850-1925), and number 4, with its tall chimney. Number 8 has a blue plaque to artist Marcus Stone (1840-1921), the illustrator of Charles Dickens's later works. It was built for him by Norman Shaw in 1875-6 in Queen Anne style with tall windows; film director Michael Powell lived here in from 1951 to 1971.

Pre-Raphaelite painter William Holman Hunt lived at number 18 in the early 20th century; between 1923 and 1924 this was the headquarters of the UK's secret intelligence service, MI6. It's been converted into flats, as has number 22, the former home of composer Benjamin Britten who lived here 1948-53, when he wrote his operas *Billy Budd* and *Gloriana*.

Further along on the left, the **Tower House** ❼ at number 29 is probably Melbury Road's most famous property. It's a striking, Grade I listed house, built in 1876-8 in the medieval French Gothic style by the Victorian art-architect William Burges as his own home. The exterior is of red brick with stone dressings, the roof grey slate with diminishing courses, the whole adorned with a profusion of stained glass windows. It's now owned by Led Zeppelin guitarist Jimmy Page, who bought it from the actor Richard Harris in 1974. Page is a Burges enthusiast and reportedly outbid fellow rock icon David Bowie. The film director Kenneth Anger lived in Page's basement at the Tower House while he was editing the film *Lucifer Rising*, and many Led Zeppelin songs were composed in its music room.

Next door, at number 31, is Woodside, looking like it should be on a small country estate. It's remarkable to have a house of this size – a 47-room mansion – in an upmarket area of central London. It was built in 1875 by Norman Shaw for the painter Luke Fildes, who wanted to outdo his friend, the above-mentioned Marcus Stone who lived at number 8, also built by Shaw. It was bought cheaply after WWII, due to bomb damage, by the parents of film director, food critic and professional contrarian Michael Winner. He grew up here and has lived in the house ever since, although it was reportedly on the market for an eye-watering £60m following Mr Winner's marriage in 2011.

Turn right along Holland Park Road, once the centre of a late Victorian artists' community. There are some fine houses here, including number 10, which was built for the painter James Shannon around the original farmhouse of Holland Farm. At number 12 is **Leighton House** ⑧, an unjustly-obscure museum in the former home of painter and sculptor Frederic, Lord Leighton, 1830-96 (daily except Tue, 10am-5.30pm, £5 adults). It's one of the 19th century's most remarkable buildings; from the outside it's elegant rather than striking, but the interior is jaw-dropping.

The first part of the house was designed in 1864 by George Aitchison and resembles an Italianate villa, built of red Suffolk brick with Caen Stone dressings in a restrained classical style. Subsequently, the building was extended over 30 years by Aitchison. The centrepiece is a remarkable, two-storey Arab Hall, designed to display Leighton's priceless collection of over 1,000 antique tiles. The whole interior of the property is opulent, with gilded ceilings, peacock blue tiles, red walls, intricate black woodwork and much else. It also boasts an impressive collection of art by various Pre-Raphaelites.

The Arab Hall in Leighton House has appeared in a number of films and television series, including Terry Gilliam's *Brazil*, and the BBC's spy drama *Spooks*. It's also provided a backdrop for music videos such as Spandau Ballet's *Gold*.

On leaving Leighton House, turn left and return to Melbury Road. Turn right and, at the end of the road, make a left along

Leighton House

St Sarkis   Iverna Court

Kensington High Street. Until the 19th century Kensington was a small country town, but developed rapidly and was consumed by London. Kensington High Street is now one of London's longest and busiest shopping streets. Cross Kensington High Street, turn right along Earl's Court Road, left along Abingdon Villas and left up attractive **Iverna Gardens** 9, which is lined with London plane trees. At the end, on the right is the jewellery box-like **St Sarkis Armenian Church** 10 (Wed and Fri, 9.30am-5.30pm).

The church was built in 1922 by businessman and philanthropist Calouste Sarkis Gulbenkian as a memorial to his parents. It was designed by Mewes and Davis, and modelled on the 13th-century bell tower of the Haghpat Monastery in Armenia; inside it's decorated with lapis lazuli, marble and onyx. Gulbenkian chose

Mewes and Davis because they also designed the permanent suite he kept at the Ritz Hotel and he liked their Beaux-Arts style.

When you leave the church, continue ahead along **Iverna Court** 11, which is lined with elegant, red-brick residential mansion blocks. At the end, turn left into Wrights Lane; this used to be a country path and was named after the houses built for Gregory Wright at its southern end in the 1770s.

Turn left along Kensington High Street, cross the road and take the first right, which is Campden Hill Road, developed in the 1860s to provide large houses for those who wanted to escape the pollution of the city. It's named after Campden House, built around 1612 for Sir Baptist Hicks who was made Viscount Campden of Campden, Gloucestershire in 1628; the house was demolished

Observatory Gardens

The Churchill Arms

around 1900. Attractive properties line the left of the road as you proceed uphill. After you pass the chunky mansion block (Campden Hill Court) on your right, turn right down **Observatory Gardens** 12, which has terraces of impressively-showy, colourful properties. The road was laid out in 1870 on the site of New Campden House, formerly Phillimore House, built in 1762 by Robert Phillimore. From 1826-67 it was owned by Sir James South, one of the founders of the Royal Astronomical Society, who had his own observatory in the garden.

Observatory Gardens leads into Campden Grove. At the end, swing a left along Kensington Church Street which links Notting Hill and Kensington. It's an attractive street with a number of interesting antique shops. At number 119 is the **Churchill Arms** 13, a pub that's a regular winner in the London in Bloom competition. This is a strange-sounding union of a Fullers pub and a Thai restaurant, which is actually a relaxing place to take a break, with decent Thai food at keen prices.

Turn right out of the pub and stroll back down Kensington Church Street. Near the end, take a short diversion to the right down Holland Street for **Ottolenghi** 14, which is the second on the left. This is a good place to buy some take-away food to eat in the gardens along **Kensington Church Walk** 15, our next destination. It's the brainchild of Israeli-born chef and restaurateur Yotam Ottolenghi, one of four London outlets. They're stylish and imaginative delicatessens, offering Mediterranean-style dishes with a Middle Eastern influence, plus beautiful cakes and snacks; the window displays alone will make your mouth water.

St Mary Abbots Church

Turn right from Holland Street down Kensington Church Street and right again into Kensington High Street, then almost immediately, take a sharp right up Kensington Church Walk. The Walk is a tranquil alley, leading to a small park and gardens, perfect for consuming your Ottolenghi victuals. While there, take a few minutes to admire elegant **St Mary Abbots** 🔟 church. There's been a church here since the 13th century, founded by the Abbot of Abingdon; the current one was built in 1869-72 by Sir George Gilbert Scott, who also built St Pancras station (see page 210).

St Mary Abbots has London's tallest spire at 278ft (85m). Scientist Sir Isaac Newton, anti-slavery campaigner William Wilberforce and author Beatrix Potter all worshipped here.

Return to Kensington High Street, turn left and just past a branch of Wagamama, turn left along **Kensington Palace Gardens** 🔟, a long, straight street of beautiful mansions. They're reputed to be London's most expensive properties, which may raise the hackles of the residents of Addison Road and Melbury Road (see above).

Kensington Palace Gardens was built in 1841-3 and was originally called Queen's Road. Its magnificent mansions date from 1844-70 and are built in the Italianate style. Most are very impressive buildings; number 18 was designed by Charles Barry and is where Julius Reuter, founder of the eponymous news agency, lived from 1867-99.

Kensington Palace Gardens is a private roadway, part of the Crown Estate, guarded by manned huts and traffic barriers at both ends. Kensington Palace itself, the London home to several members of the Royal Family, including the Duke and Duchess of Cambridge (a.k.a. Wills and Kate), is just to the east, facing Hyde Park. Many of the properties are now embassies, including those of Israel, Romania, Norway, Finland, France and Russia. Thus we end our walk in what is effectively a diplomatic enclave with exclusive connections.

To return to Notting Hill Gate tube station, when you reach the end of Kensington Palace Gardens turn left along Notting Hill Gate and it's a few hundred yards on the right-hand side.

Kensington Palace Gardens (All)

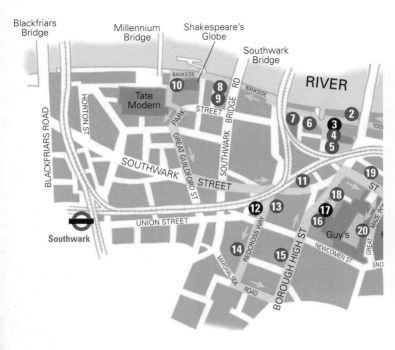

1. St Olaf House
2. Glaziers' Hall
3. The Mudlark
4. Southwark Cathedral
5. Roman soldier
6. Winchester Palace
7. Clink Prison Museum
8. Bear Gardens
9. Ferryman's Seat
10. Cardinal's Cap Alley
11. Hop Exchange
12. Boot and Flogger
13. Cross Bones Graveyard
14. Redcross Way Cottages
15. Three sculptures of blue musicians
16. Talbot Yard
17. George Inn
18. White Hart Yard
19. Old Operating Theatre
20. Great Maze Pond
21. Fashion and Textile Museum
22. Shad Thames
23. Design Museum

● Places of Interest   ● Food & Drink

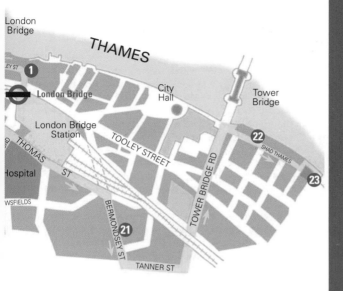

London
Bridge

THAMES

...EY ST

① London Bridge

London Bridge
Station

THOMAS

ST

Hospital

WSFIELDS

TOOLEY STREET

City
Hall

Tower
Bridge

② City Hall area

BERMONDSEY ST

②①

TANNER ST

TOWER BRIDGE RD

②② SHAD THAMES

②③

WALK 18

SOUTHWARK

WALK 18

Distance: 2.73mi (4.39km)
Duration: half to full day
Start/End: London Bridge station

SOUTHWARK

Southwark is one of the oldest and most fascinating parts of London, with a history dating back to Roman times when it marked the easiest crossing point of the Thames; modern Southwark begins on the river, facing the City and Blackfriars. Just south of here, archaeologists have found evidence of a prehistoric settlement, including burial mounds, while two major Roman roads conjoined in what is now Borough High Street. The Anglo Saxons gave Southwark its name, recorded in the Domesday Book of 1086 as Sudweca from the Old English *suth* and *weore*, meaning 'southern defensive work'.

Southwark gradually evolved into a centre for entertainment. During the Middle Ages, it was London's 'red light' district, and hosted a famous annual fair. It attractive the criminal element for being outside the control of the City, and Londoners visited for such 'amusements' as bear-baiting and to watch plays by Shakespeare and Christopher Marlowe at the Rose and the Globe. Less fortunate visitors ended up in one of Southwark's many jails, such as the infamous Clink.

What's striking about modern Southwark is how much of its history is still tangible. It has undergone huge regeneration in recent times and is home to some ultra-modern buildings, including The Shard and City Hall, but still has a genuine feeling of age. There are reminders of the past around every corner; not just the magnif cent cathedral but also riverside warehouses, historic coaching inns and narrow, claustrophobic alleyways.

Southwark coat of arms

Southwark is home to the headquarters of the Great London Authority, the administrative body for Greater London led by the Mayor of London. The GLA's base is at City Hall, an unusual, bulbous glass building designed by Norman Foster. Overlooking the Thames, east of London Bridge, it has been likened to a misshapen egg, a motorcyclist's helmet and even a testicle!

St Olaf House

Start Walking...

We begin this walk at London Bridge railway station's Tooley Street exit. The name Tooley is apparently a corruption of St Olave's, after the nearby church of the same name which once stood here. In the 17th century, Tooley Street was called Short Southwark to distinguish it from Long Southwark, now Borough High Street (see below). Directly opposite the station exit is the Grade II listed, Art Deco elegance of **St Olaf House** ❶. Built in 1928-32 as an office block for the Hays Wharf Company, it now houses the London Bridge Hospital's consulting and administration rooms (it isn't open to the public), but it has much more ancient associations. The house – and the church which stood here earlier – is named after St Olav, King of Norway 1015-28, who allied himself with Ethelred the Unready in his battle against King Canute's Danish army at London Bridge in 1014.

The building's Thames frontage bears the name of the Hay's Wharf Company in gold stylised lettering along the top, while the riverside façade's central section displays a large relief panel of gilded metal and terracotta, with three stylised figures at the top and 36 smaller abstract panels below. At first glance, the Tooley Street façade isn't as decorative, but closer examination reveals some beautiful features. The name St Olaf House appears in stylised script above the doorway and the door itself has an attractive, understated metal wave motif. St Olaf is pictured on the sleekly curved corner of the building, spelt St Olave and scripted in black and gold mosaic. The contrasting arrangement of the front windows – on the left they are grouped in parallel sets of three, while on the right they're offset in step formation – is another attractive design motif.

Walk east from St Olaf House and under London Bridge, and soon after on the right is **Glaziers' Hall** ❷, marked with an oval plaque. The Glaziers Company dates from 1328 but didn't receive its first royal charter until 1638. This Hall is recent, built in 1978, and is shared with the Scientific Instrument Makers and Launderers – unusual bedfellows!

Soon after on the left is a pub, **The Mudlark** ❸. There's been a pub here since the mid-1700s, but this building dates to 1860. The pub's interior is sleek and modern, more like an internet café than a traditional boozer, but the outdoor area has views of the splendid cathedral next door.

> The Mudlark pub is popular with filmmakers and its credits include *Bridget Jones's Diary*, *Lock, Stock and Two Smoking Barrels* and *Harry Potter and the Prisoner of Azkaban*.

Just past the pub is the impressive bulk of beautiful, historic **Southwark Cathedral** ❹. The entrance is on the opposite side and as you walk along the side of the cathedral, there's a modern sculpture of a **Roman soldier** ❺. The cathedral and The Shard rise behind it, providing an interesting contrast between the old and new; a common feature in London.

Southwark Cathedral is the mother church of the Anglican diocese of Southwark. it has only been designated a cathedral since 1905 but has been a place of worship for over 1,000 years; the site was used by the Romans, who often built on earlier settlements, therefore its use is probably much older. There are claims that a convent was founded here in 606 and a monastery by St Swithin in the 9th century, but there's no proof of either. The site's first official mention is in the Domesday Book of 1086, as the 'minster' of Southwark. The current building is mainly Gothic, dating from 1220-1420; a 12th-century Norman arch survives in the north aisle of the nave. Do go into the cathedral, the interior of which is striking and decorative. (There's no admission fee, although there's a suggested donation of £4 and a £2 fee to take photographs.)

Southwark Cathedral ❹
Mon-Fri, 8am to 6pm, Sat-Sun, 8.30am-6pm, with main visiting times 10am-5pm

Past the cathedral is a sign pointing sharp right to the Clink Prison Museum: follow it and you soon pass a full-size reconstruction of Sir Francis Drake's galleon, the *Golden Hinde*, on the right. Turn left along Pickfords Wharf leading to Clink Street and ahead on the left are the remains of **Winchester Palace** ❻. These are a rare fragment of a bishop's palace dating to 1109, consisting mainly of a tall wall topped by an elegant 13ft (4m) hexagonal rose window. It dates from the 14th century, built on 12th-century foundations. There are three doorways which once led to the buttery, kitchen and pantry.

Clink Prison Museum ❼
July to September, daily, 10am-7pm; October to June, Mon-Fri, 10am-6pm, Sat-Sun, 10am-7.30pm; adults £7

the largest and most important buildings in medieval London, and stood in a 70 acre (28ha) park fronting onto the Thames. After the bishops moved to Chelsea in the 17th century, the palace was divided into tenements and warehouses; it was mostly destroyed by fire in 1814.

Further along on the left is the **Clink Prison Museum** ❼. The Clink was the Bishop of Winchester's notorious jail (or gaol as it used

FOOD & DRINK

③ The Mudlark:
A Nicholsons' establishment offering a wide choice of beers, specialising in local and seasonal ales and good pub grub. Nice outdoor area.

⑫ Boot and Flogger:
Wine bar offering affordable wines alongside such specialities as rare sirloin and cured ox tongue cold cuts, game pie and Newlyn crab. Closed weekends.

⑰ George Inn:
An historic galleried coaching inn with a good choice of real ales and good traditional pub food.

Winchester Palace – the London residence of the Bishops of Winchester – was one of

Winchester Palace

to be called), in use from 1144 to 1780 and probably Britain's oldest prison. The prison burned down in the anti-Catholic riots of 1780 and there's now an excellent museum on the original site. The instruments of torture hanging outside the entrance paint a vivid picture of daily 'life' in the Clink.

> The name Clink is thought to come from the sound of striking metal, either the sound of the prison's metal doors as they closed or the rattle of the prisoners' chains. it has since become a slang term for prison.

Turn right at the end of the street, with the Vinopolis wine centre and exhibition to the left, then swing left along the riverbank; St Paul's Cathedral can be seen ahead. Pass under a bridge and on the left are a number of places to eat, including a Greek restaurant, The Real Greek, and a branch of Pizza Express which has panoramic views of the river from the second floor. Between these two restaurants is **Bear Gardens** ❽, once the site of a bear-baiting area, where

dogs were set on bears, bulls and sometimes other animals for 'entertainment'.

The first reference to bear- and bull-baiting in London is here at Bankside in 1546. Henry VIII enjoyed the spectacle, while later Elizabeth I entertained French and Spanish ambassadors at the bear pit. In 1604, Edward Alleyn, actor and later founder of Dulwich College, was appointed Master Overseer and Ruler of the Bears, Bulls and Mastiff Dogs – a position of some importance. As well as Bankside, there were bear gardens at Tothill Fields, the splendidly-named Hockley-in-the-Hole, Saffron Hill and Islington. They were less popular by the 17th century, but were still much visited; Cromwell tried and failed to suppress the 'sport'. Bankside bear garden was closed around 1675, but others continued and baiting wasn't outlawed until 1835.

There's no longer evidence of bear-baiting at Bankside, beyond the name of this cobbled road, but there's a historic relic of another sort on the left as you enter Bear Gardens: embedded into a side wall of The Real Greek is the **Ferryman's Seat** ❾. Its date is uncertain but it was taken from an earlier building and incorporated into this modern one. The seat was probably in use for many centuries by ferrymen who worked on the Thames. Until 1750, London Bridge was the only major crossing point in central London and their services were much in demand to transport people and goods across the river.

Ferryman's Seat

area's oldest. They're attractive, crooked houses, including one which architect Sir Christopher Wren is reputed to have lived in when he was working on St Paul's Cathedral. Henry VIII's first wife, Catherine of Aragon, is said to have sheltered at one of the houses in 1502 on her arrival in London. Neither claim can, however, be verified.

Continue along the riverbank and just before the imposing Tate Modern gallery, turn left and then right along Park Street. Head left down Great Guildford Street and turn left along Southwark Street, into an area that has improved greatly in recent years. It used to have a reputation for sleaze and crime, but now boasts a number of sleek, modern buildings, with more being built.

Continue along the riverbank and soon, on the left, is Shakespeare's Globe, a reconstruction of the circular Globe Theatre which was built by William Shakespeare's troupe and stood here from 1599 to 1642. Just past it is Cardinal's Wharf and **Cardinal Cap Alley** ⑩, a narrow alley running by the wharf with a rare surviving 17/18th-century terrace, the

Cardinal Cap Alley

Southwark Street has an impressively long line of 'Boris Bikes', the informal name for Barclays Cycle Hire, a public bicycle-sharing scheme. It was launched in July 2010 in London and 'named' after Mayor Boris Johnson. There are currently around 400 docking stations and 6,000 bikes, for which you pay an access fee and user charges (the first 30 minutes are free). See 🖳 www.tfl.gov.uk/roadusers/cycling/14808.aspx for more information.

Hop Exchange Building

Continue over the junction with Southwark Bridge Road and soon the ubiquitous Shard appears ahead to the left. You may wish to detour to see Southwark Bridge, built 1814-19 by John Rennie and replaced in 1912-21 with a bridge designed by Sir Ernest George. Back on Southwark Street, the impressive Grade II listed **Hop Exchange** ⑪ building sweeps along the left hand side of the road at number 24. Southwark had a long association with brewing, from at least the 17th century onwards, and the exchange opened in 1867 when trade in hops was at its peak; in 2012 this handsome building was empty.

Just past the Hop Exchange is the entrance to Borough Market, which is London's oldest fruit and vegetable market dating back to the 13th century, when it was a raucous affair held just south of London Bridge. The buildings at its current location were designed in 1851 and the atmospheric black brickwork and nooks and crannies create a Dickensian feel, making it a popular film location. Borough Market has expanded in recent years to sell a wide range of foods, and is where chefs, caterers and the capital's foodies go to buy everything from sausages to samphire. The main market opens on Thursdays, Fridays and Saturdays, and there are some excellent places to eat.

Cross Southwark Street and turn right, heading back the way you came for a short distance, before turning left down Redcross Way. On the right is the atmospheric **Boot and Flogger** ⑫. Though it looks like a pub, it's actually a wine bar (which sells a few bottled beers), with an attractively wood-panelled interior. It's the only place in the UK allowed to sell wine without a licence and is named after a corking device.

Directly opposite is one of London's odder and more poignant sights: the **Cross Bones Graveyard** ⑬ where Winchester Geese (prostitutes, see box) were buried. The graveyard closed in 1853 when it was full to over-flowing, with around 15,000 souls buried in unmarked graves. More recently, it has become an unofficial shrine to the prostitutes and other 'outcast dead', with thousands of notes, photos, ribbons and other items attached to the gates outside. It's an example of the public grieving that's increasingly common among the once-reserved British.

Southwark was noted for its brothels, many of which were licensed by the Bishops of Winchester who owned much of the land. They received payment for the licences, hence the prostitutes' nickname, Winchester Geese. Sadly, when the women died they were deemed unworthy of a Christian burial and had to be interred in unconsecrated ground, a spectacular example of church hypocrisy.

Near the end of Redcross Way, on the right, you'll see a short row of smart cottages fronted by a pretty, communal garden; it's an unexpectedly tranquil spot in this busy part of London. One cottage has a blue plaque to Octavia Hill (1838-1912), a Victorian reformer and social housing pioneer, who was also a co-founder of the National Trust. She wanted to help London's poor by providing decent,

affordable housing, including the **Redcross Way Cottages** 🕐. The cottages were developed in the 1880s and tenants were obliged to watch their behaviour if they wanted to keep their homes; drinking and swearing were frowned upon, and would sometimes lead to eviction. The attractive garden in front of the cottages, Redcross Garden, was planned as an 'open air sitting room for the tired inhabitants of Southwark'.

At the junction soon after, turn left along Marhsalsea Road, named after Marshalsea Prison (see below and box), which was close to the southeastern end of the road. On the left is a blue plaque marking Suffolk Place, a mansion on the west side of Borough High Street belonging to the Dukes of Suffolk. It was built in the 15th century and rebuilt in 1522; Henry VIII assumed ownership in the 1530s and in 1545 it was converted into a royal mint before being demolished in 1557.

Opposite Borough tube station, turn left up Borough High Street, an area suffused with history. Borough was one of the busiest parts of medieval London, although there's little

Redcross Way Cottages

visual evidence as much of it was destroyed in the 1676 'Little Fire of London' and later rebuilt. The High Street has always been one of London's busiest thoroughfares and in the Middle Ages it was the main route south from London Bridge and long before that the Roman road to Chichester.

Borough High Street was famed for its inns, places of entertainment and prisons, including Marshalsea which occupied two different locations, from 1373 to 1811 and then from 1811 to 1842. Charles Dickens's father was jailed for debt here in 1824, an experience the author immortalised in *David Copperfield* and *Little Dorrit*. Borough High Street was also the site of the Southwark Fair, the largest in south London, held for two weeks in September from 1462 to 1763. The street began to decline in importance with the arrival of the railway in the 19th century, which signalled the beginning of the end for its coaching inns.

blue musicians

> Many of the prisoners at Marshalsea were debtors and those who could afford to pay the prison's fees were allowed out during the day, presumably to work so they could pay of their debts more quickly.

The rather ugly Maya House on the left of Borough High Street is brightened by the **three sculptures of blue musicians** 15 clinging to its front: it's an 'art installation' called *Blue Men* (2007) by Israeli artist Ofra Zimbalista. Further along the street, a right turn takes you to **Talbot Yard** 16. There's a blue plaque on the left commemorating

the site of the Tabard Inn, which is where the pilgrims gathered before leaving for Canterbury in Geoffrey Chaucer's *Canterbury Tales*; it's also where Chaucer began work on the book in 1388. An inn was established here in 1307, named after the sleeveless jacket worn by knights over their armour. It was rebuilt in 1629 as the Talbot, burned down in 1676, rebuilt again and finally demolished around 1875.

Turn right out of Talbot Yard and continue along Borough High Street. It's worth investigating some of the narrow, atmospheric courts and passageways which lead off the main road, as they provide a glimpse of how Southwark must have appeared in days gone by.

> The name Borough derives from Burgh, which means a stronghold protecting a river crossing.

Look for the sign on the right of Borough High Street for the historic **George Inn** ⑰. This Grade I listed pub in a cobbled courtyard is Greater London's only surviving coaching inn with a gallery overlooking the yard. Coaching inns were constructed around a courtyard so that coaches could enter and be unloaded in a protected place; in its heyday the George would have received 70 or 80 coaches a week. it has been here since at least 1543 and was rebuilt in 1676 after the fire that destroyed most of Southwark. It has had some notable literary customers over the years, including Shakespeare, Dickens, Samuel Johnson and Samuel Pepys.

Turn right out of The George and soon, to the right, is **White Hart Yard** ⑱. It's a small alleyway leading to the site of the White Hart Inn, immortalised by William Shakespeare in *Henry VI* and by Charles Dickens in *Pickwick Papers*: this is where Mr Pickwick met Sam Weller. A rectangular brass plaque

marks its former site, but nothing remains of the early 15th-century inn, which was demolished in 1889. The Kentish rebel Jack Cade based himself at the White Hart in 1450 when his rebel army tried to take over London; they failed when the rebels were defeated in a battle at London Bridge and Cade was killed soon after.

Return to Borough High Street, turn right along it and take a right down St Thomas Street. Two of London's most famous hospitals were founded here: St Thomas's in the 13th century, which moved out in the 19th to make way for the railway, and Guy's, established in 1725 by Thomas Guy. On the right of St Thomas Street at number 8 is a blue plaque to poet John Keats, who lived here when he was a medical student.

On the left is the **Old Operating Theatre** ⑲, one of London's more unusual museums (10.30am-5pm, adults £5.90). It's dedicated to surgical history and is evocatively situated in one of the world's oldest surviving operating theatres. This is in the garret, i.e. roof space, of an English baroque church, which used to be attached to a hospital. The garret is where herbs were cured and stored, the top of a building being the airiest part and the least susceptible to damp. The museum is a sobering eye-opener, showing how grim and life-threatening surgery was in the days before modern techniques and anaesthetics.

Continue along St Thomas Street and admire the decoration on the gateway to Guy's and St Thomas' Hospital on the right. Shortly after, you reach the

Great Maze Pond plaque

base of The Shard, the striking 72-floor skyscraper which stands 1,017ft (310m) tall and is now the dominant feature of London's skyline. Its architect Renzo Piano compared his vision to a 'shard of glass, hence the name – its official title is Shard London Bridge. Opposite is **Great Maze Pond** 20, where there's a large blue plaque on the right detailing the area's long history. The 'maze' pond that used to be here was fed by a Thames tributary now called Guy's Creek. Archaeological investigation has revealed an early Romano-British boat and Roman timbers edging the creek.

Return to St Thomas Street, turn right and a little further on take another right along Bermondsey Street, which is a conservation area lined with attractive converted warehouses and trendy places to eat and drink; note the shop front at numbers 68 and 78, the latter dating from the 17th century.

> Bermondsey is an ancient place which could date back as far as the 8th century. The name may come from Beormund's eye, or island, which probably belonged to a Saxon 'lord'.

On the left at number 83 is the colourful **Fashion and Textile Museum** 21. Founded by Zandra Rhodes and now owned by Newham College, it's housed in a striking building designed by the Mexican architect Ricardo Legorreta. It has an eye-catching orange and pink exterior, which adds a touch of colour to Bermondsey. The museum has a small permanent collection of Zandra Rhodes's designs, while changing exhibitions exploring the world of fashion, textiles and jewellery.

Turn left along Tanner Street – the name reminds us of the area's former leather industry – and left again at Tower Bridge Road. Just on the left is a grey plaque to Thomas Guy, who built and endowed Guy's Hospital. Cross the junction with Tooley Street for good views of City Hall, Minster Court and the Gherkin. Then cross to the right-hand side of the road and when you reach Tower Bridge, take the stairway on the right which leads down to the river level.

Fashion and Textile Museum 21
Tue-Sat, 11am-6pm, adults £7

Turn right along **Shad Thames** 22, an attractive cobbled walkway fronting one of London's best-preserved stretches of 19th-century warehouses, now converted into housing. These were coffee, grain, spice and tea warehouses, and their upper floors are linked by a lattice of striking, wrought-iron bridges. The architectural critic Nikolaus Pevsner called Shad Thames 'the most dramatic industrial street surviving in London', and it has provided the backdrop for a number of films, from *Oliver!* to *The Elephant Man*. The name Shad Thames is allegedly a corruption of St John at Thames, although this seems rather tenuous.

Walk towards the river along Maggie Blake's Causeway, named after a local community activist who fought against restricting public access to the riverside. Turn right at the end along the invariably windy Butlers Wharf Pier, which runs along the riverbank. The Wharf is named after an 18th-century grain trader and contains the largest collection of warehouses on the Thames; built

in 1871-3, many were converted into apartments and studios in 1972 (David Hockney had a studio here).

Our last stop is the **Design Museum** 23 on the right (10am-5.45pm, adults £8), housed in a former 1940s banana warehouse, which was converted to resemble a 1930s Modernist building. The museum specialises in contemporary design in every form, from architecture to furniture, graphics to industrial design, mostly through temporary exhibitions. Why not end this walk with a warming cup of something in the first-floor café, while taking in the panoramic river views.

To return to London Bridge station, retrace your steps back along Butler's Wharf Pier, Maggie Blake's Causeway and Shad Thames, take the steps back up to Tower Bridge Road and turn left. Then turn right along Queen Elizabeth Street, which leads into Tooley Street, and continue until London Bridge station appears on the left.

Shad Thames

WALK 19

WESTMINSTER

Distance: 2.43mi (3.92km)

Duration: half day

Start/End: St James's Park tube station

WESTMINSTER

To many people, Westminster is synonymous with British politics and describes a political system as well as a place. The term 'Westminster Village' is sometimes used in the context of British politics, but doesn't refer to a geographical area at all; it denotes a supposedly close social circle of Members of Parliament, political journalists and other 'insiders' connected to events in the Palace of Westminster.

It has been a seat of government for much of the past 1,000 years and its landscape is still dominated by the icons of power and rule, including the Houses of Parliament, Westminster Abbey and nearby Buckingham Palace. Westminster is one of the most central parts of London, describing a small area just north of the Thames surrounding Westminster Abbey, which was founded as early as the 7th century. It became known the West Minster (monastery church) from its location to the west of St Paul's and gave the area is name.

The Abbey still dominates Westminster; it's where England's kings and queens were crowned before they moved into the nearby Palace of Westminster to rule their domain. The Palace now houses (hopefully) less autocratic leaders in the shape of the British Parliament. Our walk passes most of these bastions of power, but also highlights some of the lesser known attractions – churches, schools and homes where the great and the good lived, learned, worshipped and wed – and ends at the place from where lesser mortals were transported Down Under.

Palace of Westminster

WESTMINSTER

Start Walking…

Start exploring Westminster at St James's Park tube station, leaving by the Victoria Street exit. Turn left along Palmer Street and left again along Caxton Street. Almost immediately on the left at number 10 is the former **Caxton Hall** ❶, with its decorative red-brick frontage and green plaque to Sir Winston Churchill. The plaque reveals a tenuous connection with the great man: he didn't live in the building, but 'spoke' here between 1937 and 1942.

> Caxton Hall was a popular place for celebrities to tie the knot. Well-known brides and bridegrooms include Elizabeth Taylor (and Michael Wilding), Peter Sellers (and Britt Ekland), Diana Dors (twice), George Harrison, Ringo Starr, Joan Collins and Roger Moore.

The hall and street take their name from the printer William Caxton, who worked near here in the 15th century. Caxton Hall was designed by William Lee and F. J. Smith, and opened in 1878 as Westminster City Hall, a public meeting place and registry office. It's now home to luxury apartments.

Turn and walk east along Caxton Street, passing Palmer Street on the right. At number 23 on the left there's an unexpected delight: an elegant, early 18th-century detached townhouse of red brick, sitting among undistinguished modern office blocks. This is **Blewcoat School** ❷, built in 1709 by William Green, a local brewer, to provide education for poor children. It was a school until the '20s or '30s (there's some confusion about the exact date). During WWII it was requisitioned as an army store and in 1954 it was purchased by the National Trust which uses it as a gift shop and information centre.

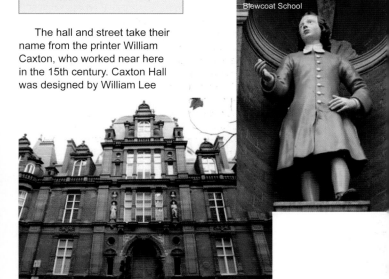

Blewcoat School

Caxton Hall

At the Caxton Street entrance is a Corinthian-columned vestibule carrying the original external clock chamber. A striking, life-sized painted wooden carving of a Blewcoat charity boy, wearing his blue coat, still stands above the doorway.

At the end of Caxton Street turn right along Buckingham Gate, which retains some handsome 18th-century houses, including number 16 (built around 1706). Prime Minister William Gladstone lived at number 20 in 1889, while *War of the Worlds* author H. G. Wells lived at number 52 in 1924. Turn sharp right along Petty France, passing the London Central Barracks on the left. Petty France takes its name from the French wool merchants who lived here; other residents included poet John Milton (1652-60) and writer and critic William Hazlitt in the early 19th century. One interesting stop is Albany House on the right where the entrance is guarded by two semi-abstract figurative **Man & Woman sculptures** ❸ by Willi Soukop, RA (1907-95).

Turn left opposite the main entrance to St James's Park tube station, along **Queen Anne's Gate** ❹. On the left is a green plaque for philosopher and social reformer Jeremy Bentham. It's affixed to the wall of the bland, modern Ministry of Justice edifice, which is in stark contrast to the lovely buildings found along the sweep of Queen Anne's Gate.

This road has some of London's best examples of Queen Anne architecture from the early 18th century: fine pink and white houses with splendidly ornate porches, delicate iron railings and interesting touches such as the cone-shaped torch snuffer outside number 26. Several houses have an elaborate wooden canopy over the front door. The area has long been popular with the good and great, as the number of blue plaques demonstrates. Liberal and Labour politician Lord Haldane lived at number 28; two-time Prime Minister Lord Palmerston was born at number 20 in 1784; MP William Smith and Admiral of the Fleet Lord Fisher both resided at number 16; antiquary and collector Charles Townley lived at number 14; and Foreign Secretary Sir Edward Grey at number 1. Number 36 is now the headquarters of the National Trust.

Soukop woman sculpture

Queen Anne style can refer to either the English Baroque architectural style popular around the time of Queen Anne's reign (1702-14) or to a revived form which found favour in the late 19th and early 20th centuries. In Queen Anne's Gate the former style prevails.

Queen Anne's Gate

Queen Anne

An elegant statue of Queen Anne graces the right side of the street. It's a copy of one at St Paul's Cathedral – Anne was the ruling monarch when St Paul's was completed – but it isn't the only sign of her presence. Her ghost is said to walk three times around Queen Anne's Gate on the anniversary of her death, July 31st, which could be an interesting date on which to visit.

Returning along Queen Anne's Gate, turn right after number 34A towards the greenery of St James's Park. Another right takes you along Birdcage Walk, enjoying views of the park to the left. James I's aviary was situated at this end of St James's Park, hence the name. Birdcage Walk itself dates back to 1660 but until 1828 only the Hereditary Grand Falconer and the Royal Family were allowed to drive along it.

At the end of the park, Birdcage Walk leads into Great George Street, built 1752-7 and now dominated by The Treasury and the Royal Institution of Chartered Surveyors. At the junction of Storey's Gate and Great George Street is **Brasserie One** ❺ in the basement of the building that houses the Institution of Civil Engineers. In an area of expensive (often expense-account) restaurants, it's known as the place to come for a reasonably priced working lunch and offers three courses for around £20.

Leave the restaurant, return to Great George Street and turn right along Little George Street towards two of London's busiest attractions: Westminster Abbey and the Houses of Parliament. These are magnets for tourists who largely ignore the equally interesting sights around them. On the right is the ornately carved entrance to the **Supreme Court** ❻ (Mon-Fri, 9.30am-4.30pm). Do go in, as it's free and you can look around the courtrooms and even sit in on trials.

It's located in the Middlesex Guildhall, which was formerly the

Supreme Court

headquarters of Middlesex County Council and later a Crown Court. It was built in 1912-3 by J. S. Gibson in what architectural commentator Nikolaus Pevsner called an 'Art Nouveau Gothic' style. The building is charmingly decorated with medieval-style gargoyles and other sculptures, and is Grade II* listed. On leaving the Supreme Court turn right into lively, traffic-choked Parliament Square – the heart of Westminster. The square was built in 1868 by Sir Charles Barry who had slum properties demolished to make way for it.

Parliament Square features a large number of statues of ex-Prime Ministers and notable foreign figures. Alongside Sir Winston Churchill, Benjamin Disraeli and Abraham Lincoln, there's a 9ft (2.7m) bronze of Nelson Mandela, unveiled in 2007 in the presence of the great man himself.

On the right, behind Westminster Abbey, and overshadowed by it, is pretty, historic **St Margaret's Church** ❼. It was built in 1485-1523 and is the third church to stand on the site, which has been occupied for around 900 years. Since 1614, it has been the official church of the House of Commons (but don't let that put you off!). St Margaret's has long been a popular venue for society weddings, including MP and diarist Samuel Pepys in 1655; poet John Milton in 1656; and Winston Churchill in 1908. Printing pioneer William Caxton and soldier and explorer Sir Walter Raleigh are buried here. On leaving the church, turn left and left again, so that the church is on your left and the Abbey on your right, with the Houses of Parliament directly ahead.

Swing right along Abingdon Street, which dates from at least 1593. A mansion stood here from the late 17th century and later became the home of the Earl of Abingdon. Civil engineer Thomas Telford lived at number 24 from 1820 until his death in 1834. Pass Old Palace Yard on the right, named after a yard in Canute's 11th-century Palace of Westminster. Poet and 'father of English literature' Geoffrey Chaucer lived here when he was Clerk of the King's Works in the 14th century, and dramatist, poet and actor Ben Jonson also had a house here. The Gunpowder Plot was partly hatched in the house of Thomas Percy on Old Palace Yard, and Guy Fawkes and his co-conspirators were hanged in the

St Margaret's Church 7
Mon-Fri, 9.30am-3.30pm, Sat, 9.30am-1.30pm, Sun, 2-5pm

Yard, as was Sir Walter Raleigh in 1618. Sadly, the yard and its houses were lost during the 1834 fire that destroyed much of the medieval Palace of Westminster.

Opposite the Sovereign's entrance to the current Parliament buildings is the **Jewel Tower** 8 (10am-5pm, adults £3.50).

Jewel Tower

Dating from around 1365, it's the only significant remains of the medieval Palace of Westminster, along with Westminster Hall. The three-storey building is surrounded by a moat and was built from Kentish ragstone as a store for Edward III's treasure. From 1621-1864, it housed the House of Lords' records and from 1869-1938 was home to the Weights and Measures office. It's now a museum run by English Heritage.

Next to the Jewel Tower is Abingdon Street Garden, which was built in 1963-6 and contains a 1962 Henry Moore bronze, *Knife Edge Two Piece*. Cross Abingdon Street and just past Parliament, turn left into the triangular-shaped **Victoria Tower Gardens** 9 which border the Thames between the Parliament buildings and Lambeth Bridge. This is an excellent vantage point from which to view the river, the

The Burghers of Calais

Jeté

London Eye and Lambeth Palace. It also contains one of London's best pieces of public art. Rodin's statue **The Burghers of Calais** ⑩, which commemorates the heroism of six citizens of Calais at the town's surrender to Edward III in 1347. It's one of 12 cast from the original, which is the maximum allowed under French law, and has been here since 1915.

In the middle of the gardens is the **Gothic Buxton Memorial** ⑪, which used to stand in Parliament Square. It remembers Sir Thomas Fowell Buxton, brewer, social reformer and abolitionist, and commemorates the emancipation of slaves in the British Empire. Leave the gardens and turn left along Millbank; in the 14th-century, the Abbey's mill house stood at this junction. Modern Millbank is noted for some large and striking buildings, including Thames House, the home of MI5; the 387ft (118m) tall Millbank Tower, which used to be the Labour Party HQ; and the Tate Britain art gallery. The last is named after the 19th-century

sugar tycoon Henry Tate and is now somewhat overshadowed by its younger sibling, Tate Modern, which opened on the South Bank in 2000.

> The two Tates are linked by a riverboat service which departs from the Millbank Millennium Pier. They're serviced by boats which were decorated by the artist Damien Hirst.

Further along Millbank, there are some interesting works of art. On the corner of 45-57 Millbank is an elegant sculpture called **Jeté** ⑫ by Enzo Plazzotta (1921-81), an Italian-born sculptor. Based on the dancer David Wall, it was sculpted in 1975 and unveiled in 1985; a *jeté* is a leap in ballet in which one leg is extended forward and the other backward. Further along in Riverside Walk Gardens facing Vauxhall Bridge, there's a large sculpture by Henry Moore (1898-1986) called **Locking Piece** ⑬ (1963-4), which is owned by the nearby Tate Britain. Just past it, is another piece of public art, **Search for Enlightenment** 🄐 (2010) by Simon Gudgeon, consisting of two large bronze human heads, male and female, standing next to each other facing the river. The space inside each head is hollow and there are peaceful expressions on their faces; the search for enlightenment is presumably going well.

Directly opposite the sculptures is **The Morpeth Arms** 🄕, a comfortable Victorian pub. It was built for the warders at the nearby Millbank Penitentiary, on whose site Tate Britain now stands. The prison was built in 1816 under the guidance of social reformer Jeremy Bentham and was in operation until 1890. In its heyday it was the world's largest jail, and was used mainly to house those awaiting transportation to Australia. The prisoners would take their last step off British soil onto ships moored on the Thames; a bollard on the edge of Riverside Walk Gardens marks the exact spot. This is something to contemplate over a drink at one of the pub's outdoor tables, with their sweeping river views.

FOOD & DRINK

5 Brasserie One (☎ 020-7665 2340): Restaurant serving reasonably-priced creative modern European food. Only open for lunch, noon-2.30pm, Mon-Fri.

15 The Morpeth Arms: Stylish Young's pub with traditional cask ales and home cooked food.

Leave the pub and head up Ponsonby Place. At the end, turn right along John Islip Street, which is named after an Abbot of Westminster (d 1532). Continue along it as it becomes Dean Ryle Street and into **Smith Square** 🄖. This is an important Westminster square, built in 1725-6 and named after landowner Henry Smith; the northern side has some elegant Georgian houses. The Conservative Party headquarters was based at number 32 until 2004.

The centre of Smith Square is dominated by **St John's** 🄗, one of London's finest examples of Baroque architecture and an

St Johns

Lord North Street

excellent small concert venue. It began life as a church, St John the Evangelist, designed by Thomas Archer (1668-1743) and built 1713-28. At the time, it was one of 50 new churches built under the 1711 Act of Parliament to serve London's expanding population; with a cost of almost £41,000, then a colossal sum, it was also the most expensive.

> St Johns was nicknamed 'Queen Anne's footstool'. When consulted by its designer, the Queen supposedly kicked over her footstool so the legs faced upwards, like the church's four towers, and instructed him to build it 'like that'. The towers were also an effort to stabilise the building which was built on marshy ground. It still stands at a slight slant.

The church opened in 1728 but wasn't a popular building: in *Our Mutual Friend*, Charles Dickens described it as 'a very hideous church... resembling some petrified monster'. It was gutted by fire during the Blitz in WWII and wasn't restored to its former glory until 1965-9. St John's, Smith Square (as it's now called) is no longer a church but a highly regarded concert hall.

Turn right off Smith Square to admire the attractive elegance of **Lord North Street** 18, one of London's best preserved Georgian streets and popular with Westminster's wealthier politicians, as it's just a short stroll from Parliament. It was built in the late 18th century as North Street and became Lord North Street in 1936; Lord North was Prime Minister when America won the War of Independence. It has been home to some famous people over the years, including socialite and interior designer Lady Sybil Colefax, theatre manager and producer Hugh 'Binkie' Beaumont, Prime

Barton Street plaque

Cowley Street

Minister Harold Wilson and MP and jailbird Jonathan Aitken. Look out for the painted signs on some of the houses pointing to their underground air-raid shelters.

At the end of Lord North Street cross Great Peter Street into **Cowley Street** 19 and then **Barton Street** 20, two beautifully preserved early 18th-century streets. Both are named after the actor Barton Booth, who had a house at Cowley, near Uxbridge, and owned land in this area. Cowley Street was built in 1722 and is still mainly 18th century; like Lord North Street, the houses here are coveted by MPs, and the Liberal Democrat headquarters is at number 4. There are blue plaques to Director General of the BBC Lord Reith at 6 Cowley Street, and to soldier, writer and adventurer T. E. Lawrence at 14 Barton Street.

Great College Street is thought to mark the southern boundary of Thorney Isle, an islet at the mouth of the Tyburn on which the first church at Westminster was built.

At the end of Barton Street, turn left along Great College Street, a quiet thoroughfare running along one side of the Abbey grounds. Built

Cowley Street

249

in around 1722, it's named after Westminster School; poet John Keats lived at number 25 in 1819.

Between numbers 26 and 16 Great College Street is a gated walkway; take it into the often-ignored **Dean's Yard** 21, a leafy garden square owned by the Abbey, where we end this walk. It feels like a village green but is surrounded by important educational and religious buildings, including Church House and Westminster School. On the right of the yard is the ancient Westminster School Office and there's a beautifully-weathered entrance soon after with a bright coat-of-arms.

Westminster School is one of Britain's most prestigious seats of learning, founded in the mid-14th century following a papal decree that urged all monasteries (in this case, Westminster Abbey) to support a school. It was originally a charitable establishment,

providing free education to the sons of local traders, but became independent of the Abbey in 1868. Pupils have included dramatist Ben Jonson, architect Sir Christopher Wren, actors John Gielgud and Peter Ustinov, MP Tony Benn, Chancellor of the Exchequer Nigel Lawson and composer Andrew Lloyd-Webber. The school's buildings are of various ages and architectural styles.

Further along Deans Yard, just before the Chapter Office at number 20, is another old doorway and shortly after are some expressive stone heads around an ornate entrance to the Abbey. Soon after this, veer to the left and turn right out of Deans Yard, with number 1 ahead.

To reach St James's Park tube station, cross Victoria Street ahead and turn left along Tothill Street, leading into Broadway.

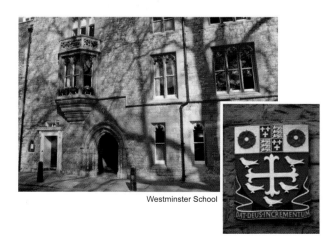

Westminster School

Westminster Abbey

1. Cleopatra's Needle
2. Lion's heads
3. Best views
4. Laurence Olivier statue
5. Royal Waterloo Hospital for Children and Women
6. Roupell Street
7. The King's Arms
8. Imperial War Museum
9. Tibetan Peace Garden
10. The Marine Society
11. The Garden Museum
12. Lambeth Palace
13. London Fire Brigade Headquarters
14. MI6 building
15. Vauxhall Bridge
16. Battersea Power Station
17. Pizza Express

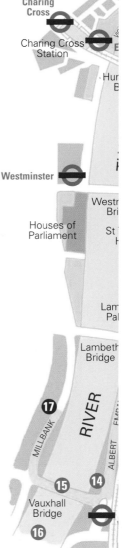

Places of Interest ● Food & Drink

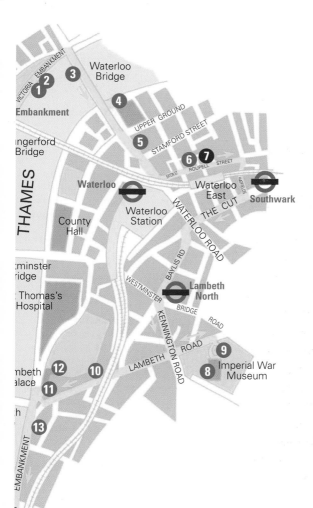

Waterloo
Bridge

① ② ③

④

Embankment

ngerford
Bridge

⑤ UPPER GROUND

STAMFORD STREET

⑥ ⑦ ROUPELL STREET

BRENT STREET

THAMES

Waterloo Ⓣ

Waterloo
Station

Waterloo
East

THE CUT

HATFIELDS

Southwark Ⓣ

County
Hall

WATERLOO ROAD

BAYLIS RD

:minster
ridge

WESTMINSTER

Lambeth Ⓣ
North

: Thomas's
Hospital

BRIDGE

ROAD

KENNINGTON ROAD

ROAD

⑨

mbeth
alace

⑫ ⑩

LAMBETH ROAD

Imperial War
Museum

⑧

⑪

⑬

LAMBETH

Vauxhall

WALK 20

WALK 20

Distance: 3.25mi (5.23km)
Duration: half to full day
Start: Embankment tube station
End: Vauxhall tube station

Lambeth is the area (borough) of London on the south bank of the Thames directly opposite Westminster, bordered by Waterloo Bridge to the north and Vauxhall Bridge to the south, with Kennington marking its easternmost edge; it's one of 14 local authorities which make up Inner London, measuring 7mi (11.3kn) north to south, and around 2.5mi (4km) east to west.

Its history stretches back at least 1,000 years; early records from 1062 show it as Lambethitha meaning a 'landing place for lambs', although other historians believe the name is derived from loamhithe (a muddy bank). Until the mid-18th century, much of north Lambeth, including the area now occupied by Waterloo Station, was marshland know as Lambeth Marshe, which was drained in the 18th century but is remembered in the Lower Marsh Street name. Sometime after the opening of Waterloo railway station in 1848 the area around the station and Lower Marsh became known as Waterloo.

Lambeth has a thriving and expanding arts and leisure industry, the most visible element of which is The South Bank complex, plus internationally famous theatres such as the Old Vic, the Young Vic, the National Theatre, the Royal Festival Hall and the National Film Theatre. It's also home to the iconic London Eye.

The best-known building in Lambeth is Lambeth Palace, London home of the Archbishops of Canterbury since the 13th century. Our walk takes a wider loop, from the curious landmark of Cleopatra's Needle to the iconic 'towers' of Battersea Power Station.

Start Walking…

To begin this version of the Lambeth walk, leave Embankment tube station by the Embankment exit and turn left to walk east along the river. Cross the road to admire **Cleopatra's Needle ❶**, an ancient Egyptian monument that fits snugly next to the Thames in damp, grey London. Many people will have noticed the needle – it's difficult to miss an 59ft (18m) granite obelisk weighing 186 tons – but few stop to examine it closely, which is a pity.

Cleopatra's Needle

The obelisk is actually much older than Cleopatra, who ruled over Egypt during the Roman era. It dates from around 1,475BC, when it was cut from quarries at Aswan and transported down the Nile to be erected at Heliopolis. It was taken to Alexandria in Roman times and stood there for centuries before toppling into the sand. The obelisk was presented to Britain in 1819 by the Turkish Viceroy of Egypt but was left where it was for the next 58 years due to the monumental task of transporting it. It finally arrived in London in 1878, towed on a specially designed barge, after an eventful journey in which six seamen drowned during a Bay of Biscay storm and the obelisk itself almost sank. It was originally destined to be erected in front of the Houses of Parliament, but the site was found to be subsiding, so it ended up on Victoria Embankment instead.

This is a good vantage point from which to examine the **lion's heads ❷** that line the riverbank in central London; look along the embankment's wall to see them.

It's said that if the lions along the Thames drink, London will flood. Policemen patrolling near the river in the 19th century were instructed to be alert to this and to sound the alarm if the level of the water approached the lions' mouths.

lion's heads

Sculpted in bronze by Timothy Butler in 1868-70, they run along both sides of the Thames, their mouths holding mooring rings to secure river craft.

Cross the road and continue ahead towards Waterloo Bridge. Once you pass the statue of Michael Faraday outside the Institution of Electrical Engineers, and Savoy Street, both on the left, take the steps up to Waterloo Bridge. One of London's least architecturally interesting bridges, it provides some of the **best views** ❸, which inspired one of the finest songs written about London: *Waterloo Sunset* by the Kinks. The song was apparently written after the band's leader, Ray Davies, was taken outside by a nurse while he was a patient in a hospital here in the early '60s.

The first bridge on this site was built 1811-19, designed by John Rennie. It was so attractive that the French artist Monet captured it on canvas more than 40 times

between 1899 and 1905, but it became structurally unsafe and was demolished in 1936. The current bridge, built 1937-42, is a bland affair made of cantilevered reinforced concrete box girders. Even so, as you cross it to the south bank, you have wonderful views of St Paul's Cathedral, the City, Canary Wharf, the Oxo Tower and The Shard to the left and the London Eye, Houses of Parliament and Cleopatra's Needle to the right.

Just before the end of the bridge, turn left down a flight of steps towards the National Theatre. On the left at the bottom of the steps is an endearingly kitsch statue of theatrical knight **Laurence Olivier** ❹ playing Hamlet. It's by Angela Connor and was unveiled in 2007, though many think it doesn't resemble the great actor. The National Theatre opened in 1976 and also divides opinion as to its aesthetic value: the harsh, stark construction is

Thames at night from Waterloo Bridge

Royal Waterloo Hospital for Children and Women

imposing IMAX cinema which dominates the roundabout. On the left is the impressive **Royal Waterloo Hospital for Children and Women** ⑤. It was founded in 1816 and moved here in 1823, operating under various names until settling on this one; it closed in 1976. The handsome building (Grade II listed) is built of red brick with brown terracotta dressings, with a Doulton-ware porch and a three-tiered terracotta loggia with attractive lettering bearing the institution's name.

cutting-edge modern architecture to some, but a grubby, concrete eyesore to others. It's Grade II* listed, so presumably it must have some merit.

The National Theatre was designed by Denys Lasdun and the foundation stone laid by Princess Elizabeth in 1951, although it didn't actually open until a quarter of a century later. There are three theatres – the Cottesloe, the Lyttelton and the Olivier – as well as bars, a bookshop, cafés and gallery spaces.

Like Waterloo Bridge, the National Theatre is a splendid vantage point for panoramic views of the river, especially from its bar which is best visited during a performance, when you may have it pretty much to yourself.

Return up the steps to the bridge and turn left, heading into Lambeth on the south bank of the Thames. As you leave the bridge, don't take the underpass but continue over ground towards the

Pass Stamford Street on the left and continue past the James Clark Maxwell Building, part of King's College London and named after the physicist (1831-79), a professor at the college from 1860. Turn left down Exton Street and at the end continue almost straight ahead into **Roupell Street** ⑥, a characterful, elegant street of terraced houses with high chimneys, redolent of Victorian London. John Palmer Roupell developed the area as the Lambeth Estate from the 1820s-40s, with uniform terraced houses, incorporating corner shops and a pub. Roupell Street, Theed Street and Whittlesey Street are little-altered since, and the surrounds were designated a conservation area in 1976.

The **King's Arms** ⑦ is at number 25 Roupell Street, on the corner with Windmill Walk. It's a cosy pub, winner of the Best London Freehouse Award in the

Great British Pub Awards 2011. There's traditional wood panelling, old photos on the walls and two bars, as well as a great selection of beers; the only drawback is that it can become crowded at peak times.

At the end of Roupell Street, turn right along Hatfields and at the bottom turn right again along The Cut, passing the Young Vic Theatre on the right and the Old Vic Theatre on the left at the end. Cross Waterloo Road and continue ahead along Baylis Road, which is named after Lilian Baylis (1874-1937), a theatrical producer and manager who ran the Old Vic. On the left is the Duke of Sussex, a popular real ale pub, which is a civilised place to stop for refreshment; it has a distinctive Truman, Hanbury, Buxton & Co exterior sign.

At the end of Baylis Road, cross the busy junction and head straight on down Kennington Road. This area was once a royal manor, and the name is thought to come from the Saxon *kyning-tun*, the town or place of the king; the Domesday Book calls it Chenintun. Walk along the left-hand side of the road and just past the Three Stags pub you'll come to a sign for the **Imperial War Museum** 8 (10am-6pm). Turn left along Lambeth Road and the museum is about 150m (164yd) along on the right.

> Number 100 Lambeth Road was once home to Captain William Bligh, commander of the ill-fated *HMS Bounty*, and a blue plaque commemorates this. Bligh was buried at St Mary-at-Lambeth church, now the Garden Museum (see below).

Imperial War Museum

This excellent museum was founded in 1920 and has been housed in various buildings; the current one was designed by James Lewis in 1815 and was formerly part of Bethlem Royal Hospital (the original 'Bedlam'). It covers the period from 1914 to the present day and attracts more than 1m visitors every year. Walk through the gates and the massive guns outside the front entrance are a striking sight, flanked by large artillery shells painted yellow. They're British 15-inch (381mm) naval guns, weigh 100 tons each and can fire a shell up to 16.25mi (26km). Inside the large atrium there's a display of military vehicles – including artillery, jeeps and tanks – plus fighter aircraft hanging from the ceiling.

The surrounding gardens are called the Geraldine Mary Harmsworth Park, after the mother of Viscount Rothermere, and contain the Soviet War Memorial and the **Tibetan Peace Garden** ❾ – it's over to the right as you leave the main building and is often overlooked but well worth visiting. The Tibetan Garden of Contemplation and Peace, or *Samten Kyil*, was opened in 1999 by the Dalai Lama. It's simple and tranquil, a poignant plea for peace in the shadow of a museum that records the history of modern warfare.

FOOD & DRINK

7 King's Arms: Popular traditional pub serving a wide choice of decent ales on tap and tasty Thai food.

17 Pizza Express: One of the first outlets of the ubiquitous chain, a cut above the average.

The main monument is a bronze cast of the Kalachakram Mandala, traditionally associated with world peace. It's surrounded by eight meditation areas and has four modern sculptures sitting to the north, south, east and west, representing Air, Fire, Earth and Water. A language pillar is inscribed with a message from the Dalai Lama written in Tibetan, English, Chinese and Hindi, which promotes communication between cultures. The garden also has planting from Tibet and the Himalayas, and contemplation seats.

Leaving the museum's grounds, turn left and walk back up Lambeth Road, following the signs for Lambeth Bridge. Pass under a railway bridge and on the right at number 202 is the attractive, red-brick building of **The Marine Society** ❿. It was founded in 1756 by James Hanway to encourage men and boys to volunteer for the navy during the Seven Years' War. It obviously worked as 10,000 were sent to sea as a result. The Society has since joined forces

The Marine Society

Garden Museum

gardeners and plant hunters, John Tradescant, father and son; five members of this family are buried in St Mary's graveyard. Elizabeth Boleyn, Anne's mother, also rests here. The churchyard has a restored 17th-century knot garden, in a formal, geometric style with authentic period planting.

> Between them, John Tradescant the elder and younger introduced many foreign plants to British gardens, including the magnolia, aster and phlox. The flowering genus *Tradescantia* is named in honour of them.

with the Sea Cadets and still supports people wanting to work to sea; it moved to this site in 1979.

Just before Lambeth Bridge, **The Garden Museum** 11 is on the right (Mon-Fri, 10.30am-5pm, closed first Monday of the month, Sat-Sun, 10.30am-4pm, adults £6). Described by the *Daily Telegraph* as 'one of London's best small museums', it's sometimes overlooked as it sits next to Lambeth Palace and almost opposite the Houses of Parliament. Founded in 1977, it has over 9,000 exhibits/specimens and is the world's first museum dedicated to the history of gardening.

It's set in the deconsecrated church of St Mary-at-Lambeth, which dates from the 14th century and was restored in 1850. This was chosen as an auspicious location after the discovery of the graves of two 17th-century royal

Next to the museum and overlooking the river is the impressive red-brick façade of **Lambeth Palace** 12. Visits are by pre-arranged guided tour, but are so popular that you must wait for around a year to secure a place on one! The Palace is one of the most distinctive sights on the banks of the Thames and has been home to the Archbishops of Canterbury since 1200. It was originally right on the river, with the Archbishops coming and going by barge, but the late 19th-century Thames embankment put an end to this. Lambeth Palace contains a number of London's few remaining Tudor buildings, some of which are visible from the outside; most obvious is the red-brick gatehouse dating from 1495.

Turn left out of the Garden Museum and walk south along the Albert Embankment. On the left is the large, Grade II listed **London Fire Brigade**

London Fire Brigade Headquarters

Headquarters ⑬, with gilded designs above the entrance and Art Deco reliefs. It was the fire brigade's base from 1937 to 2007 when the organisation relocated to Southwark. In late 2011, a proposal to turn the building into 265 new homes was vetoed by Lambeth Council.

Further along, right on the river, is a '60s tower block of exclusive apartments called Peninsula Heights (formerly Alembic House). Its most famous resident is 'colourful' novelist and former politician Jeffrey Archer; he owns the penthouse, where he keeps his impressive art collection and hosts shepherd's pie and Krug parties for movers and shakers. Other celebrated residents have included entertainer Tommy Steele and composer John Barry.

Continue along the river path and where it briefly diverts left around a slipway, stop to admire the large **MI6 building** ⑭ on the left. Opened in 1994, it's an ostentatious pile with nods to Egyptian pyramids and Mayan temples in its design; indeed, it has been nicknamed the Aztec Temple. It was designed by postmodernist architect Terry Farrell and houses the part of the secret service concerned with overseas intelligence. Large Art Deco-style lamps decorate the wall along this part of the riverbank.

> Some people refer to the MI6 building as Ceaucescu Tower, after the late Romanian dictator who was fond of large, self-aggrandising building schemes.

MI6 Building

At low tide, a wide expanse of riverbed is exposed in front of the MI6 building, which was the site of an interesting discovery in 2010: the piles of a structure dating back some 6,000 or 7,000 years. Armed police arrived to quiz archaeologists examining the find after an onlooker saw them poking around in the silt and mistook their equipment for weapons. The piles are Mesolithic, i.e. Middle Stone Age, and structural finds from this period are rare anywhere in Britain. Tools and Neolithic (New Stone Age) pottery were also found. The site is around 600m downstream from a Bronze Age timber bridge or jetty which was discovered in the '90s.

Next to the MI6 building is one of London's most attractive, colourful bridges, **Vauxhall Bridge** 15. The name Vauxhall comes from a house built here in the reign of King John which was formerly known as Fulke's Hall, after Falkes de Breaute who built it. Over time, the name changed to Faukshall and Foxhall, with the current name becoming popular when Vauxhall Pleasure Gardens opened in the 17th century. Originally called Regent's Bridge, Vauxhall Bridge was opened by the Prince Regent in 1816; it used to be a toll bridge but charges ceased in 1879. The old bridge was replaced by the current one, designed by Sir Alexander Binnie, in 1895, featuring five steel arches on granite piers. F. W. Pomeroy and Alfred Drury were responsible for the bronze figures along the sides, which represent Pottery, Engineering, Architecture and Agriculture upstream, and Science, Fine Arts, Local Government and Education downstream.

The riverside path passes under Vauxhall Bridge, with excellent views of the majestic **Battersea Power Station** 16. One of London's most iconic structures, it was designed by Sir Giles Gilbert Scott, opened in 1933 and closed as a working operation in 1983. Since the '80s, this striking building has had an uncertain future. There were plans to turn it into a leisure park, but the scheme ran out of

Vauxhall Bridge

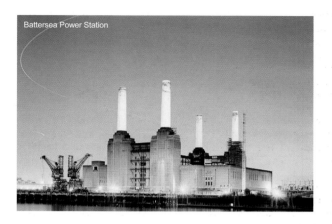

Battersea Power Station

money and it's still seeking a new lease of life.

> In 1977 Battersea Power Station was famously featured on the cover of the Pink Floyd concept album *Animals*, with a large inflatable pig floating above it. The pig was originally tethered to one of the southern chimneys but broke free of its moorings and drifted into the flight path to Heathrow Airport, later coming to ground in Kent.

It's something of a culinary desert around the southern end of Vauxhall Bridge, but cross it to the north bank and turn right to end the walk at **Pizza Express** ⓱, which is just past Tate Britain at 25 Millbank. It offers the chain's usual good quality and value, in a bright, high-ceilinged premises with partial river views, a civilised way to end the walk.

To reach Vauxhall tube and railway station, re-cross Vauxhall Bridge to the south bank of the river and the station is just past the junction ahead.

1 Maida Vale tube station

2 Spanish and Portuguese
   Synagogue

3 The Warrington Hotel

4 Alexandra Court

5 Clifton Gardens

6 Cab shelter

7 Bridge over a canal

8 Puppet Theatre Barge

9 Westbourne Terrace Road
   Bridge

10 Maida Avenue

11 Café Laville

12 Window Cleaner sculpture

13 Patogh

14 Tyburn Tree

● Places of Interest   ● Food & Drink

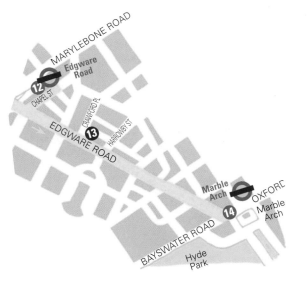

MARYLEBONE ROAD

Edgware
Road

12 CHAPEL ST

CRAWFORD PL

EDGWARE ROAD **13** HARROWBY ST

Marble
Arch

OXFORD

14 Marble
Arch

BAYSWATER ROAD

Hyde
Park

MAIDA VALE

WALK 21

Distance: 2.57mi (4.14km)
Duration: half day
Start: Maida Vale tube station
End: Marble Arch tube station

Maida Vale is one of west London's most attractive areas, remarkable for its wide avenues, solid red-brick mansion blocks and colourful houseboats. The Regents and Grand Union Canals meet here at the charmingly named Little Venice, where the poet Robert Browning once lived. Maida Vale is the area bounded by Maida Vale Road to the northeast, Kilburn Park Road to the northwest, Maida Avenue and the Regent's Canal to the south and Shirland Road and Blomf eld Road to the southwest. Maida Vale is the triangular area bordered by St John's Wood to the east and Kilburn to the north and west, with its southern reaches following the line of the canals. It's only a few tube stops from central London but is a tranquil, tree-lined retreat.

The area was developed by the Ecclesiastical Commissioners – purse holders for the Church of England – in the early 19th century to provide middle-class housing, and is still resolutely middle class. Its residents include artists, writer, actors and assorted media types – one of the BBC's earliest studios still broadcasts radio shows from Maida Vale. It takes its name from a pub, the Hero of Maida, which stood on nearby Edgware Road. The pub was named in honour of General John Stuart, later Count of Maida, who led the victory against the French at the Battle of Maida in Italy in 1806, during the Napoleonic Wars. The Hero of Maida opened soon after in the area f rst called Maida Hill and later known as Maida Vale (the building is still there, but it's no longer a pub).

Our walk takes us along tree-lined streets and canal paths before heading south along Edgware Road, grittier and more urban, but one of London's more interesting places to eat, especially if you enjoy Middle Eastern cuisine.

Start Walking…

This walk departs from **Maida Vale tube station** ❶ and it's worth pausing to admire this small, well-preserved station; it's Grade II listed and one of a number of tube stations awarded heritage status. In 2009, it won a National Railway Heritage Award in the London Regional category, for the successful modernisation of a historic station. Turn left along Elgin Avenue, a residential street of three- and four-storey terraces and mansion blocks, then take a second left down tree-lined Ashworth Road. The unusually high number of Mercedes, Range Rovers and Porsches parked outside the well-kept houses mark this area out as an upwardly-mobile place to live.

Turn left into Lauderdale Road to see the attractive, red-brick, Grade II listed **Spanish and Portuguese Synagogue** ❷ or Sha'ar Hashamayim (☏ 020-7289 2573 for information about visiting). It was built in 1896 in a Byzantine style by architects Davis and Emanuel, and is one of only three Sephardic Jewish synagogues in London; the others are the Bevis Marks Synagogue in the City (see page 49) and another in Wembley.

In the late 19th and early 20th centuries, Maida Vale was a predominantly Jewish district, and once counted among its residents David Ben-Gurion, who became the first Prime Minister of Israel. He lived at 75 Warrington Crescent, within sight of the Spanish and Portuguese Synagogue.

At the end of Lauderdale Road, turn right and cross Sutherland Avenue, heading towards **The Warrington Hotel** ❸ at 93 Warrington Crescent. Noted for its attractive, colourful Art Nouveau

Warrington Hotel

WALK 21

Alexandra Court

entrance, it was formerly a hotel and also, reputedly, a brothel. More recently it has been a bar and restaurant, and was owned for a time by f-word celebrity chef Gordon Ramsey who sold it in 2011. The Warrington currently receives mixed reviews, but merits a visit for its visual appeal. The entrance is flanked by two large, rare lamps and the exterior columns and walls are covered in glazed tiles. Inside, there's an impressive, marble-topped, semi-circular bar, with cherubs above, while the room is decorated with Art Nouveau glasswork and other exotic detailing.

Leave the hotel and turn right along Sutherland Avenue and right again at the traffic lights into Maida Vale itself which, like many streets around here, is lined with attractive, understated mansion blocks. Some are Art Deco or Art Nouveau in style, such as **Alexandra Court** ❹, a beautiful block with lots of period features. By a set of traffic lights on the left of Maida Vale, a sign points to Warwick Avenue tube station; follow it, turning right along Clifton Road. This is another affluent area, with delicatessens and

an organic butcher and grocer. Continue as Clifton Road becomes **Clifton Gardens** ❺, with its distinctive cream-coloured houses and mansion blocks; the name probably comes from Isambard Kingdom Brunel's suspension bridge at Clifton, completed in 1864, around the same time the street was built. The last stretch of the road, leading down to the canal, is called Clifton Villas, and tucked away behind it is garden supplier Clifton Nurseries. Founded in 1851, it claims to be London's oldest garden centre.

At the end of Clifton Gardens, turn left along Warwick Avenue, which is one of the area's first roads, built in the early 1840s and lined with large mansions. Numbers 2 to 16 are thought to have been designed by George Ledwell Taylor, architect to the Bishop of London's estate. On the traffic island to your right there's a green, wooden cabin. This is one of London's 13 surviving **cab shelters** ❻, funded by the

cab shelter

Little Venice

According to some sources, the name Little Venice was coined by local resident and poet Robert Browning; others attribute it to Lord Byron. Either way, it didn't come into general use until after WWII.

FOOD & DRINK

3 **The Warrington Hotel:** A handsome historic pub, good ales and reasonable food.

11 **Café Laville** (☎ 020-7706 2620): Charming café (licensed) serving rustic Italian and contemporary food with great views of Little Venice.

13 **Patogh:** Iranian café serving delicious authentic Persian food. No alcohol license.

Cabmen's Shelter Fund and all Grade II listed, where cabbies can find rest and refreshment without being tempted to visit a pub (see page 106).

The sign to Little Venice is outside the entrance to Warwick Avenue tube station; follow it down the avenue until you reach a **bridge over a canal** 7, with attractive blue and gold railings and a coat of arms. There are impressive views along the canal from either side of the bridge. The term Little Venice is used fairly loosely, particularly by estate agents, but it properly describes just one square mile of Maida Vale, around the junction of the Grand Union Canal and its spur to the Paddington Basin. This area comprises around ten streets, lined with weeping willows and majestic white stucco houses, designed by noted architect John Nash. Some of the most desirable directly overlook the water.

Just before the bridge, turn right along Broomfield Road and skirt around a large, triangular 'pool' of water (also called Little Venice). To the left is the red and yellow **Puppet Theatre Barge** 8, which opened in 1982; its patron is the comedian, actor and writer Michael Palin. The 'theatre' can seat 55 and stages imaginative, skilful shows at reasonable prices (adults £10, children and concessions £8.50). The barge usually has performances in Little Venice from October to June, and spends the summer moored at Richmond-upon-Thames (for information, see 🖥 www.puppetbarge.com).

Continue around the pool and cross **Westbourne Terrace Road Bridge** 9, noting the attractive Borough of Paddington coat of arms. It was erected by the eponymous Metropolitan Borough, which existed from 1900-65. The blue background comes from the arms of Paddington's first mayor, Sir John Aird (1833-1911), and has also been used on the bridge railings. The bridge's old toll house dates from 1812.

Turn left along Warwick Crescent, with a barge café to the left – a convenient spot to re-caffeinate and soak up the local atmosphere. The crescent was demolished and rebuilt in 1966, and the former number 19 was the home of poet Robert Browning from 1861-87. He's said to have had

trees planted on what's now called Browning's Island, an islet in the middle of the canal. Turn left along Harrow Road and left again along Warwick Avenue, and to the left is Rembrandt Gardens, a small green area with benches and a pleasant place from which to contemplate the surroundings. The gardens also contain free public conveniences.

Take the first right down **Maida Avenue** 10, with a long, straight section of canal to the left. Only low railings separate you from the water here, making it one of the best places from which to admire the many houseboats moored alongside (Virgin owner Richard Branson used to live on one). They're a striking, colourful spectacle, and lovely properties line the streets on both sides of the canal.

If you cannot afford to invest in a houseboat – prices start at around £100,000 and don't include mooring fees – you can take a trip with the London Waterbus Company (🖥 www.londonwaterbus.co.uk) which runs a service linking Little Venice to Camden Lock via London Zoo.

Just before **Café Laville** 11, at the end of Maida Avenue, there's a blue plaque on the right to comic actor Arthur Lowe who played Captain Mainwaring in *Dad's Army*. The café sits atop the 250m Maida Vale Tunnel, into which the canal disappears for a stretch. Boats were once 'legged' through the tunnel; the crew would lie on their backs on the boat's roof and 'walk' along the tunnel's roof to move the boat through. The tow horses would

Westbourne Terrace Road Bridge plaque

meet up with the boat on the other side of the tunnel.

Turn right into Edgware Road, a long, straight thoroughfare which was originally a Roman road. It's the capital's Arab corner, and most of its shops and restaurants are Middle Eastern, many Lebanese; the southern end of the road is sometimes called Little Beirut or Little Cairo. It isn't the loveliest part of London – the architecture is bland and the traffic heavy – but it's an excellent place to soak up a different kind of atmosphere and also to eat.

As you reach the (ugly) Marylebone flyover, on the left in Chapel Street is Edgware Road tube station. Outside the station is a rather splendid sculpture, **The Window Cleaner** 12, by English sculptor Allan Sly. It depicts a flat-capped figure carrying a ladder and looking up to survey the daunting number of windows in the surrounding buildings.

Return to the Edgware Road, turn left and shortly afterwards swing a left into Crawford Place for **Patogh** 13 at number 8, a small, wonky, slightly scruffy Iranian café. There are shared tables and it's known for its large portions of robust street food at low prices: grilled meats, mezze, vegetables and breads. No alcohol is served but you can bring your own. If you want to savour the authentic flavour of a Tehran café, this is the place to come.

Return to the Edgware Road and turn left, continuing to the end, where we finish this walk by contemplating a plaque on a small traffic island near Marble Arch, at the junction of Edgware Road, Park Lane and Oxford Street. It claims to mark the site of the **Tyburn Tree** 14, a gallows that was a place of public execution from 1196 to 1783, when executions were moved to Newgate prison. It's estimated that between 40,000 and 60,000 people died at Tyburn. Huge crowds gathered to watch the executions, and it was believed that the bodies of the dead had curative properties. People paid the hangman for the chance to stoke the hands of the just-executed across their faces or injuries. Something to ponder as you stand on the spot where so many died.

To reach Marble Arch tube station, head along Oxford Street. The station is a short distance on the left.

The Window Cleaner

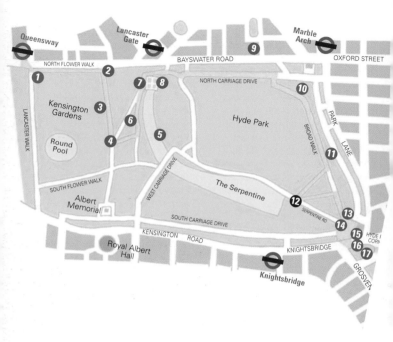

1. North Walk
2. Lancaster Gate
3. Lancaster Walk
4. Physical Energy statue
5. Long Water
6. Peter Pan statue
7. Italian Garden
8. Jenner statue
9. Tyburn Convent
10. Speakers' Corner
11. Joy of Life fountain
12. Serpentine Bar and Kitchen
13. Arthur, Duke of Wellington
14. Queen Elizabeth Gate
15. Apsley House
16. Statue of Wellington
17. Wellington Arch
18. Queen Victoria Memorial
19. Canada Gate
20. Bridge
21. Duck Island
22. Red Lion

● Places of Interest ● Food & Drink

Green
Park

PICCADILLY

Green Park

Admiralty
Arch

PARK
NER

CONSTITUTION HILL

18 **19**

Buckingham
Palace

THE MALL

HORSE GUARDS ROAD

WHITEHALL

21

20 St James's
Park

KING CHARLES ST

PARLIAMENT ST

BRIDGE ST

22 Westminster

PLACE

BIRDCAGE WALK

St James's
Park

ROYAL
PARKS

Distance: 3.94mi (6.34km)
Duration: full day
Start: Queensway tube station
End: Westminster tube station

ROYAL PARKS

The Royal Parks are lands originally owned by the monarchy of the United Kingdom for the recreation (mostly hunting) of the royal family and are part of the hereditary possessions of the Crown. With the increasing urbanisation of London in the 19th century, some were preserved as freely accessible open space and became public parks with the introduction of the Crown Lands Act, 1851.

There are eight 'London' royal parks in total – which include the largest green spaces in central London – covering a total area of almost 4,900 acres (2,000ha). The four featured in this walk (see below) plus Regent's Park in north London (see Walk 16), Richmond and Bushey Parks in southwest London, and Greenwich Park in southeast London.

For such a crowded city, London is unusually rich in parks and four of the best known form a verdant chain through the capital's centre. This walk takes in the beautiful sweep of parkland which links Bayswater to Westminster. Surprisingly, you can walk the length of four royal parks – Kensington Gardens, Hyde Park, Green Park and St James's Park – and only cross one busy road junction at Hyde Park Corner.

Our walk takes in some of the lesser known highlights of the parks – f ora and fauna, monuments and views – but is also an opportunity to enjoy these green oases that are often aptly referred to as the city's lungs.

Lancaster Gate

Start Walking…

Leave the lift at Queensway tube station and take the exit to the left onto Bayswater Road. This was once part of the Roman road, *Via Trinobantia*, and is one of London's more attractive major thoroughfares, tree-lined and with a variety of architectural styles. Bayswater Road really comes alive on Sundays when artists use the south side as an impromptu gallery to showcase their work.

Cross at the traffic lights and almost directly in front is an entrance to Kensington Gardens (6am-dusk), the first of our four royal parks. Originally part of Hyde Park, it has been a separate green space since the 1730s and covers 275 acres (111ha). The official boundary with Hyde Park is West Carriage Drive and the bridge which crosses the Serpentine (lake); the western section, Long Water, lies within Kensington Gardens.

The gardens were formerly the grounds of Nottingham House, which became Kensington Palace when it was acquired in 1689 by William III. Kensington Gardens first opened to the public in 1733, but only on Saturdays or Sundays, and there was a strict dress code. In 1997, they became the focus of national grief after the death of Diana, Princess of Wales, whose official London residence was at Kensington Palace.

As you enter Kensington Gardens, take the path to the left, the **North Walk** **1**. Almost immediately there's a sense of calm, with the elegant white terraces along nearby Bayswater Road adding to the air of tranquillity. Continue along the North Walk until you reach the second entrance gate on the left, **Lancaster Gate** **2**, and then take the path to the right, called **Lancaster Walk** **3**.

> Lancaster Gate – thought to be named after the Duchy of Lancaster – is a mid-19th century development to the north of Kensington Gardens, consisting of two long terraces of houses, plus a square with a church.

Kensington Gardens

As you stroll down Lancaster Walk, the muted traffic noise from Bayswater Road fades and you soon forget that you're in the middle of a city of over 7.5m people. On the left is one of London's more underwhelming monuments, commemorating a huge achievement. The plain, brown obelisk by Philip Hardwick, dating from 1864, honours explorer John Hanning Speke's discovery of the source of the Nile, with the words 'Speke, Victoria Nyanza and the Nile 1864'.

Ahead, in the middle of the path, is the much more impressive **Physical Energy** ❹ by George Frederic Watts, OM RA (1817-1904). It's a large bronze sculpture of a naked man astride a horse, shielding his eyes from the sun and is based on an equestrian monument Watts made in 1870 of Hugh Lupus, an ancestor of the Duke of Westminster. Behind the sculpture, the Royal Albert Hall is visible through the trees.

Take the second of the two paths leading left from of the statue, i.e. *not* the one that heads back towards the road. There are views of the top of the Telecom Tower to the left. At the next junction, head sharp left towards Long Water. This quiet and secluded part of the gardens has some particularly attractive trees, some of them intriguingly gnarled and mangled by time, wind and lighting strikes.

Continue ahead with **Long Water** ❺ to your right. This is the northern 'tail' of the Serpentine, the lake which links the gardens with Hyde Park; the lake was created in 1730 for Queen Caroline from a string of ponds along the River Westbourne. Look out for the famous bronze statue of **Peter Pan** ❻ – playing his pipe, surrounded by fairies and woodland creatures – on the left overlooking the lake, in a part of the gardens rich in birdlife, including ducks and herons. The statue by Sir George Frampton

Physical Energy

Peter Pan

(1912) was commissioned and paid for by *Peter Pan* author J. M. Barrie. Barrie chose the location himself, claiming it's the spot where Peter landed in *Peter Pan in Kensington Gardens*. Some MPs objected to its presence, saying the statue was effectively an advertisement for Barrie's work. Today it's one of London's most popular statues, beloved by generations of children.

Sir James Barrie lived at number 100 Bayswater Road from 1902 to 1909. It was during this time that he wrote *Peter Pan* (or *The Boy Who Wouldn't Grow up*). It was first published as a play and made its stage debut in 1902. It was published as a novel, *Peter and Wendy*, in 1911.

Jenner

Ahead, at the top of Long Water, the fountains of the **Italian Garden** ⑦ are visible. The garden – constructed in 1860-1 at the instigation of Prince Albert – is a nicely over-the-top confection of fountains and urns, plus an Italian summer house and Queen Anne's alcove. On the far side there's a large bronze statue of **Jenner** ⑧. Dr Edward Jenner (1749-1823) was the pioneer of the smallpox vaccine and is often called 'the father of immunology'. The statue is by W. Calder Marshall and was originally erected in Trafalgar Square in 1858 before being moved here in 1862.

With the Italian Garden behind you, turn right and walk east, with Bayswater Road on your left, to enter the western reaches of Hyde Park (5am-midnight). This is the largest of the royal parks, covering 350 acres (142ha). It was created in 1536 when Henry VIII seized land belonging to Westminster Abbey to use as a deer park. The Manor of Eia had been bequeathed to the Abbey shortly after the Norman Conquest and comprised three separate properties: Ebury, Neate and Hyde. Henry VIII sold Ebury and Neate, but retained Hyde for hunting, and deer were hunted in Hyde Park until 1768. The park was opened to the public by James I in the early 17th century. The Parliamentarians assumed control of it for military use during the Civil War and Charles II enclosed the park for the first time after the Restoration of the monarchy in 1660.

Shortly after entering Hyde Park, skirt left around a traffic roundabout and continue ahead, along the grandly-named North Carriage Drive, a straight, tree-lined, rather featureless section of park. After several minutes, the attractive **Tyburn Convent** 9 is visible to the left across Bayswater Road (tours daily at 10.30am, 3.30pm and 5.30pm). This Catholic convent was founded only in 1901 and is dedicated to the martyrs executed for their Catholic faith at nearby Tyburn gallows between 1535 and 1681, most notably during the Reformation. The convent crypt has a series of relics of these executions and a model of the gallows – the infamous 'Tyburn Tree' – and is one of London's more poignant and grimly fascinating exhibits.

Tyburn was a place of public execution from 1196 to 1783, after which the grisly business was moved to Newgate prison. It's estimated that between 40,000 and 60,000 people were executed here. The spot is marked by a plaque on the traffic island at the junction of Bayswater and Edgware roads, overlooking the northeast corner of Hyde Park.

After passing the convent, continue on to Marble Arch, a white Carrara marble monument designed by John Nash, which stands on a traffic island at the junction of Oxford Street and Park Lane, almost directly opposite Speakers' Corner (see below). Completed in 1833, the Arch stood in front of Buckingham Palace until 1851, when it was moved here. In front of the Arch is a changing display of statues, which in 2012 included a giant bronze statue (27ft/8.2m, weighing 6 tons) of a Marwari Horse Head by Nic Fiddian-Green (installed in June 2009) and a 16ft/5m bronze sculpture of Mongolian warrior Genghis Khan by Dashi Namdakov (April 2012). Both are supposed to be temporary installations, although the 'horse's head' has been here for over three years.

A few short steps away in the northeast corner of Hyde Park is **Speakers' Corner** 10, which became a favourite place of protest in the mid-19th century, although the gatherings were illegal and often dispersed. However, in 1872 the area was recognised as a legitimate place where people could publicly state their opinions, provided they weren't blasphemous, seditious or likely to incite violence. Speakers' Corner became famous – indeed it became an institution – and crowds gathered to hear the speakers. Heckling and banter were expected as part of the spectacle, but the crowds began to dwindle in the late 20th century.

as congested Hyde Park Corner emerges ahead. There was once a toll gate here marking the entrance to London from the west; Kensington and Knightsbridge were then small villages outside London.

Around 400 yards further south along the Broad Walk (on the left) is the **Joy of Life fountain** 11, with Park Lane behind it. The fountain is by T. B. Huxley-Jones (1963) and was donated by the Constance Fund, an organisation founded in 1944 by Mrs Constance Goetze in memory of her husband. Two bronze figures holding hands seem to dance above the water, while four bronze children emerge from the pool. Around 60,000 daffodil bulbs are planted near the fountain, creating a spectacular early spring display.

Park Lane has been a sought-after and upmarket address since the 1820s and nowadays is one of London's most fashionable streets. In the 20th century, many of the great houses that lined the road were demolished and it's now mainly offices and hotels.

Soon after the fountain, turn right into the park and head to the far southeast of the Serpentine for the **Serpentine Bar and Kitchen** 12, which serves good seasonal food at reasonable prices in an attractive garden setting. When you leave, return to the path running along the east of the park, parallel to Park Lane, and turn right along it. Keep walking south

FOOD & DRINK

12 Serpentine Bar and Kitchen:
This iconic café/restaurant serves delicious seasonal English classics. Good value, no bookings.

22 Red Lion:
Another lively, historic Fuller's pub offering breakfast, lunch and dinner, platters and fine ales.

On the left, just before Hyde Park Corner, is a large statue called **Arthur, Duke of Wellington** 13. It's actually of Achilles, the Greek hero of the Trojan War, although the head is said to be modelled on the Duke of Wellington's. Achilles is carrying a sword and shield, with his armour beside him, and the statue is an imposing 20ft (6m) high. It's by Sir Richard Westmacott (1822) and was originally completely naked but there was a public outcry and a fig leaf was added to cover Achilles' appendage (it isn't recorded whether this was modelled on the Duke's).

Just past the statue, look to the left for the decorative **Queen Elizabeth Gate**  to the park, also called the Queen Mother Gate, opened in 1993 to honour the Queen Mother's 93rd birthday. The gate, railings and lamps are by Giusseppe Lund, and made of forged stainless steel and bronze, while the central screen is by David Wynne. Lund's design is intended to incorporate and span the various styles of the 20th century.

Cross the road, heading towards the low arch ahead, go through it and immediately to the left is attractive, honey-coloured **Apsley House** (10am-4pm, adults £6.30). Grade I listed and run by English Heritage, this was the Duke of Wellington's London home, now a museum and art gallery, although the 8th Duke still uses part of the building as his London residence.

The house was originally built in red brick by Robert Adam 1771-8 for Lord Apsley and was acquired in 1817 by the Duke of Wellington, who faced the brick walls with Bath stone. The interior has changed little since the Iron Duke's time and is a dazzling example of the Regency style. There's also a fine art collection, including works by Brueghel the Elder, Goya, Landseer, Murillo, Rubens, Van Dyck and Velasquez.

> Apsley House is also known as Number One, London, as it was the first house which visitors saw when passing through the tollgate at Knightsbridge.

Wellington Arch
Wed-Sun, 10am-5pm in summer, 11am-4pm in winter, adults £3.90

Ahead on a traffic island is a **statue of Wellington** and the **Wellington Arch**. Cross to the island to view them – it's easiest to use the traffic lights by the exit from Hyde Park. The bronze statue of Wellington set on a polished granite plinth is by Sir Joseph Edgar Boehm (1888) and depicts the Duke in uniform on his favourite horse, Copenhagen, while at each corner are bronze figures of soldiers from various regiments.

The Wellington Arch was designed by Decimus Burton and built in 1826-30; much of the intended exterior decoration was omitted in order to save money after George IV overspent on the refurbishment

Duke of Wellington

Go through Wellington Arch, cross at the traffic lights and walk along the southern edge of Green Park (unrestricted access), with Constitution Hill to the right. The name may derive from the habits of Charles II who took his 'daily constitutional' walks along the route, although other monarchs found it dangerous. Three attempts were made on Queen Victoria's life while travelling along Constitution Hill, in 1840, 1842 and 1849. It now divides Green Park from Buckingham Palace's walled gardens, and has many splendid plane trees.

of Buckingham Palace. The Arch commemorates Wellington's victory over Napoleon and was originally crowned with a massive statue of the Duke. It was 28ft (8.5m) high and weighed 40 tons, but attracted ridicule as its vast size made the Arch look like a footstool!

The statue wasn't removed until after the Duke's death to avoid offending him. It was relocated to Aldershot in Hampshire and replaced in 1912 by a large bronze quadriga (a chariot drawn by four horses) – Europe's largest bronze sculpture – depicting the angel of peace descending on the chariot of war. The Arch is now owned by English Heritage and has exhibits detailing its history; visitors can ascend to the top where there are terraces on both sides affording panoramic views of London. Creative floodlighting makes the Arch an impressive sight at night.

The title London plane tree is misleading. The trees in the capital are a hybrid of *Platanus orientalis*, from western Asia, and *Platanus occidentalis* (North America). They were introduced to Britain in the early 16th century, but have only been commonly planted in London since the mid-18th century. They're well suited to cities as they shed their bark, thus protecting the tree from the pollution the bark has absorbed.

Green Park

Green Park – its name reflects its verdant grass and trees – is the smallest of the royal parks, covering just 47 acres (19ha). Some people find it rather austere, as it has few of the floral displays which distinguish nearby St James's Park. Henry VIII enclosed the park in the 16th century, and Charles II designated it a Royal Park. It was once a favourite spot for duels.

As you walk east through Green Park, the majestic bulk of Buckingham Palace is visible on the right, with the magnificent, if sometimes overlooked, **Queen Victoria Memorial** 18 on the roundabout in front of it. Designed by Aston Webb and erected in 1914, it's Grade I listed, 82ft (25m) high and cut from a single block of marble. As you stand with the memorial behind you, facing up The Mall, the large, impressive golden gate on the left is the **Canada Gate** 19. Made from gilded wrought iron, it was presented to London by Canada as a memorial to Queen Victoria, who died in 1901. The gate was installed in 1911 and bears the emblems of the seven Canadian provinces at the time.

Cross to the right side of The Mall and head into St James's Park (5am-midnight). Slightly

larger than Green Park at 58 acres (23ha), this is London's oldest royal park. It's named after the St James's Hospital for female lepers, which was rebuilt in 1531-36 as St James's Palace. The park was originally a marshy field by the hospital where the lepers fed their pigs, but Henry VIII had it drained to use as a nursery for his deer. James I kept a menagerie in the park, including camels, crocodiles and elephants, as well as an aviary of exotic birds on what's now called Birdcage Walk, which runs along the south of the park. Today, St James's Park is home to over 30 bird species, including duck, geese, gulls and pelicans. It's the only large London park that isn't enclosed by railings.

The park is long and narrow with a lake running down the middle. Walk along the path to the left of the lake until you reach the **bridge** 20. From here you can enjoy some of London's best views: west for Buckingham Palace; east for Horse Guards Parade and the towers, turrets, spires and domes of Whitehall.

Queen Victoria Memorial

In Henry VIII's day, Horse Guards Parade was a tiltyard where jousting tournaments took place. Today it's best known as the venue for the Trooping the Colour ceremony which celebrates the Queen's Official Birthday in early summer (May or June), and is named after the practice of parading flags and banners to familiarise troops with their battle colours.

Continue along the path and as you reach the end, **Duck Island** 21 is in the middle of the lake. This tranquil spot is but a short walk along the Mall from Charing Cross station. The lake here is rich in birdlife, including St James's famous colony of pelicans which were a gift from Russia in the 17th century. Arrive between 2.30 and 3.30pm and you may be lucky enough to see them being fed.

Proceed ahead to the end of the park, turn right along Horse Guards Road and left along King Charles Street. At the end is Parliament Street, with the traditional Fuller's pub the **Red Lion** 22 at number 48 (Mon-Sat, 10am-11pm, Sun, 10am-9pm), across the road from the Houses of Parliament, where we end the walk.

To reach the nearest tube station (Westminster), proceed south along Parliament Street and turn left down Bridge Street.

Canada Gate

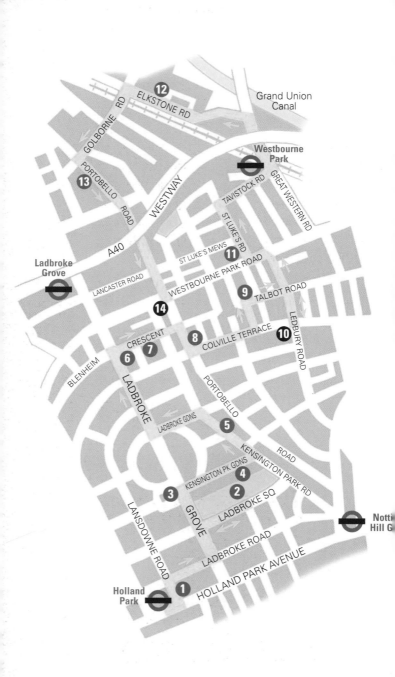

WALK 23

NOTTING HILL

Distance: 2.80mi (4.51km)
Duration: half to full day
Start: Holland Park tube station
End: Ladbroke Grove tube station

NOTTING HILL

Notting Hill has had a see-saw reputation since it became a London suburb. Built as a district to rival 19th-century Kensington in the fashion stakes, it became known more for its slum housing and race riots in the mid-20th century. Today, it's back on an upward trajectory, once more a highly desirable place to live.

The name Notting Hill f rst appears in records from 1356 as the rather charming Knottynghull, although the name's origin is uncertain. Until the 19th century, it was mainly farmland. Gravel and sand extraction took place from the 17th century onwards, and later the clay soil was used to feed London's insatiable demand for bricks.

When building began in earnest in the 1830s, rows of smart terraces with hidden garden squares went up alongside shabby slums where the brick makers and pig keepers lived – the so-called Potteries and Piggeries which bordered today's Holland Park. By the end of WWII, many of Notting Hill's grand houses had been divided into f ats and bedsits, and the area took on a seedy air. It became notorious for the murders at 10 Rillington Place (now demolished) where John Christie killed at least eight women between 1943 and 1953. And as Afro-Caribbean immigrants poured into the area in the '50s, so did the prostitutes and slum landlords, and racial tensions began to brew.

Since the '60s, Notting Hill has attracted media and creative types, which has given it a bohemian edge (further enhanced by the Notting Hill Carnival established in 1965). The process of regeneration and gentrif cation continued and by the '80s it was becoming an expensive place to live. The 1999 f lm *Notting Hill* helped to reinforce the area's increasingly upmarket image. Its characters were attractive, creative and wealthy, although the f lm was criticised for ignoring the black population.

Start Walking…

To explore this interesting, vibrant area, turn left out of Holland Park tube station and left again along Lansdowne Road. This is part of the Ladbroke Estate (see below), developed in the 1840s by James Weller Ladbroke. As with other thoroughfares on the estate, it was named after a member of the House of Lords, Lord Lansdowne, Lord President of the Council.

Much of the property on the Ladbroke Estate dates back to the mid-19th century, and comprises stuccoed terraces set around large, private garden squares. Many are enclosed by houses – like large communal back gardens – and hidden away from the street. The houses were designed by architect, landscaper and surveyor Thomas Allason, who took his inspiration from John Nash's work in Regent's Park, although lack of funds scaled back his original vision; a number of other designers were also involved. The majority of the Ladbroke Estate still remains and is now a conservation area.

On the right of Lansdowne Road is attractive **Lansdowne House** ❶, built in 1904 to William Flockhart's design. It has a blue plaque to six artists who worked in studios here: Charles Ricketts, Charles Shannon, Glyn Philpot, Vivian Forbes, James Pryde and F. Cayley Robinson.

Number 9 Lansdowne Road is one several local properties to 'star' in the film *Notting Hill*. It's the house where Hugh Grant's character William Thacker surprises his friends by bringing superstar actress Anna Scott (Julia Roberts) to a birthday dinner.

Lansdown House

Turn right along Ladbroke Road and left up Ladbroke Grove, named after banker Sir Robert Ladbroke who purchased the land the estate is built on in 1750. It's north Kensington's main thoroughfare, running north from Holland Park towards Kensal Green; at around 2mi (3.2km), it's one of London's longest roads. Ladbroke Grove was begun in the 1830s and completed in the

Ladbroke Square

church **3** (☎ 020-7727 4262 for opening hours), designed by J. H. Stevens and G. Alexander as the centrepiece of the Ladbroke Estate. It was built in 1845 in the early neo-Gothic style. A plaque next to it marks the fact that this was once part of the ill-fated Hippodrome racecourse. In 1836 an entrepreneur, John Whyte, leased around 200 acres (81ha) of land from James Weller Ladbroke to create a racecourse which he hoped would rival Ascot. His venture was a failure for several reasons: the heavy clay soil became easily waterlogged, making it dangerous for horses and jockeys, while local people objected to the interruption to their rights of way. The racecourse closed in 1841 to make way for new housing, but the Hippodrome lives on in a way, as its curved outline is still evident in the crescent-shaped roads around Notting Hill, namely Blenheim Crescent, Elgin Crescent, Stanley

1870s; a varied, interesting road, with striking villas and stucco terraces in the southern part, giving way to shabbier buildings and council estates towards the north. It became a Mecca for bohemians, artists and musicians from the '50s onwards and many rock bands began their careers here, notably space rockers Hawkwind – Lemmy's band before Motorhead – and punk rockers The Clash.

Turn right into the impressive (Grade II listed) **Ladbroke Square** **2**, one of 16 green spaces on the Ladbroke Estate. At 7.4 acres (3ha), it's London's largest private communal garden square. The square was originally on the site of the Hippodrome racecourse (see below) before development began on the estate, and has some interesting architectural styles.

Return to Ladbroke Grove and turn right. Soon, on the left, is Grade II listed **St John's**

St John's Church

Crescent, Cornwall Crescent and Lansdowne Crescent.

Take the right turn in front of the church, **Kensington Park Gardens** ④, an attractive residential street with a variety of architectural styles, mainly cream and white terraces. There's a blue plaque for scientist Sir William Crookes, who lived at number 7 from 1880 until his death in 1919; this was one of the first houses in Britain to be lit by electricity.

St Peter's

> Kensington Park Gardens and neighbouring Kensington Park Road were allegedly so-named in the 1840s in the hope that an upmarket-sounding name would encourage people to want to live in them – it certainly worked!

At the end of Kensington Park Gardens, turn left along Kensington Park Road and continue to Stanley Gardens. On the right is the attractive, warm orange hue of **St Peter's Notting Hill** ⑤ (☎ 020-7792 8227 for opening hours), a Grade II listed, Victorian Anglican church. It was designed in the classical style by Thomas Allom, a founding member of what became the Royal Institute of British Architects, and built in 1855-7. The interior is elaborate, with gilded capitals on some of the pillars. Allom also designed parts of the Ladbroke Estate and worked on the Houses of Parliament with Sir Charles Barry.

When you leave the church, turn right, go left along Ladbroke Gardens and right up Ladbroke

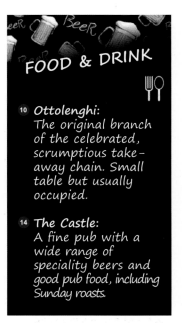

FOOD & DRINK

10 Ottolenghi: The original branch of the celebrated, scrumptious take-away chain. Small table but usually occupied.

14 The Castle: A fine pub with a wide range of speciality beers and good pub food, including Sunday roasts.

Grove. Glance up the side streets as you walk to see the splendid residential terraces. Turn right along Blenheim Crescent, passing

Electric Cinema

Books for Cooks

attractive, cobbled Codrington Mews on the right, then cross Kensington Park Road into the next stretch of Blenheim Crescent, with its parade of interesting shops and restaurants. Marc Bolan of rock band T. Rex lived at number 57 from 1968-70, just before he became successful.

The **Notting Hill Bookshop** 6 is on the right, but isn't – as many believe – the actual bookshop (which was in Portobello Road) where the scenes were filmed for the eponymous film starring Julia Roberts and Hugh Grant. On the left at number 4 is **Books for Cooks** 7 founded in 1983, which has been described as the world's best-smelling shop; recipes from some of its wealth of cook books are tested daily in the small kitchen at the back.

Turn right a short distance along Portobello Road and at number 191 is the **Electric Cinema** 8. One of Britain's oldest purpose-built cinemas, it dates back to 1910 and is Grade II* listed. Despite its slightly down-at-heel appearance, it's air-conditioned and has a full-size wide screen, a bar and restaurant, and an upstairs private members club, and is one of London's favourite cinemas.

Turn left along Colville Terrace, before taking a second left turn into Powys Square. The understated elegance of the houses here belies the area's former notoriety. Many of the immigrants who arrived in the '50s ended up living in cramped conditions in Colville Terrace, which at one time was estimated to have Britain's second-highest population density after Glasgow. At the same time, Powys Square was a red light district populated by prostitutes and pimps. Not surprisingly, this small area saw some of the worst violence during the 1958 Notting Hill race riots.

Tabernacle   Ottolenghi

This corner of Notting Hill was once the haunt of notorious slum landlord Peter Rachman who owned and let out many of the properties here, often to immigrants who had no choice but to pay his high rents.

Walk to the northern end of Powys Square for the **Tabernacle** ❾ (9.30am-10pm) on Talbot Road, a Grade II listed building with a curved Romanesque façade of red brick and terracotta, and towers with spires on either side. It was built in the 1880s as a Christian evangelical place of worship and used to be known as the Talbot Tabernacle, after the Talbot family (see below). It's now better known for its role in the history of London's rock music scene: Pink Floyd and the Rolling Stones rehearsed here and The Clash played gigs. It's still a performance venue, and has a bar and caféteria with outdoor seating.

Turn left out of the Tabernacle along Talbot Road; the Talbot family owned a large estate until the '50s, much of it in Kensington. Turn right along Ledbury Road for a branch of the excellent **Ottolenghi** ❿ at number 63. It's the brainchild of Israeli-born chef and restaurateur Yotam Ottolenghi, one of four outlets; the others are in Kensington, Islington and Belgravia. They're stylish, imaginative, takeaway delicatessens, offering Mediterranean-style dishes with a middle Eastern influence and delicious cakes and snacks; the window displays of food are beautiful and enticing. The Islington outlet is also a restaurant and Ottolenghi has a new (2011) restaurant in Soho called NOPI.

Return the way you came along Ledbury Road, continue to the end and turn left along Westbourne Park Road. Number 280 was where Hugh Grant's character William

Thacker lived in *that* film, behind a famous blue door (now black). It was the home of the film's writer Richard Curtis during filming, although he sold it soon after. Turn right along St Luke's Road and immediately on the left is **St Luke's Mews** . This pretty mews has some sad history: television presenter Paula Yates was found dead at number 4 in 2000, aged just 41. The ex-wife of occasional singer and poverty campaigner Sir Bob Geldof and girlfriend of the late INXS singer Michael Hutchence died from a heroin overdose.

On leaving the mews, turn left up St Luke's Road towards the northern section of Notting Hill. The properties here are still large and impressive, but slightly shabbier; a lot of renovation work is in progress. Turn right down Tavistock Road and left along the Great Western Road, with Westbourne Park tube station on the left. Continue under the Westway flyover in this less salubrious part of town and turn left along Elkstone Road, with a railway line to the left.

Trellick Tower

The bleak, imposing bulk of **Trellick Tower** ⑫, a 31-storey tower block of 219 flats, rises 322ft (98m) on your right. When completed in 1972 it was London's tallest block of flats and was designed for the Greater London Council by Erno Goldfinger and Partners.

> Mr Goldfinger (1902-87) was a famously arrogant, Hungarian-born architect, said to have been the model for the Bond villain of the same name. It's rumoured that Ian Fleming used the name following a dispute over a Goldfinger building in Hampstead, where they both lived.

The style of Trellick Tower is much influenced by Le Corbusier's Unite d'Habitation in Marseilles. There's a separate service tower with lifts, linked to the main tower by walkways. It's a stark, brutally modernist building and was portrayed as embodying the worst excesses of high-rise living. The walkways attracted muggers and junkies, and the block came to be called Terror Tower. Residents were often effectively prisoners in their flats due to the drug dealers and muggers prowling the stairwells. Life in the Trellick Tower improved from the late '80s and into the '90s, partly because of better surveillance and the recruitment of a concierge. It was Grade II listed in 1998 and a few of the flats are now privately owned and quite sought-after, not least for the stunning views.

Turn left over the railway line and along Golborne Road into a buzzy, slightly scruffy area. It has a lot of places to eat, many Middle Eastern

The Royal Borough of Kensington and Chelsea

PORTOBELLO ROAD, W.11

some fascinating shops and places to eat on either side.

> Portobello Road was originally named Porto Bello Lane, after the Spanish port Puerto Bello (now in Panama), which was captured by Sir Edward Vernon for Britain in 1739. Many pubs and streets in the British Empire were subsequently named after the admiral or the port.

or Indian, a number of junk shops and some antiques outlets; the surroundings become tidier and more upmarket as you continue. Turn left into Portobello Road and soon on the right is the impressive building of the **Instituto Español** 13, somewhat obscured by the wall in front; it's a Spanish school in a former Franciscan convent built in 1862. The school moved here in 1982 in an area that has long had Spanish connections: after the Spanish Civil War in the 1930s, political exiles and refugees settled locally.

Portobello Road is Notting Hill's best known street, once a rural lane to Portobello Farm. Much of the road was built in the Victorian era and the famous Portobello Market began in the mid-19th century, when gypsies met to trade horses and herbs. The northernmost section sells second-hand goods, while the middle part majors in fruit and vegetables. The further south you walk, the more upmarket the wares become, with the southern end of the market specialising in antiques, collectables, and arts and crafts. The market is busy at weekends, with over 1,000 stalls, and there are

We end the walk at one of Portobello Road's pubs, **The Castle** 14, which is at number 225, near the door that featured in *that* film. The pub has a wide choice of beers, decent pub food (not quite gastro, but good) and is known as a people-watching spot. It has a plain, open-plan interior and its bohemian atmosphere befits the area, making it an ideal spot to finish the walk.

To reach the nearest tube station (Ladbroke Grove), return north up Portobello Road and turn left along Lancaster Road.

houses on Portobello Road

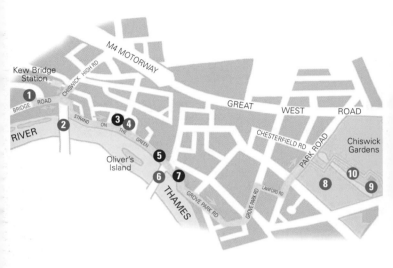

1 Kew Bridge Steam Museum
2 Kew Bridge
3 Bell and Crown
4 The Dutch House
5 City Barge
6 Railway bridge
7 Bulls Head
8 Chiswick Gardens
9 Chiswick House

10 Ionic Temple
11 Hogarth's House
12 St Nicholas Church
13 Chiswick Mall
14 Bedford House
15 Said House
16 Kelmscott House Museum
17 The Dove
18 Hammersmith Bridge

Places of Interest ● Food & Drink

WALK 24

GREAT WEST ROAD
Furnival Gardens
RIVER THAMES
CHISWICK MALL
Chiswick Eyot
Nature Reserve
PAXTON RD
BURLINGTON LANE
CHURCH ST
11
12
13
14
15
16
17
18

CHISWICK

WILLIAM HOGARTH
LIVED AND WORKED HERE FOR 15 YEARS

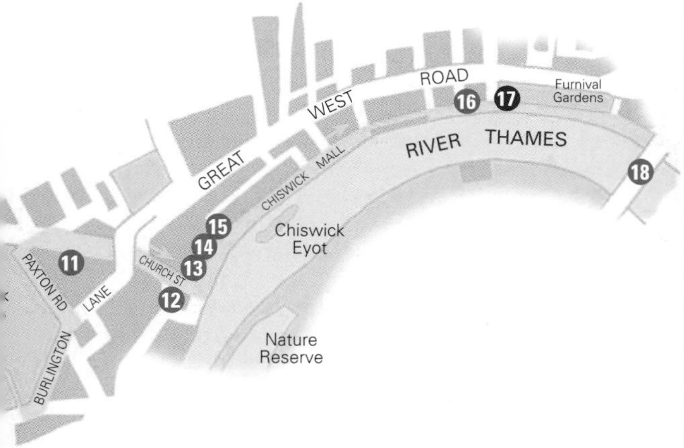

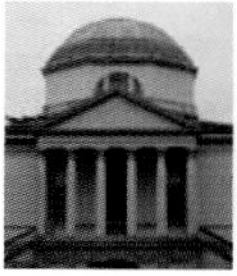

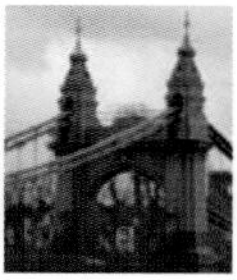

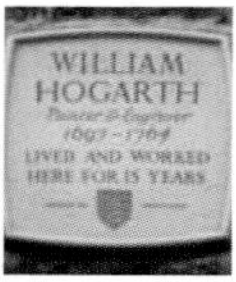

Distance: 3.59mi (5.78km)
Duration: half to full day
Start: Kew Bridge railway station
End: Hammersmith tube station

CHISWICK

The west London suburb of Chiswick sits on a meander of the River Thames, with Hammersmith to the east and Kew to the west. It f rst gets a mention in around 1,000AD as Ceswican. This is reputedly Old English for 'cheese farm' and may derive from the annual cheese fair held here until the 18th century. Other etymologists claim that Chiswick means 'the village by the stony beach'. Until the early 19th century, it was a rural outpost relying on agriculture and f shing, but increasing river pollution saw the latter decline – apparently, contamination was due not only to industry but also to the invention of the f ush toilet!

Originally, Chiswick was part of Middlesex and for a long time it was a popular country retreat from London. Chiswick House was where the Earls of Burlington went to escape Piccadilly's summer heat. The area began to develop into a suburb in the late 1800s and the population increased almost tenfold during the 19th century. It has become an increasingly attractive and sought after place to live, for its large houses (a mixture of Georgian, Victorian and Edwardian), wealth of green spaces and proximity to the Thames. It has also managed to retain its village atmosphere in places, not least along the riverbank where it's hard to imagine central London is just a 30-minute train ride away.

Chiswick House Park

Start Walking…

To explore Chiswick, leave Kew Bridge railway station and cross the road. Facing the station, look to your left to see the tower of **Kew Bridge Steam Museum** ❶, which is housed in a 19th-century riverside pumping station (Grade I and Grade II listed). Past the traffic lights bear left towards Kew, and then veer left towards the river and the quaintly named Strand-on-the-Green; this runs alongside the Thames and has some attractive 18th-century houses and good pubs fronting on to the river.

To the right at the beginning of Strand-on-the-Green is elegant, Grade II listed **Kew Bridge** ❷. There's been a bridge here since the mid-18th century; the current one dates from 1903 and is by Sir John Wolfe-Barry and Cuthbert Brereton.

> Modern Chiswick grew out of four villages which gradually merged to create the suburb. One village was Strand-on-the-Green; the others were Little Sutton to the east, Turnham Green to the northeast and Chiswick itself (see below).

As you stroll along the riverbank, the surroundings feel semi-rural and it's easy to forget that central London is so close. On the left, a branch of Café Rouge with outside tables upstairs provides an excellent vantage point for river-watching, although there are three good pubs a bit further on. Just past the restaurant are some attractive cottages which reinforce the impression that you're in the countryside.

Keep to the right which takes you along the riverside walk. The first pub you come to is the **Bell and Crown** ❸, a Fullers pub with tasty food and a good selection of real ales. Smugglers used to land their contraband here but had to get their timing right as the river falls several metres at low tide, exposing a treacherous, muddy bed.

Just past the pub the river path narrows and the attractive houses lining it are separated from the water only by a shallow bank. **The Dutch House** ❹ is eye-catching, its shutters painted in the Dutch

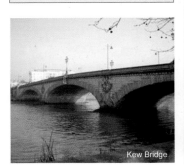
Kew Bridge

Dutch House

style with a split-diamond design, although in blue and white rather than the red and white favoured in The Netherlands; the house's gable is also of Dutch design. As several warning signs confirm, the properties along this narrow river path are at risk of flooding when the Thames rises at high tide – the price to be paid for living in this idyllic spot.

Bulls Head

FOOD & DRINK

3 **Bell and Crown:** Good Fuller's pub with their usual fine ales and traditional pub grub.

5 **City Barge:** Welcoming pub with well-kept real ales and good food.

Further along is another recommended riverside pub, the slightly weather-beaten **City Barge** 5. Parts of the building date from the late 15th century, although a WWII bomb destroyed much of the original. The steel door and high window ledges reflect the fact that the river can rise a couple of feet up the pub's walls. The elegant, pale green **railway bridge** 6 crosses the river at this point.

Last, we come to the **Bulls Head** 7. Like many old pubs,

it's attractively wonky, with low ceilings and creaking floorboards. Opposite the pub is the eyot, sometimes called Oliver's Island after Oliver Cromwell, who made his headquarters at the inn a number of times during the Civil War. He's also said to have taken refuge on the island, although this is unconfirmed.

> The word eyot comes from the Old English for a small island in a river or lake. Eyots are often long and narrow, and the term is used especially for islands in the Thames and its tributaries.

Soon after, leave the river and its excess of tempting pubs, and turn slightly inland along Grove Park Road into an attractive residential area. At the roundabout, which is a white painted affair, veer left then take another left at the next junction (still on Grove Park Road) and

The Cascade, Chiswick House

Ionic Temple

left again over a railway bridge signposted towards Chiswick railway station.

Turn right along Lawford Road, opposite the end of the bridge, and make a left along Park Road, lined with understated semi-detached and detached houses in a quiet residential area. Just before Chesterfield Road on the left, turn right through a gated entrance into **Chiswick Gardens** 8 (7am-dusk). Follow the path ahead and the signs for **Chiswick House** 9 (April to October, Sun-Wed, 10am-5pm); turn left over an attractive bridge and the house is on the right.

There's an **Ionic Temple** 10 on the right as you follow the path leading to the rear of the house. Further along, the path is lined with pillars displaying sphinxes and urns. Turn left at the rear of the house and go through an archway, where there's a large café on the left. Turn right to reach the front of the house, with its impressive entrance pillars and more sphinxes.

Chiswick House is an imposing suburban neo-Palladian villa built in 1727-9 and modelled on an idealised ancient house by the 3rd Earl of Burlingham, a noted authority on architecture and patron of the arts. The gardens were originally intended to resemble those of Ancient Rome, but were redesigned from the early 18th century in the geometrical style by Charles Bridgeman, to include ornamental buildings at the ends of vistas. Other parts of the gardens are in a much more natural style, designed by Samuel Lapidge for the 5th Duke in 1784. Many of the ornamental buildings were later demolished, but some remain, including the above-mentioned Ionic Temple, a Doric column, three statues of

Romans, two obelisks, a cascade, the avenue of urns and sphinxes, a bridge, a deer house, a rustic house and a conservatory – so there's plenty to see and explore in the gardens!

> The Beatles shot two of their earliest music video promos in the gardens of Chiswick House, for *Paperback Writer* and *Rain*, in 1966. A number of films and television series have also made use of the house and gardens, from Dirk Bogart's *The Servant* in 1963 to the BBC's *Horrible Histories*.

Leave the gardens by the exit directly in front of Chiswick House and turn left along Burlington Lane. Swing left along Paxton Road, with its attractive, characterful terraced houses; at the end, it branches to the right as Sutherland Road. Turn right at the end into the traffic-choked Great West Road, which comes as a shock after the riverside and verdant tranquillity enjoyed up to this point. Soon, on the right, is **Hogarth's House** ⑪ (Tue-Sun, noon-5pm), an attractive brick house which the artist William Hogarth (1697-1764) used as a retreat from 1749 until his death. It first opened as a museum in 1909, was damaged during WWII and restored in 1997 for the tercentenary of Hogarth's birth. The nearby Hogarth Roundabout and Flyover are named after the great man – a dubious honour.

Turn right out of Hogarth's House and cross the large roundabout ahead, using the underpass unless you wish to risk life and limb. Turn right along Church Street, which resembles a high street in a country town and is a pleasant change from the Great West Road. Fuller's Brewery is on the left as you enter the street; beer has been brewed in Chiswick for over 350 years. Further on, a sign saying that the road is 'liable to flooding' sign shows that we're heading back to the river.

At the end of Church Street on the right is an ancient right-of-way, Powell Walk, and **St Nicholas Church** ⑫ (☎ 020-8995 4717

Hogarth's House

St Nicholas Church

for opening times), where William Hogarth and fellow artist James McNeill Whistler (1834-1903) are buried. The old village of Chiswick grew up here by the river, around St Nicholas's and along what is now Church Street. The saint the church is dedicated to marks the fact that Chiswick began as a fishing village: St Nicholas is the patron saint of fishermen and sailors, among others. The church's ragstone tower dates from 1446 and is the only reminder of the medieval church; the rest was completely rebuilt in 1882 by John Loughborough Pearson, one of Britain's best Victorian architects.

Chiswick Mall, eyot

with large, attractive houses, some of which, unusually, are separated from their riverside gardens by a road. The houses look to be from the 17th to 20th centuries, but it's likely that some are older and have been refaced. The properties include large, impressive **Bedford House** 14 and, next to it, **Said House** 15, with its red urn. Bedford House and nearby Eynham House were originally one property, dating from the mid-17th century, while Said House was the home of Sir Nigel Playfair, the actor-manager.

The island in the Thames is Chiswick Eyot which can be reached on foot at low tide. Ahead, the path deviates briefly from the river and leads to another worthy pub, the Black Lion – allegedly haunted by 'the Hammersmith ghost' – offering a selection of well-kept real ales and good food.

FOOD & DRINK

7 **Bulls Head:** Traditional Chef & Brewer pub – good place for a pint and meal while listening to live jazz at weekends.

17 **The Dove:** Another quintessential historic pub in a great location with Fuller's ales and tasty food.

Turn left at the end of Church Street for **Chiswick Mall** 13, which runs along the Thames to the border of Hammersmith. The Mall is lined

The 'Hammersmith ghost' may be that of bricklayer Thomas Milward, victim of a strange case of mistaken identity. The story goes that a tall white ghost had been terrifying Hammersmith residents and that a vigilante took matters into his own hands, tracked the spectre down and shot it. But the 'ghost' turned out to be the unfortunate Milward, covered in pale brick dust. His body was taken to the Black Lion pub and, it's said, haunts it to this day.

Pick up the Thames side path again in front of the pub; there's a short stretch of modern housing here but once past Linden House – number 60 on what is now Upper Mall – there's a return to older, more characterful properties. Built in 1733, Linden House is a fine brick property with an entrance flanked by Ionic columns, home to the London Corinthian Sailing Club (founded 1894) since 1963.

At number 26 is **Kelmscott House Museum** ⑯ (Thu-Sat, 2-5pm), home of the William Morris Society, a striking Georgian building where artist, designer and man-for-all-seasons Morris lived from 1879 until his death in 1896. It was built in around 1780 and originally called 'The Retreat', but William Morris renamed the house after his Oxfordshire home Kelmscott Manor. He sometimes travelled between the two by boat – those were the days! In 1891, Morris established the Kelmscott Press at 16 Upper Mall. Today, the William Morris Society occupies the basement of Kelmscott House, the entrance to which is down steps leading from the driveway; it has a small, interesting museum with a collection of Morris designs and memorabilia.

Slightly further along is the pretty 18th-century pub, **The Dove** ⑰. It used to be a coffee house, but is now the quintessential English pub; it claims to have the smallest bar in England and its riverside terrace is a coveted place from which to watch the University Boat Race. Charles II and Nell Gwyn apparently had assignations at the Dove, and it has inspired writers and musicians. In 1740, the poet James Thomson wrote *Rule Britannia* in an upstairs room, while Gustav Holst used to compose music at the pub – the beer must be inspirational!

Hammersmith Bridge has the dubious distinction of being London's most bombed bridge. There have been three attempts by IRA terrorists to blow it up – in 1939, 1996 and 2000.

The Dove

Kelmscott House Museum

Turn right out of the pub and continue along the river to end the walk by admiring the elegant, decorative bulk of **Hammersmith Bridge** ⑱, with its 423ft (129m) central span. The original bridge was built in 1824-7 by William Tierney Clarke and was London's first suspension bridge. It was replaced in 1883-7 by the (stronger) present suspension bridge, designed by Sir Joseph Bazalgette, who reused the old piers and abutments. Pass under the bridge and the path curves to the right into Queen Caroline Street. Walk to the top for the large Broadway shopping centre and Hammersmith tube station.

Hammersmith Bridge

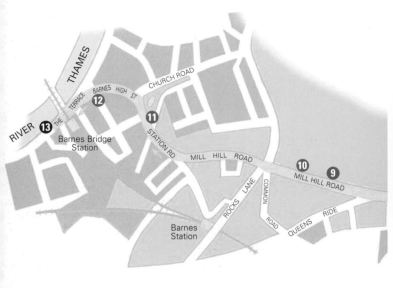

1. Fulham Pottery
2. Footbridge to Putney
3. Sir Abraham Dawes Almshouses
4. Boathouse
5. St Mary's Church
6. Putney Bridge
7. Kenilworth Court

8. Duke's Head
9. Putney Lower Common Cemetery
10. Barnes Common Local Nature Reserve
11. Barnes Green
12. The Terrace
13. Ye White Hart

Places of Interest ● Food & Drink

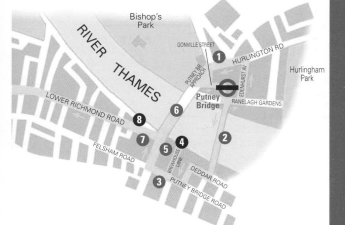

Bishop's
Park

RIVER

THAMES

GONVILLE STREET

HURLINGTON RD

PUTNEY BR
APPROACH

EDENHURST AV

Hurlingham
Park

**Putney
Bridge**

RANELAGH GARDENS

LOWER RICHMOND ROAD

1

2

6

8

7

5

4

3

FELSHAM ROAD

BREWHOUSE
LANE

DEDDAR ROAD

PUTNEY BRIDGE ROAD

BARNES &
PUTNEY

WALK 25

Distance: 3.06mi (4.93km)
Duration: half to full day
Start: Putney Bridge tube station
End: Barnes Bridge railway station

Barnes and Putney are tucked into an upward loop of the River Thames, on the southern bank opposite Chiswick and Hammersmith to the north. Together, they're two of the most affuent and desirable suburbs of southwest London.

Barnes was once in Surrey and appears in the Domesday Book of 1086 as Berne, meaning barn; it's now within the borough of Richmond-upon-Thames. The heart of Barnes still feels like a village, with the requisite village green and duck pond, much of which is protected as a conservation area. A short distance away, The Terrace has some of London's oldest, most desirable riverside housing – a row of exquisite Georgian mansions facing the Thames.

Nearby Putney is less of a village, more of a suburban sprawl, but is still a sought-after destination for young, upwardly-mobile Londoners. Its proximity to the river made Putney a strategic spot for many centuries. Its Anglo-Saxon name was Putelei, which translated as 'Putta's landing place', and the opening of Putney Bridge in the early 18th century marked it as an important river crossing. It also had political signif cance – at the end of the Civil War it hosted the Putney Debates (see below) to decide England's political future.

For many years, farming and f shing were the main occupations, but it also provided well-to-do Londoners with clean air, open spaces and many leisure pursuits, from hunting and hawking to bowling. These days, it's one of Britain's leading centres for rowing and provides the starting point for the annual University Boat Race which ends just after Barnes.

BARNES & PUTNEY

Start Walking…

Our final walk departs from Putney Bridge tube station; on leaving the station, turn left and left again along Ranelagh Gardens, passing under a railway bridge. Turn left up Edenhurst Avenue, which is lined with attractive Victorian semi-detached houses, and left again along Hurlingham Road. Pass under a bridge and ahead, across New Kings Road, is the **Fulham Pottery** ❶, sitting anomalously next to a modern tower block.

What we see today is a 19th-century kiln, but the pottery was established in 1672 by John Dwight. A former lawyer, he was also a skilled artist and was the first in England to successfully produce Continental-style, salt-glazed domestic ware. A fire in 1918 destroyed most of the old pottery buildings and only some late 19th-century structures remained, most of which were demolished in the '70s.

The name Fulham is said to come from a personal name and to mean Fulla's settlement in a low-lying bend of the river.

Head southwest along Putney Bridge Approach, turn left along Gonville Street and right to cross Ranelagh Gardens, heading towards a sign for the **Footbridge to Putney** ❷. Climb a flight of steps to reach the footbridge, which runs parallel to a railway bridge; the latter provides reassurance and a physical barrier for those (like the author) who don't necessarily enjoy crossing large bodies of water on narrow pedestrian bridges. The railway bridge was built 1887-9 by William Jacomb, Brunel's assistant on the ship *Great Eastern*; it has five spans of lattice-girder construction and now serves the District tube line.

Turn right at the end of the bridge, left along Merivale Road and right along Putney Bridge Road. Soon, on the left, are the attractive **Sir Abraham Dawes Almshouses** ❸, named after their founder, a collector of customs' duties. He lived in Putney from

Fulham Pottery

Almshouses

1620 until his death in 1640, and his house, built 1634-36, stood on the site now occupied by Putney station. Sir Abraham provided the almshouses in 1629 for '12 poor indigent decayed and decrepit almsmen and almswomen'; the present buildings date back to 1861 and still house local people.

Turn right down Brewhouse Lane to admire the river from the walkway in front of the gleaming, recently-refurbished **Boathouse** ❹ restaurant on Putney Wharf, with an al fresco dining area on the first floor, offering elevated views of Putney Bridge and the footbridge. Return up Brewhouse Lane and turn right along Putney Bridge Road and right again into Putney High Street. Just before the bridge, **St Mary's Church** ❺ (Mon-Sat, 9am-6pm) is on the right and has a welcoming café.

It occupies a lovely position, right on the riverside, where there's been a church since at least the 13th century. Parts of today's structure are medieval, including the tower and some of the nave arcading, which is mid-15th century, while the Bishop West Chapel is early 16th century. The rest was rebuilt in 1836 and renovated in the '70s and '80s following an arson attack. Oliver Cromwell's New Model Army had its headquarters at the church in autumn 1647, where they discussed England's new constitution in talks around the communion table – the so-called Putney Debates. There's an exhibition about this in the church.

> Since 1845 Putney Bridge has been the starting point of the University Boat Race (between eights from Oxford and Cambridge). The race finishes just before Chiswick Bridge, 4.2mi (6.8 km) upstream.

On leaving the church, turn right and cross the approach road to **Putney Bridge** ❻, negotiating a couple of sets of lights in the process. Attractive lamps line the sides of the bridge, which is Grade II listed and has some of London's best river views. The first bridge was a timber structure built in 1727-9 and until 1750, when Westminster Bridge opened, it was the only bridge across the Thames west of London Bridge. Before that, travellers wanting to cross the Thames had to use the services of the local ferrymen. The present bridge is a five-span granite structure, built in 1882-6 by Sir Joseph Bazalgette. It's the only bridge in Britain to have a church

St Mary's Church

at both ends: St Mary's on the south bank, All Saints, Fulham on the north.

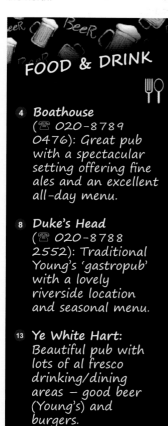

FOOD & DRINK

4 Boathouse (☎ 020-8789 0476): Great pub with a spectacular setting offering fine ales and an excellent all-day menu.

8 Duke's Head (☎ 020-8788 2552): Traditional Young's 'gastropub' with a lovely riverside location and seasonal menu.

13 Ye White Hart: Beautiful pub with lots of al fresco drinking/dining areas — good beer (Young's) and burgers.

Putney Lower Common Cemetery

Victorian pub with great Thames views. This Young's pub has been a popular spot to watch the University Boat Race for some 150 years.

Turn right out of the pub and continue along Lower Richmond Road, heading inland from the river, with its mix of attractive residential properties, shops and restaurants. After around ten minutes, you reach the green expanse of Putney Common. This is part of a reserve which stretches from the London Wetland Centre in the north to Barnes Common to the west, and has been a popular retreat for centuries. It's a haven for rare wildlife and plants.

Take the right-hand fork towards Mill Hill Road; with grass and trees on both sides, it's like walking along a country lane. Soon, on the right, is **Putney Lower Common Cemetery** **9** (Mon-Sat, 8am-dusk, Sun 10am-dusk). Like most London cemeteries, it's well worth visiting to see some attractively weathered memorials. The cemetery, founded

With the bridge behind you, turn right along Lower Richmond Road which runs parallel with the river. Attractive, red-brick **Kenilworth Court** **7** is on the left, a prestigious mansion block built in 1901-3. On the right soon after, close to the river, is the **Duke's Head** **8**, a Grade II listed

309

Turn right along Station Road towards **Barnes Green** ⑪. This tranquil spot has a large pond and resembles a village green. Opposite is a house once occupied by the author of *Tom Jones*, Henry Fielding (1707-54), marked by a blue plaque; it's one of the area's oldest properties, with parts dating from the 16th century.

The parakeets spotted around southwest London and further afield are thought to be descended from a flock that escaped from Shepperton Studios in Surrey during filming of the Humphrey Bogart film *The African Queen* in 1951.

in 1858 and covering around 3 acres (1.2ha), has a number of interesting historic tombs, including that of Sir Alfred Dryden (died 1912), a descendent of the poet John Dryden.

Further along, also on the right, is **Barnes Common Local Nature Reserve** ⑩. Barnes Common covers around 120 acres (49ha) and was mainly marshland until being drained in the late 19th century. It now attracts plenty of wildlife, including flocks of parakeets, which have colonised parks and back gardens in southwest London, Surrey and Kent. There are estimated to be around 30,000 of these adaptable colourful birds, although there are plans to cull them as they pose a threat to native wildlife.

At the busy road junction, cross over Rocks Lane and continue ahead, as the open space gives way to a residential area.

Turn left along Barnes High Street and when you reach the river, take another left along **The Terrace** ⑫, which is lined with characterful Georgian houses in a variety of architectural styles dating from 1720 and overlooking a wide and peaceful stretch of the Thames. There's a blue plaque to the English composer Gustav Holst (1874-1934), who lived at number 10 from 1907-13 when he was head of music at St Paul's Girls' School. The house has a large music room on the top floor

and a terrace where Holst and fellow composer Ralph Vaughan Williams would watch the Boat Race.

Go under Barnes Bridge – the railway station is here – and continue to the end of The Terrace to conclude this walk at **Ye White Hart** ⑬. This excellent Young's pub has a large bar, dark wood interior, Chesterfield sofas by the fire and wonderful river views.

Barnes Bridge & oarsman at dusk

INDEX

T

U/V

W

Y

PHOTO CREDITS

Graeme Chesters

© Pages 15 (all), 18, 19 (both), 20 (both), 21, 22 (all), 23 (both), 24, 25 (both), 26 & 27 (top photos), 29 (all), 31 (both), 32 (all), 33, 35 (all), 36, 39 (all), 41 (both), 42 & 43 (all), 44, 45 (bottom), 47 (all), 51 (all), 53 (left), 54 (both), 55 (bottom two), 59 (top two), 60, 61, 63 (all), 65 (both), 66 (all), 67, 68, 71, 72 (top three), 73 (top left, top right), 75 (all), 77 (both), 78 (top left), 79 (top right), 81, 82 (both), 83, 85 (bottom left), 87 (all), 89 (all), 90, 91 (both), 92 (left), 93 (top and bottom left), 95 (top right and bottom), 99 (all), 101 (bottom left and top right), 102 (left), 104 (top), 107 (top), 108, 109 (both), 113 (all), 117 (top left), 119 (top and middle), 120, 121 (top), 122 (both), 123 (both), 125 (all), 127, 130 (top), 131 (right), 132 (both), 133 (both), 136, 139 (all), 141 (both), 142, 143 (both), 144 (both), 147 (right), 148 (top), 149 (top), 150, 151, 153 (all), 155 (bottom), 161 (top), 163 (small), 165 (all), 167, 168, 169 (both), 173 (both), 179 (all), 185 (all), 186, 187 (middle), 188, 191 (all), 194 (bottom), 195 (both), 198, 200, 203 (all), 208, 209 (left), 213 (all), 219 (left), 221 (left), 225 (all), 229 (bottom), 230, 231 (bottom three), 233 (both), 234, 236 (top), 239 (all), 241 (both), 248 (right), 249 (bottom), 250 (small), 253 (all), 265 (all), 267 (both), 268 (bottom), 270, 273 (all), 276 (right), 277, 278, 279, 285 (all), 287 (left), 290 (right), 291 (right), 295 (all), 302 (right), 305 (all), 307 (both), 308, 309, 310 (both), 311 (top).

Miscellaneous

© Pages 6 © olavs, 16, 23, 27 © William Attard McCarthy, 9 (top), 59 (bottom), 73 (centre top), 85 (top), 92 (right), 110, 111 (both), 119, 121 © Argironeta (box), 145 (both), 146, 171, 174 © docbrown.info, 180 © St James's Hotel & Club, 204 © Flickr, 226 © ngw.nl, 251 © Forgiss, 263, 269 & 283 © Flickr, 296 © English Heritage, 309 © only-melancholy, 311 © Flickr.

Wikipedia

© Pages 17 (hat), 17, 26 (bottom), 33, 34 (both), 37, 45 (top), 46, 49 (bottom), 53 (right), 55 (top), 56 (both), 57, 58 (both), 67, 70 (all), 72 (bottom), 73 bottom, 78 (top right), 79 (top left and bottom), 80, 84 (both), 85 (bottom right), 93 (bottom right), 94 (both), 95 (top left and top centre), 96 (both), 97, 100 (bottom right and top left), 102 (right), 103 (all), 104 (bottom), 105 (both), 106 (both), 107 (both bottom), 115, 116, 117 (top right and bottom), 129 (all), 130 (bottom), 131 (left), 134, 135 (both), 137, 145 (box), 147 (left), 148 (bottom), 149 (bottom), 155 (top), 156, 157, 158, 159 (both), 160 (both), 161 (bottom), 162, 163 (large), 170 (both), 172 (both), 174 (both), 175 (both), 176, 177 (both), 181, 182 (both), 183, 184, 187 (top and bottom), 189, 192, 193, 194 (top), 197 (both), 199, 201, 204, 205, 206, 207 (both), 209 (top and bottom right), 210 (both), 211, 215 (both), 216, 217 (both), 218, 219 (right), 220 (both), 221 (right), 222, 223 (all), 227, 228, 229 (top), 231 (top), 232, 235, 236 (bottom), 237, 240, 242, 243 both, 244, 245, 245 (both), 246 (both), 247, 248 (left), 249 (top left and right), 250 (large), 251, 255 (both), 256, 257, 258, 259, 260, 262 (both), 262, 263, 268 (top), 269, 271, 274, 275, 276 (left), 280, 281 (both), 282 (both), 283 (both), 287 (box), 288 (both), 289, 290 (left), 291 (left), 292, 293 (both), 297 (both), 298, 299 (both), 300 (both), 301, 302 (left), 303, 311 (bottom).